Key Issues
in the Arts and
Entertainment Industry

Key Issues
in the Arts and Entertainment Industry

Edited by Ben Walmsley

(G) Goodfellow Publishers Ltd

(G) Published by Goodfellow Publishers Limited,
Woodeaton, Oxford, OX3 9TJ
http://www.goodfellowpublishers.com

British Library Cataloguing in Publication Data: a catalogue record for this title is available from the British Library.

Library of Congress Catalog Card Number: on file.

ISBN: 978-1-906884-47-5

Design and typesetting by P.K. McBride, www.macbride.org.uk

Printed by Marston Book Services, www.marston.co.uk

Cover design by Cylinder, www.cylindermedia.com

Contents

Acknowledgements

I would like to dedicate this book to everyone who works, or is aiming to work, in the arts and entertainment industry. I have always been struck by the passion of the people who make this industry so unique, and this book is hopefully a tribute to the creativity and tenacity of these people, who are currently in the process of transforming their organisations and steering them through some of the most difficult times they have ever experienced. In particular, I'd like to thank all the organisations who gave us permission, and often actively helped and encouraged us, to use them in this book as a case study. The reason they are here as case studies is because they are beacons in the industry which illuminate the way forward.

I would also like to thank the small and dedicated team at Goodfellow, for their unfailing support and encouragement and for their student and lecturer-friendly approach to academic publication. Finally, I'd like to acknowledge my students and colleagues at Leeds Metropolitan University, who have shaped and supported this publication, and my partner, family and friends, who have been as encouraging as ever.

Ben Walmsley, Editor

Contributors

David Bollier is an author and activist who studies the commons as a new paradigm of economics, politics and culture. He blogs at Bollier.org, collaborates with the Commons Strategy Group, and has written ten books. He is also Co-founder of Public Knowledge and Senior Fellow at the Norman Lear Center at the USC Annenberg School for Communication and Journalism.

Douglas Brown has taught Arts and Cultural Management at Queen Margaret University, Edinburgh since 1999. He has recently moved on from his position as the Senior Lecturer in Cultural Management to continue to lecture, research and work in the arts and cultural sector in Austria.

Anna Franks has worked in a variety of marketing and communications roles including for Abbey National and a Leeds-based housing association, where she established a communications function for the trust. Anna joined the Leeds-based cultural marketing agency &Co in 2004, and as Client Services Director she oversees membership, events and consultancy services, working with a range of arts and cultural organisations.

John Holden is a Visiting Professor at City University, London and an Associate at the think-tank Demos. His publications include *Democratic Culture, Culture and Class, Cultural Diplomacy* and *Cultural Value and the Crisis of Legitimacy*. John is a member of the Advisory Boards of the Clore Leadership Programme, the Arts and Humanities Research Council and the Institute for Cultural Diplomacy in Berlin.

Chantal Laws is a Senior Lecturer at the University of Gloucestershire, where she teaches Events, Music and Festival Management. Chantal's research interests focus on cultural experiencescapes and liminal events and she regularly presents and publishes work on these topics. Chantal has previous professional experience in the cultural industries and is a regular festival-goer.

Stuart Moss is a Senior Lecturer, Teacher Fellow, and Course Leader for the BA (Hons) Entertainment Management at Leeds Metropolitan University. Stuart has had two books published: *Employability Skills* (2005) and *The Entertainment Industry: An Introduction* (2009) and also maintains an academic blog at http://www.entertainmentplanet.eu. He has made numerous conference presentations globally about employability, entrepreneurship and the entertainment industry.

Simon Mundy is a Cultural Policy Adviser who regularly works with UNESCO and the Council of Europe. He has been a judge for the Sony Radio Awards, was Broadcasting Correspondent of *Classical Music Magazine* and Director of the National Campaign for the Arts in the 1980s and 1990s, and a frequent presenter on BBC Radios 3 and 4. He is an Associate Fellow of the Conflict, Security and Development Group at King's College, London.

James Oliver is a social anthropologist who researches spaces and practices of culture, identity and place. Currently a Research Fellow at the University of Melbourne, he has extensive experience in Scotland and Australia across a range of arts practices, social and cultural policy issues and arts development. He has a particular interest in the development of practice-led research, and creative and reflexive methodologies.

Daragh O'Reilly is a Lecturer in Marketing at the University of Sheffield where he teaches modules on branding and the creative industries. His research interest is in the relationship between markets and culture and he is the co-editor of *Marketing the Arts: A Fresh Approach* (Routledge, 2010), as well as of special issues on Arts Marketing in the journals *Consumption, Markets and Culture* (2009, 3), the *International Journal of Culture, Tourism and Hospitality Research* (2010, 1), *Journal of Marketing Management* (26, 7/8) and the *European Journal of Marketing* (forthcoming).

James Roberts is a Research Fellow at Leeds University Business School, where he specialises in innovation and strategic management. Before his academic career he spent 12 years as a strategy consultant, latterly with Oliver Wyman, working with large media and entertainment companies including the BBC, Sony Corp., Viacom, Warner Bros and Walt Disney.

Ben Walmsley is a Senior Lecturer in Arts and Entertainment Management at Leeds Metropolitan University with a background in theatre producing. Before taking up a managerial post at the new National Theatre of Scotland, he managed the leading Scottish touring company, Benchtours. Ben is a Fellow of the Higher Education Academy, an Artistic Assessor for Arts Council England and an active member of the Academy of Marketing and the Arts Marketing Association. His research interests are related to the qualitative value and impact of theatre.

Introduction

The idea for this book came from my surprise and frustration at the lack of high quality literature available in the academic field of arts and entertainment management. After two years of exhaustive (and exhausting) searches for up-to-date teaching material for a module exploring contemporary issues in the arts and entertainment industry, I decided that the only way to bring together my disparate collection of newspaper and journal articles, conference papers, consultants' reports and guest speakers' lecture slides was to edit a book myself.

My principle aim in editing this book was to create a publication that would speak to a wide range of stakeholders in the arts and entertainment industry – students, academics, practitioners and policy makers alike. I therefore strove to bring together a diverse mix of authors with specialist interests, knowledge and practical experience in a range of complementary fields. I was delighted by the desire of the academic and industry colleagues I approached to contribute towards this publication; and if this book does achieve its aim, it is because of the quality, passion and commitment of its authors.

The book is constructed around one core underlying thesis: namely that we are witnessing a fundamental change in the way that the arts and entertainment are produced, experienced and consumed, and that this phenomenon is revolutionising traditional relationships between producers, consumers and audiences. While for centuries, the arts and entertainment industry has striven to safeguard its role as gatekeeper, pushing its products down to its audiences, the advent of digitisation and global interconnectivity, which have fanned the flames of accessibility and cultural democratisation, is challenging this power dynamic and gradually transforming modern arts and entertainment organisations into facilitators and conduits.

Every chapter in this book provides an example of this transformation. In Chapter 1, Anna Franks and I explore the benefits and implications of audience development and co-creation, illustrating what can happen when organisations hand over artistic control to their audiences. Chapter 2 considers how this shift in control is impacting on business models in the industry, illustrating in particular how technology can be harnessed to add value for both providers and consumers of content. In Chapter 3, James Oliver outlines the challenges of cultural funding in a climate of cuts in public spending, reconfiguring the terms of the funding debate and reassessing the concept of public value.

Chapter 4 provides a highly critical perspective on the traditionally commercial approach to branding the arts and entertainment, with Daragh O'Reilly advocating a culturalist interpretation of brands as signs or 'meanings' informed by the ideologies, values and interaction of producers and consumers alike.

Chapter 5 is equally polemical, with David Bollier arguing for a 'sharing economy', where the primary function of copyright is to advance public knowledge, education and culture.

In Chapter 6, the relationship between producer and audiences again comes under the microscope as James Oliver and I critique reductive, quantitative and benefits-based approaches to understanding the value of the arts in favour of richer, qualitative methods which explore and express value in audiences' terms. Chapter 7 continues in the same vein, tracing the history of arts and entertainment venues and illustrating how they are adapting to new ways of working, with Douglas Brown providing an illuminating glimpse of how modern venues are opening up to audiences.

In Chapter 8, James Roberts traces the rise of home entertainment, illustrating how the convergence in technology is reshaping the relationship between consumers and content providers, impacting differently on the supply and demand sides of the equation to shape the future of the industry. Chapter 9 focuses similarly on the impacts of technology and on the possible challenges of cannibalisation; but here, Simon Mundy considers how technology is shaping the future of broadcasting, bringing it online and thereby transcending traditional barriers of culture, geography and class.

Chapters 10 and 11 explore the topical issues of cultural entrepreneurship and leadership, illustrating how successful entrepreneurs and leaders are adapting to the challenges of the new and emerging relationships between producers and consumers or audiences. First, Stuart Moss provides a deeply personal insight into what makes a cultural entrepreneur by probing the childhood, influences and career history of music entrepreneur Morgan Khan. Then John Holden scrutinises modern cultural leadership in a case study of organisational change at the RSC.

I felt it was appropriate to conclude the book with one of the hottest topics currently affecting the industry – namely the hot potato of sustainability. So in the final chapter, Chantal Laws tackles the various arguments of the responsibility debate, dissecting the terminology and providing a diverse range of illustrative examples of how the festivals and events sector is responding to the increasingly urgent calls for change.

I am confident that this book will provide an illustrative and critically analytical snapshot of what is happening now in the arts and entertainment industry. But overall, I hope that the ideas and case studies within it will inspire those of you who read it to continue to invest your time and passion in the sector in the difficult times that inevitably lie ahead.

Ben Walmsley, Editor.

1 The Audience Experience: Changing roles and relationships

Ben Walmsley and Anna Franks

Introduction

This chapter will focus on the changing role of the modern-day consumer and audience member and explore the implications of this development for arts and entertainment organisations. It will begin with an exploration of the 'experience economy' (Pine and Gilmore, 1999), demonstrating how the changing needs, abilities and expectations of audiences and consumers are effecting a revolutionary shift in behaviour from the traditional push from producers towards a creative dialogue, where consumers have at least a voice and sometimes even an equal role as artist and co-producer.

The chapter will go on to discuss the rise of what we'll call 'creative interaction', the intermediary space where professional artists, producers, venues and content providers join their audiences and consumers to create or experience something new together. This discussion will be underpinned by a focus on the changing role and mission of arts and entertainment organisations from privileged gatekeepers to facilitators. It will also discuss the various factors and developments that are effecting this change.

The evolving role of audiences will then be explored in detail through a review of the theory and practice of audience development. The changing focus and practice of audience development will be illustrated by case studies on Audiences Central's Big Picture project and York Theatre Royal's TakeOver Festival.

The experience economy

The term 'experience economy' was famously coined by Pine and Gilmore (1999: 2) to describe the new environment of customer focus where 'experiences are a fourth economic offering, as distinct from services as services are from goods'. Pine and Gilmore trace product development from basic commodities through goods and services to the complex modern realm of the experience. This development is illustrated in Table 1.1.

Table 1.1: Economic distinctions

Economic offering	Commodities	Goods	Services	Experiences
Economy	Agrarian	Industrial	Service	Experience
Economic function	Extract	Make	Deliver	Stage
Nature of offering	Fungible	Tangible	Intangible	Memorable
Key attribute	Natural	Standardised	Customised	Personal
Method of supply	Stored in bulk	Inventoried after production	Delivered on demand	Revealed over a duration
Seller	Trader	Manufacturer	Provider	Stager
Buyer	Market	User	Client	Guest
Factors of demand	Characteristics	Features	Benefits	Sensations

Source: Pine and Gilmore (1999: 6)

The terminology employed in Table 1.1 illustrates the different expectations demanded of organisations by consumers in the experience economy. Notable developments from services to experiences include a focus on the personal, an expansion of distribution from short-term to long-term and a shift in demand from benefits to sensations. The implications of this semantic shift are far-reaching and they highlight the need for today's organisations to create long-term, personal relationships with their 'guests' by appealing to their senses and creating a sense of occasion.

Developing their thesis that successful products must also be memorable and meaningful experiences, Pine and Gilmore (1999: 20) urge organisations to 'draw the consumer into the process' of designing, producing and delivering their products to maximise the impact of their experience, claiming that consumers enjoy the acquisition process as much as the end result. They also highlight the need to enrich the consumer experience, evoking the concept of the 'sweet spot' to denote the holy grail of the experiential product, the 'distinctive place' where the realms of aesthetics, escapism, education and entertainment overlap

(Pine and Gilmore, 1999: 43). In this ideal experience, the consumer is fully immersed and becomes an active participant.

Pine and Gilmore use theatre as an exemplar for the staged experience required of businesses in the new economy, and it seems therefore that the arts and entertainment industry is ideally placed to excel in this new experience economy. According to some commentators, this is essentially because the industry has always functioned in a constant state of creative flux: 'Having thrived as a permanent "industry" with inherently temporary arrangements, in a dynamic, multicultural and project-oriented environment, the arts context is the epitome of organisation for the "new economy"' (Butler, 2000: 343). Touring arts organisations are perfect examples of these dynamic, project-based initiatives. In the next chapter, we will move on to consider how organisations' types and models are changing; what we are interested in here is how they can better connect with their guests to deliver more memorable and sensational experiences.

Imagineering

One technique which can help organisations to deliver such experiences is 'imagineering'. Imagineering is a blend of the words 'imagination' and 'engineering' and the term was first coined by Alcoa (the Aluminium Company of America) in the 1940s as part of an internal programme to drive up demand for the public use of aluminium by encouraging imaginative uses for the product. According to Alcoa (1942: 59), imagineering is about 'letting your imagination soar, and then engineering it down to earth'.

The Imagineering Academy (2010) defines the concept as 'value creation and value innovation from the experience perspective'. This essentially means creating (or co-creating) novel experiences which tangibly increase guests' satisfaction. The Imagineering Academy is a Holland-based community of academics and practitioners who strive to 'energise and transform the process of value creation' by applying the key imagineering principles of 'experience, co-creation, inspiration and transformation' to a whole range of organisations in what they call the 'creative knowledge economy'. These principles lie at the heart of the audience experience and we will revisit them time and again in this book to explore how the relationship between producers and consumers is evolving on an almost daily basis.

The Imagineering Academy uses Cirque de Soleil as a prime example of world-class providers of creative content. Its mission is to encourage other businesses and industries (and even entire towns and cities) to emulate the imagination and creativity of established experience providers like Cirque de Soleil and apply it to their own context (or 'bring it down to earth', as Alcoa would have said). Imagineering has most successfully been adopted and employed by Walt Disney Imagineering – Disney's world-leading research and development (R&D) arm. The employees of this department are referred to as 'imagineers' and they are renowned for their ability to blend creativity, expertise, and technological advancements.

One of the earliest examples of Disney's use of imagineering can be found in its 1940 film Fantasia, which 'exemplifies the combination of science and creativity, engineering and imagination that Disney's term represents. Fantasia is literally an imagineering of music. Its images and stories introduce layers of signification to sound that add meaning to and comment on music' (Clague, 2004: 96). What's interesting here is Clague's assertion that imagineering can 'add meaning' and 'layers of significance': this again highlights the importance of the audience experience and indicates how producers can transform a cultural good into a significant and memorable experience. One of Disney's other achievements in Fantasia was to introduce classical music to a mainstream cinema audience via a familiar and accessible platform. The film therefore provides a good case study of how imagineering can be used to successfully grow and develop a market.

Creative interaction

At the beginning of this chapter, we defined creative interaction as the intermediary space where professional artists, producers, venues and content providers join their audiences and consumers to create or experience something new together. We also discussed how consumers and audience members can become fully immersed and actively participate in an experience by being drawn into the creative process.

In order to appreciate how the producer–audience relationship is changing, we should first remind ourselves how the arts and entertainment industry traditionally operates. Despite the recent social inclusion, arts education and audience development agendas, whose communal aim is partly to open up the creative process; and despite the increasing popularity of the academic discipline of arts and entertainment management, the creative process itself often remains a mystery. There are various reasons for this. First, many artists, producers and audiences would contend that the mystery behind the process is precisely what gives arts and entertainment experiences their overriding appeal. The powerful image and symbolism of a curtain slowly revealing a stage hints at a closed, mysterious and escapist world, which can briefly transport its audience from one side of the curtain to the other. Second, the creative process itself is inherently complex, requiring a diverse body of creative agents coming together to stage a new experience. This involves many intangibles such as human and artistic chemistry, which are forced into a crucible to produce an unknown new element for the audience. Finally, like many other professional activities, writing, composing, choreography, filming, rehearsals and other related creative activities generally take place behind closed doors so that writers, directors and artists can experiment, focus and work in a spirit of artistic freedom and confidentiality.

So traditionally, the arts and entertainment industry has functioned on a product-led model, pushing its products down to its audiences to entertain, challenge and educate them. However, in recent years, whether responding to evolving audience expectations, changing artistic processes or acting under pressure from funders and other stakeholders, many arts and entertainment organisations have gradually begun to open up their processes. The case studies at the end of this chapter will illustrate the challenges and benefits of this creative interaction, but even a brief survey of the industry soon reveals a burgeoning hive of audience interaction and involvement in the creative process. Some excellent examples here include the Royal Shakespeare Company and Mudlark's Such Tweet Sorrow, a real-time adaptation of Romeo and Juliet built on audience responses to current events and cast tweets; Contact Theatre's Freestyle Mondays and Mixed Movement nights, which offer young audiences unrivalled opportunities for spontaneous performance; Tate Modern's Your Tate Track competition, which invited non-signed musicians to compose a piece of music inspired by any painting in the gallery and submit it to a public vote; and Scottish Opera's Baby O – a new interactive commission aimed at babies and toddlers comprising puppetry, a tactile garden and singing (or gurgling) along (Musolife.com, 2010).

When discussing audience involvement, we need to distinguish between active and passive participation. Active participants are those who want to try out or join in arts activities themselves. A typical example of active participation is a community show, where local people act, dance, sing, make costumes and even direct and market the show. Passive participation refers to audience members who may be highly engaged and loyal, but prefer to spectate rather than take part. There is also a significant group of consumers who just want to turn up and be entertained. It should be noted that the majority of arts and entertainment consumers are passive participants. Organisations which strive to increase loyalty through active participation must therefore be wary of alienating people who are happy to leave the art to the artists.

In any case, for the reasons highlighted above, involving audiences in the creative process is a highly controversial proposition, and this is why it is an important contemporary issue in the arts and entertainment industry. It could even be argued that creative interaction is a passing trend, and certainly the recent debate on excellence initiated by Sir Brian McMaster in the arts seems to have tipped the funding agenda back towards quality from its recent focus on inclusion. Many artists, writers, directors, producers, choreographers and filmmakers still fervently believe in the product-led model and advocate an audience-focused over an audience-led approach. They argue that they are the professionals and that funders and audiences should therefore trust them and give them the time and space to create work of the highest quality.

Audience development

The arts and entertainment industry can be divided into two main sectors: commercial and non-profit. While both these sectors face the constant challenge of growing their audience base, non-profit organisations generally have quite specific demands placed on them to reach out to new and diverse groups. There are several reasons for this. One of the main drivers of audience development is the fact that many art forms are subsidised by taxpayers, especially in European cultures. In the UK, they are funded via local councils and through the national Arts Councils, quangos of the Department of Culture, Media and Sport (DCMS). So the general public has the right to feel a sense of ownership of subsidised music, opera, dance, theatre and visual art. The problem is that the majority of the population still don't take part in these activities, and there remain significant barriers to attendance, both financial and psychological, which are still putting people off attending artistic events.

Another reason why funders are increasingly encouraging the general public to take part in the arts is because research has clearly established direct links between participation in the arts (both active and passive) and improved health, wellbeing and community or social capital. The personal and social value of the arts and entertainment will be discussed in detail in Chapter 6, but the link between tangible benefits and audience development initiatives is an important one in this context, which is currently shaping local and national government agendas.

The audience experience: changing roles and relationships

So far, we have explored how arts and entertainment organisations can better connect with their guests to deliver more memorable and sensational experiences. But before organisations can truly unpack the changing roles and relationships that are shaping the audience experience, it is essential to understand what relevance the term 'experience' has within the sector.

Individuals experience many things on a daily basis in the course of their work lives, home lives, interests and hobbies. For centuries, arts and culture have been built on creating an experience that consumers will want to engage with. This engagement takes place on many levels: physical, social, intellectual, emotional, sensual and even spiritual. It is infinitely complex, rich and multi-dimensional.

Audience development, co-creation, audience engagement, participation, public engagement (or whatever the favoured term may be) are increasingly becoming part and parcel of creating a great arts experience. However, none of these approaches will work unless the whole organisation is committed to putting the audience at the heart of the experience.

There is much debate at the moment about co-creation and audience development and it is important to consider these different processes separately in order to understand the way roles and relationships with audiences can form and evolve.

Co-creation, audience development or wanting a day out?

Co-creation is one of the most in-depth ways an audience member can engage with an organisation. Louise Govier (2009: 3) describes co-creation as follows:

> For me, this means working with our audiences (both existing and new) to create something together: it could be meaning or interpretation; a space or exhibition; an online resource or collective response – there are many possibilities. I prefer 'co-creation' to 'co-production', as the former implies slightly more openness about where the collaborative journey might take all of the participants: rather than producing something that may be relatively defined, we are creating something new.

Co-creation, however, is a process – it does not automatically turn an organisation into being audience-focused. It certainly opens the doors of trust and collaboration and develops a deeper relationship with some audience members.

But it is only one way of doing this and it is important to reiterate here that not every audience member wants to be so actively or heavily involved.

Nowadays, it almost seems that any form of interaction is labelled 'co-creation' and many important questions remain about co-creation: is co-creation merely the exchange of any value or should we stick to the idea of end users pooling their intellectual and creative assets in pursuit of a common goal? What is the reality behind the so-called best practices? Are these merely a cosmetic make-over of the traditional suggestion box? Do audiences really become part of a collective creative process? Are organisations genuinely ready and prepared to deliver their part of the co-creative bargain?

The philosophy of audience development seems to demand a less intensive commitment from the audience member. Arts Council England (2010) defines audience development as '[t]he activity which is undertaken specifically to meet the needs of existing and potential audiences and to help arts organisa-tions to develop on-going relationships with audiences. It can include aspects of marketing, commissioning, programming, education, customer care and distribution.' This definition gets closer to identifying how audience develop-ment needs to be at the heart of creating the experience when it concludes that: 'As an ethos audience development places the audience at the heart of every-thing the organisation does.' This widens the challenge for arts and entertain-ment organisations to commit to being truly audience-focused by ensuring that every touch point in a visitor's experience is exceptional.

Finally, let's not forget the audience groups who don't distinguish between active and passive participation – they don't think about the creative process, they are not highly engaged, not loyal to any particular venue or organisa-tion, but are simply looking for a good night out. Their approach to cultural engagement is no less valuable but adds a purely social layer to the audience experiences.

Managing all these layers of engagement is challenging in a world where audi-ences are consumers, opinion-makers and creators of art. However, both the co-creation and audience development approaches enable audience members to decide how they want to experience the cultural product on their own terms. Both approaches ultimately require strong leadership from the organisation; an understanding of audiences' motivations and reasons for connecting in the first place; and the creation of opportunities to allow audiences to control their depth of engagement in the cultural experience.

Leading the change

The importance of leadership in cultural organisations is explored further in Chapter 11, but it is important to note here that the role of leadership in successful co-creation and audience development is vital. Educational, outreach and learning departments are often seen as the functions which participate most directly with their audiences. But there are many rewards to be gained by leaders taking a fundamental risk by approaching audience development as a holistic, company-wide ethos. Audience development is often seen as a challenging task that is under-estimated and under-resourced, and regarded as a cost rather than an investment. Worse, it is sometimes even regarded as a set of short-term publicity tactics rather than a long-term strategy to achieve fundamental artistic, financial or social objectives. This commitment from leadership is not an easy task because successful audience development requires a delicate combination of relationship building, skills development, leading by example and openness.

The challenges of changing these perceptions and creating a new generation of cultural leaders open to embracing the differing patterns of audience engagement are being met in a number of ways. As early as 2003, arts consultants Morton Smyth rolled out a programme called Not for the Likes of You. This programme reviewed how cultural organisations could become more accessible to a broader audience by changing their overall positioning and message, rather than just by implementing targeted audience development schemes or projects. It championed the development of a holistic approach to building relationships with audiences, starting from the top of the organisation and obtaining buy-in from everyone else within it.

In developing the programme, Morton Smyth worked with 32 organisations from across the cultural sector at a variety of levels, but always including, and led by, the chief executive. Having chief executives involved was absolutely key in changing the way organisations engaged with their audiences and developed meaningful experiences and relationships. The next stage of the programme focused on harnessing the skills and understanding of every team member from the cleaner to box office manager, curator to outreach co-ordinator, to achieve a truly memorable experience for the audience.

More recently, &Co, Yorkshire's cultural marketing agency, has been working on a cultural leadership programme project called 'Audience Influencers'. This has involved working with seven Yorkshire-based organisations that have either recently been through, or are currently going through, capital redevelopments. The participating organisations are focusing on a number of key management issues, such as financial models; governance; stakeholder engagement; programme diversity and audience engagement; buildings and operations management; and brand perceptions. The programme is distinctive because it approaches each of these issues with audience engagement as a key influence and its ultimate aim is to support a group of cultural leaders to develop as 'audience influencers', committed to focusing all areas of their organisations on impactful relationships with audiences.

Understandably, in advocating for true audience engagement, there is often concern from organisations about relinquishing control. According to Nadine Andrews of Culture Probe, who has evaluated many participatory museum projects: 'True co-production probably hasn't been attempted … the big issue is the control of meaning and how prepared museums are – or individuals within museums – to give up control …. A lot of museums haven't had the internal conversation as to what co-production means to them. There may be individuals who have that aspiration but lack strategic support from the organisation as a whole' (quoted in Mulhearn, 2008: 22).

Both of the examples above illustrate how ensuring that the audience experience is exceptional has to be a vision that everyone commits to and is a part of. It needs to start with a clear vision by the leader at the top about what makes the audience experience exceptional; it also needs to be supported by ongoing research with the audiences at the end of the consumer journey; and finally this intelligence and understanding needs to be shared across the whole organisation in order to create a truly audience-focused organisation.

Walking in your audiences' shoes

To truly understand the audience experience – from the first encounter right through to how it evolves into a loyal and inspiring relationship – research is absolutely essential. Many arts and entertainment organisations understand the power of audience research in helping to identify new audiences, inform what creates an excellent experience, and in some cases even determine what art or experience gets created in the first place. However, some organisations continue to develop their artistic processes and experiences internally and just hope that the audience will come. In these cases, the cultural conversation is more of a monologue and the art or experience is sometimes presented with no true engagement or understanding about the audience or visitor experience that brings it to life.

Research does not have to be expensive. The Sandwich Glass Museum in Cape Cod, USA, gets one of its staff members to pose as a tourist in its car park, asking people leaving the museum if it's worth a visit. This gives the museum first-hand insight into the experiences that their visitors have just had; getting the organisation out of the building and into the shoes and minds of their visitors. What is probably most significant about audience and visitor research is how it helps to develop an understanding about the relationship they want to have with the organisation, which will differ in many ways. As we have seen, some audience members want to be up close and personal, co-creating the work or participating behind the scenes. They want to feel part of the community. Other audience members just want a fun night out. Neither is wrong – but successful organisations need to understand which audiences want what type of experience in order to truly fulfil their expectations. And if you don't ask, how can you possibly know?

Levels of engagement

Understanding your audiences and consumers is the starting point for any successful engagement, and this involves empathising with the barriers they face in engaging with your offer as well as appreciating what motivates them. In *Culture, Class, Distinction*, Bennett (2009) explores the crossover between class and cultural engagement in great detail. Informed by over 200 in-depth interviews, this extensive mapping of British cultural practices and preferences provides a fascinating insight into the role of class in cultural engagement. Building on the work of Bourdieu, Bennett's research frequently refers to 'legitimate culture' (such as classical music and visual art), perhaps more commonly portrayed as 'high art' as opposed to 'popular culture'. This terminology raises an important point for arts and entertainment organisations to consider: the boundaries of artistic creation, engagement and communication are blurring and organisations can therefore no longer restrict their focus to what has previously been considered 'legitimate' culture.

Chan and Goldthorpe's (2007) work offers an interesting alternative to understanding cultural engagement by dividing cultural consumers into four groups: Univores, Omnivores, Paucivores and Inactives. In discussing the findings of their research, the authors claim they are 'unable to identify any numerically significant group of cultural consumers whose consumption is essentially confined to high cultural forms and who reject, or at least do not participate in, more popular forms' (Chan and Goldthorpe, 2007: 375). They also note that status counts rather than class, and that status is defined by income rather than culture: 'Status is now attached to material consumption, not cultural consumption. People with status show who they are through expensive cars and houses rather than by going to museums and the like'. They conclude that people are 'self-excluded' rather than 'socially excluded' from culture.

Whichever camp you take, it seems that cultural experience is subjective and legitimate to each individual and should not be judged by any organisation. In fact, in the digital world, our traditional understanding of participation and engagement continues to be challenged. More and more 'producers' of art and entertainment are creating it in their own homes and engaging and partici-pating in quite an isolated, but fulfilling way to them. Indeed Arts Council England (2009) has even assigned a whole new segment to this group, referring to them as 'Bedroom DJs'. According to Arts Council England, Bedroom DJs express low levels of interest in the arts and do not currently attend any arts event. Instead, they engage with the arts by actively taking part in creative activities. The most popular activities among this group include computer art and animation, playing a musical instrument, painting and drawing, writing music, stories or poetry and dancing. Many of these activities are typically soli-tary and home-based.

Expert versus participant in the creative process

Andrew Keen's book *The Cult of the Amateur* explores some similar chal-lenges organisations face in becoming facilitators rather than gatekeepers of the cultural experience. With the rise of participation on Web 2.0, arts and entertainment organisations need to consider the impact of opening up their process and experience for public consumption and interaction. The ultimate endeavour may always remain the creation of great art and experiences, but with the flood of amateur, user-generated free content, we must ask ourselves what the repercussions will be on quality and artistic integrity.

It is not about devaluing what is created by amateurs and people wanting to engage in the creation of art and entertainment, but it is about the need to recognise that there is a skill in creating great art. Keen (2007) argues that we live in a 'self-broadcasting culture' which blurs the distinction between trained experts and uninformed amateurs. So in an era when anyone, unconstrained by professional standards or editorial filters, can present themselves as crea-tors of art, it is important that arts and cultural organisations continue to place value on the artistic direction and skill that is required to produce a cultural product that leads to a meaningful experience.

Creating the superlative visitor experience

Simon (2010) argues that museum professionals need to focus on encouraging audience participation by creating an excellent visitor experience rather than promoting audience development or education. She notes that there is a lot to learn in this regard from performing arts organisations. One such example is York Theatre Royal, which recently developed its TakeOver Festival.

Case study 1: York Theatre Royal's TakeOver Festival

TakeOver Festival grew from the Labour Government-funded initiative 'A Night Less Ordinary' (ANLO), which distributed grants through Arts Council England enabling theatres to offer free tickets to under-26s. In order to engage with ANLO's intended market as deeply as possible, York Theatre Royal decided to do something different. The theatre was already dedicated to working with young people through its large youth theatre programme. It was already selling £5 tickets to under-25s and had a vibrant outreach programme. But the TakeOver Festival took audience participation and co-creation to another level.

TakeOver was not only a first for York, but a groundbreaking festival for the theatre industry. With over 50 under-26-year-olds involved in the running of the theatre, this model had never been tried anywhere else in the country. TakeOver provided young people with the opportunity to work in a professional environment, supported by the staff of the theatre. The festival engaged audiences that wanted to take their relationship and role in the theatre to the next level – many going on to secure professional arts roles after the festival. However, it also had a huge impact for York Theatre Royal in building their under-26 audience.

Belt Up Theatre, which programmed some of the work in the festival, has now been granted an 18-month residency at York Theatre Royal. As one of Belt Up's founding directors, Jethro Compton, reflected: 'TakeOver '09 has been all about taking a massive risk to try out something that could transform York Theatre Royal and make it an accessible venue to a wider demographic' (Compton, 2010). Of course this example takes co-creation to the extreme, with audiences joining forces with professionals not just in the development of the artistic product itself but also across all the back office functions of the organisation.

Case study 2: The Big Picture

Another case study illustrating the role of co-creation in developing audience engagement is The Big Picture project, which took place in Birmingham in 2008. This was a project funded by Arts Council England West Midlands, supported by the BBC and managed by Audiences Central. The aim of the project was to inspire and encourage people in the Midlands to engage with

and experience art at a local and personal level, by taking, using, viewing and manipulating photographs. It was specifically designed to increase arts attendance and participation amongst people from the lower socio-economic groups in the region.

The project invited the general public to submit photographs to create a snapshot of the region and become part of an ambitious world record attempt. A winning photograph was chosen and then a huge mosaic of the winning image measuring 30 × 30 metres was created from the 112,896 submitted images and displayed outside the Think Tank Museum in Birmingham. All participants were given a Guinness Book of Records Certificate and during the project, 547,134 people from the West Midlands attended galleries involved in the project including Ikon and Birmingham Museum and Art Gallery, driving up attendance significantly.

The Big Picture, 2008, © Audiences Central 2011

Conclusion

Ultimately the audience experience can range from passive engagement through to co-creation of the product itself. Neither of these sits in isolation and neither is less valuable than the other. As we have seen, successful arts and cultural organisations embrace the opportunity to work with their audiences on whatever level they want to and offer different and varied points of engagement.

The role and relationship that audiences have with culture, arts and entertainment will continue to evolve. Creating a memorable and shared experience involves a two-way dialogue between professional creative teams on one side and their audiences, consumers and visitors on the other; a co-created experience goes one step further and unites these two sides under a common goal.

The key point here is that contemporary arts and entertainment organisations need to think not just about developing their audiences, but about listening, engaging, and opening up a variety of avenues to their audiences, so that everyone involved has an unforgettable experience. Everyone is the architect of their own experience, and at some stage in the creative relationship, responsibility and control have to be shared or handed over.

References

Alcoa (1942) 'The place they do Imagineering'. *Time*, 16 February, p.59.

Arts Council England (2009) 'Bedroom DJs', London, Arts Council. Available from: http://www.artscouncil.org.uk/about-us/research/arts-based-segmentation-research/13-segments/bedroom-djs, accessed 1 June 2010.

Arts Council England (2010) 'Audience development and marketing', London, Arts Council. Available from: http://www.artscouncil.org.uk/information-sheet/audience-development-and-marketing-grants-for-the-arts, accessed 2 June 2010.

Bennett, T. (2009) *Culture, Class, Distinction*, London: Routledge.

Butler, P.D. (2000) 'By popular demand: marketing the arts', *Journal of Marketing Management*, 16 (4), 343–364.

Chan, T.W. and Goldthorpe, J.H. (2007) 'The social stratification of cultural consumption: some policy implications of a research project', *Cultural Trends*, 16 (4), 373–384.

Clague, M. (2004) 'Playing in 'toon: Walt Disney's "Fantasia" (1940) and the imagineering of classical music', *American Music*, 22 (1), 91–109.

Compton, J. (2010) 'TakeOver Evaluation Study 2010'. York: Belt-Up Theatre.

Govier, L. (2009) 'Leaders in co-creation: why and how museums could develop their co-creative practice with the public, building on ideas from the performing arts and other non-museum organisations', Leicester, University of Leicester. Available from: http://www.le.ac.uk/ms/research/Reports/Louise%20Govier%20-%20Clore%20Research%20-%20Leaders%20in%20Co-Creation.pdf, accessed 2 June 2010.

Imagineering Academy (2010) 'What is imagineering?', Breda, the Netherlands: Imagineering Academy. Available from: http://www.imagineeringacademy.nl/what_is_imagineering, accessed 8 April 2010.

Keen, A. (2007) *The Cult of the Amateur: How Today's Internet is Killing our Culture and Assaulting our Economy*, London: Nicholas Brealey.

Mulhearn, D. (2008) 'Joint accounts: asking for input from members of the public seems like a good idea in principle, but it is often quite a delicate process', *Museums Journal*, 108 (9), 22–25.

Musolife.com (2010) 'Scottish Opera plans opera for babies', Musolife.com. Available from: http://www.musolife.com/scottish-opera-plans-opera-for-babies.html, accessed 13 April 2010.

Pine, B.J. and Gilmore, J.H. (1999) *The Experience Economy: Work is Theatre and Every Business a Stage*, Boston, MA: Harvard Business School.

Simon, N. (2010) *The Participatory Museum*, Santa Cruz, CA : Museum 2.0.

Further reading and research

Bourdieu, P. (1986) *Distinction: A Social Critique of the Judgement of Taste*, London: Routledge and Kegan Paul.

Chan, T.W. (ed.) (2010) *Social Status and Cultural Consumption*, Cambridge: Cambridge University Press.

Hench, J. and Van Pelt, P. (2009) *Designing Disney: Imagineering and the Art of the Show*, New York: Disney Editions.

Imagineering Academy website: http://www.imagineeringacademy.nl/what_is_imagineering

Leadbetter, C. (2008) *We-think: Mass Innovation, not Mass Production: The Power of Mass Creativity*, London: Profile.

McMaster, B. (2008) 'Supporting excellence in the arts: from measurement to judgement', research report for DCMS. Available from: http://www.culture.gov.uk/images/publications/supportingexcellenceinthearts.pdf

Pitts, S.E. (2005) 'What makes an audience? Investigating the roles and experiences of listeners at a chamber music festival', *Music and Letters*, **86** (2), 257–269.

Websites of featured organisations

Contact Theatre: http://www.contact-theatre.org/whats-on/categories/get-involved.htm

http://museumtwo.blogspot.com/

http://suchtweetsorrow.com/

Tate Modern: http://www.tate.org.uk/modern/tatetracks/yourtatetrack/

http://www.andco.uk.com/

http://www.audiencescentral.co.uk/

http://www.beltuptheatre.com/

http://www.takeoverfestival.co.uk/

http://www.yorktheatreroyal.co.uk/

2 The 21st Century Business Model

Ben Walmsley

Introduction

> The art of organization is not to create organizations but to multiply our effectiveness.
>
> (Reiner, quoted in: Byrnes, 2009: 155)

In the opening chapter, we saw how relationships between producers and audiences are undergoing a fundamental shift, with audiences becoming increasingly more involved in the creative process. In this chapter, we will move on to consider the repercussions of this phenomenon by exploring how traditional business models are evolving in the arts and entertainment industry. To achieve this, we will focus in depth on two very different sectors: popular music and the performing arts.

We will start by defining the term 'business model' itself, as it is a term which incorporates many elements and which is therefore often confused with related terms and concepts such as 'strategy' and 'structure'. We will then apply these business concepts to the popular music and performing arts sectors and consider the range of existing and emerging models across these diverse industries. By deconstructing concepts of value and audience engagement, we will explore how modern arts and entertainment organisations are adapting their business models for the 21st century. Finally, a case study on Watershed will illustrate both the process and the benefits of transforming a business model to meet modern audiences' needs.

What is a business model?

A business model can be regarded as a series of relationships participating in the creation of value (Rayport and Sviokla, 1995) and therefore as the engine and framework of a business which informs all of its activities (Falk and Sheppard, 2006). Effective business models should therefore maximise value (usually by minimising costs and generating income as efficiently as possible) and provide a holistic and effective structure to the day-to-day processes of business. Most importantly, they should reflect the drivers and values of their customers. This is what distinguishes a modern, marketing-orientated business model from the traditional production or sales-driven models.

Business models in the arts and entertainment industry

The correct interpretation of the concept of 'value' is imperative within the context of the arts and entertainment industry. In a purely commercial context, value creation is indelibly linked with profit: commercial organisations exist to create wealth for their owners, partners and/or shareholders and achieve this by maximising their profit margins. But in the non-profit, public sector and more product-led industries, value is much more subjective and therefore harder to define. In education, for example, it might be linked simplistically to a quantitative assessment of exam results, whereas a more holistic and qualitative approach might consider factors such as students' wellbeing and even transformation. But in any sector of any industry, value creation should refer back to an organisation's fundamental mission. So in the arts and entertainment industry, if an organisation's mission is to 'delight and surprise audiences' rather than to maximise profit, then value will be created (and hopefully judged) by the impact a product, event or service has on the people who engage with it.

From a marketing perspective, an effective business model should address and add tangible customer value to each of the four Ps of the marketing mix: the product, price, place and promotion. Let's now take each of these in turn and apply them to the music industry to illustrate how emerging business models have transformed the customer experience while maintaining or even generating addition revenue for the industry as a whole.

Popular music

First of all, new and emerging business models have fundamentally transformed the core product in multiple ways. What was a physical, collectable product packaged and delivered in a glossy sleeve with song lyrics and branded artwork (a CD) has become a digital, transferrable product which populates the playlist of a laptop, iPod or other mobile device. This product transformation has enabled a rigid pricing structure (the £10+ CD album and the £3.99 CD single) to morph into a flexible and cheaper pay-per-track strategy with tighter profit margins and a reduced augmented product. Apart from cheaper products, consumers have also benefited from greater choice and control, as they are no longer forced to purchase any supplementary tracks against their will.

Place and promotion have been similarly transformed. Before legal downloads and illegal file-sharing graced the scene, consumers were bombarded with mass market sales and advertising campaigns on television and radio, on billboards and buses, in newspapers and magazines and in-store. They were obliged to commute to their nearest town, track down their CD in an over-spilling rack in a crowded record store, and finally queue at the till to pay. As click-and-mortar models emerged, consumers were slowly able to order online and wait for the CD to drop through the letterbox a few days later.

Nowadays, consumers have been re-branded as fans. They communicate with each other online via blogs and dedicated fan sites, participate in online competitions to win free downloads and receive intelligent recommendations for new bands and songs they might like, based on previous purchases and their general musical tastes. A good example of this is iTunes' Genius, which suggests future purchases and builds automatic playlists based on customers' current libraries.

Interestingly, the record store is also making a comeback as an experiential alternative to the online models. Fans young and old can don a pair of DJ-style headphones and sample their favourite tracks, before chatting to an 'expert' vendor and finally bagging a CD together with the latest accessory merchandise. So what we are left with is a complex, multi-platform model, where legal competes with illegal, physical with digital, mass with customised and efficient with experiential. But the competition is between companies and business models: the net result for music fans is a convenient range of affordable options, catering for their varying budgets, demographics and moods.

The problem with these new models is that they have arguably tipped the balance too far in favour of the fans, leaving even the biggest record labels fighting for survival and the former gatekeepers of the industry scrapping over rapidly diminishing profits. This might not be so much of a problem if it only affected the intermediaries or middlemen. But illegal downloading and ever tighter margins have affected the industry as a whole, making it difficult for new and emerging bands to enter the market and challenging even the most established. According to the International Federation of the Phonographic Industry (IFPI), global music sales peaked in 1995 at US$48 billion and by 2005 had fallen by a third (Connolly and Krueger, 2006). Artists, producers and business experts have even gone as far as to sound the death knell for the entire industry.

In the 21st century, artists have slowly started to respond to this threat. According to Alanis Morissette's manager, Scott Welch, only the top 10 per cent of artists make a living from selling records; the rest go out on tour (Connolly and Krueger, 2006). This increasing necessity to tour has become known as the Bowie Theory, after Davie Bowie's prediction that recorded music would become a commodity just like any other. So for the majority of artists, the core product has shifted from the record itself towards the live performance of it; and for fans, saturated with virtual and digital products, this live experience has become increasingly rare and coveted. It is therefore perhaps no coincidence that leading global artists such as The Black Eyed Peas, Lady Gaga and Rihanna are becoming increasingly theatrical in their performance styles and that in another, albeit less cited, example of convergence, music and theatre are blurring their traditional boundaries and morphing closer together.

But there are challenges with the business model even in the live performance sector. Live performance is a slow productivity growth industry with relatively rigid fixed costs. This means that efficiency gains are hard to come by, as it takes the same number of people about the same amount of time to stage a concert today as it did 30 years ago. To increase profit margins, therefore, bands have to either tour more often, tour for longer, play bigger venues or increase ticket prices. According to Connolly and Krueger (2006), what most bands are doing is raising ticket prices; and because attendance at concerts has been steadily decreasing in the past four decades, they have taken a 10 per cent hit on their tour revenues since 2000 alone. Another challenge is that the popular music industry is heavily skewed in favour of celebrity bands, with the result that a small minority of the most popular bands earn a large proportion of the available revenue.

Bands' responses to these challenges and to the threats posed by illegal file sharing have been diverse and creative, and some innovative new business models are slowly starting to emerge. A good example of this is the pay-what-you-like model initiated by the English band Radiohead. In 2007, when their contract with EMI expired, Radiohead chose to release their seventh studio album independently via their own website, inviting consumers to pay what they felt appropriate. This model has since been much imitated, with a significant number of artists releasing their work for free in collaboration with media partners. The results have been mixed. Revenue has generally suffered, but this has on occasion been compensated for by positive PR, which has led to increased popularity on the tour and festival scenes.

Another emerging model is the aggregator model. Aggregators are digital distribution agencies, who negotiate national and global licensing deals and sell their clients' music via online and mobile channels. In the UK, the leading aggregators include Emu Bands, 7 Digital Media, Consolidated Independent, Indie Mobile and Artists Without A Label. As this last name indicates, aggregators are starting to replace established music companies and labels, representing new and emerging artists who would otherwise find it difficult to break into the market. Within this model, there are different micro models at play: while some aggregators take an annual subscription and grant artists 100 per cent royalties from their sales, others take an agreed cut of royalties.

Again, aggregators are having mixed levels of success depending on the platforms they specialise in. For example, they are struggling to make money in the lucrative ringtone market, where the big labels are dealing directly with wireless carriers. But in the blogosphere, music blog aggregators such as The Hype Machine have successfully harnessed RSS technology to track and display the latest blogs on their home pages, making it easier for fans to keep up to date with the latest industry knowledge and news.

Product placement, endorsement and brand affiliation are other successful alternative models. Product placement in the music industry has been around for decades and it can work in one of two ways. In the first model, artists include and therefore endorse products in their songs, usually in return for payment. The most famous recent example of this model at play is probably hip-hop artist Busta Rhymes' song *Pass the Courvoisier*, which radically increased the cognac company's short-term sales and led to a further deal. Industry experts anticipate that in the very near future, brands will be funding the entire production costs of an album. The second model works the other way round, with agents and managers placing their artists' work in films, television dramas and soap operas. A simple version of this is of course the old-fashioned film track, which often breathes future life into flagging song and album sales, or complements a current marketing campaign.

Brand affiliation is an extended version of product placement and is a more reciprocal model. The model works by matching an artist or album with a product according to their respective brand values and image. This is generally a harder proposition than a straightforward product placement, but when it does work it can reinforce both brands and widen their appeal. A recent success story here is Bacardi's deal with Groove Armada, whereby Bacardi agreed to fund the band's new releases in return for using their tracks and live performances to promote its brand. The main problems with these types of model are their dependence on other models to sustain them (no band has yet survived from this kind of deal alone) and potentially the loss of artistic control inherent to a band being temporarily 'bought' by a commercial enterprise with its own mission and agenda.

One of the most radical and innovative approaches to the challenges facing the industry is Bandstocks. As the name suggests, Bandstocks works by offering fans the opportunity to invest in the bands of the future. Founded by Andrew Lewis and supported by the teams behind Kaiser Chiefs and Primal Scream, it works like this: fans buy stocks in new bands or artists in increments of £10, and once the investment fund has reached a certain level, the money is released to the artist(s) so they can record an album. The model basically works as a venture capital fund invested in by fans. In return for their investment, fans receive a copy of the album and a percentage share of its profits, together with benefits such as priority booking for concerts and access to special editions. The benefit for artists is that they enjoy a higher royalty than with the major record labels and have more control over copyright and licensing. They also develop a strong core fan base, who literally have a vested interest in their success and who are likely therefore to become vocal and effective ambassadors for them.

The performing arts

The performing arts sector has its own, very different challenges. One of the strengths (and arguably weaknesses) of this sector is that its products cannot be digitised without losing their essential characteristic – the live experience that they offer. For this reason, the sector has not been forced to transform its business model in the way the music industry has. Instead, performing arts organisations have been able to adapt more gradually to the demands of modern audiences. But this process has inevitably left some organisations behind; and while the flexible and mobile music industry has been able to emigrate online, the performing arts sector, with its fixed, historical buildings, has had to work with what it's got. So if we repeat the exercise of mapping changes to the performing arts sector's business model against the four Ps, this picture of gradual change starts to emerge. This is illustrated in Table 2.1.

It can be seen here that the major impact of evolving business models in the performing arts sector has fallen on the place element of the marketing mix – i.e. where productions are paid for and enjoyed. Unlike in the music industry, the core product itself has remained intact and there has been no significant impact on price. Again, this is a both a strength and a weakness for the sector – a strength because its core product has remained competitive, withstood the technology revolution and been able to maintain its income base; but a weakness because little value has been added to organisations or audiences.

Table 2.1: Impact of evolving performing arts business models on the marketing mix

Element of the marketing mix	Impact of evolving business models
Product	Minimal change to the core product but increasing focus on audience involvement and interactivity
	Emergence of new and development of existing augmented products (e.g. online rehearsal footage; CDs and DVDs of live performances)
Price	No major impact on price
Place	The digital box office: online ticketing and seat selection
	Increasing popularity of live streamed events (e.g. National Theatre's plays and New York's Metropolitan Opera productions)
	Development of site-specific, site-sensitive and open air performances
	Emergence of visionary venues which open up the creative process (see Chapter 7)
	Rise in performing arts festivals
Promotion	Online trailers and e-marketing techniques
	Blogs, tweets and audience reviews

Let's now consider how and why business models are evolving in the sector. The structure of the performing arts sector is extremely complex. It has developed organically over centuries and is characterised by piecemeal strategy, financial instability and artistic inter-dependence. Traditional models in the sector include subsidised producing and receiving theatres and concert halls; commercial producing venues; commercial receiving venues and chains; and producing touring companies. But there is increasing evidence of evolution, with innovative models such as Artsadmin's producer model and the national touring models championed by the National Theatre of Scotland and National Theatre Wales attracting increasing attention. There are also signs of a newfound strategic integration and commercialism, as evidenced by Royal Opera House's diversification into the DVD market through its recent acquisition of Opus Arte.

The wider socio-political context is also impacting on the way the sector operates. It has been argued that there are currently too many under-funded arts organisations operating close to breaking point both financially and operationally; and as there is insufficient evidence to measure and evaluate the impact of the arts, it is difficult to determine whether public money is being spent wisely (Knell, 2005). With the recent cuts in government funding to the arts in the UK, this situation is unlikely to get any easier. Knell (2005) argues that the current portfolio of arts organisations in the UK is too fixed and that the funding system favours existing companies over new entrants. In other words, there are significant barriers to entry. Because arts organisations compete against one another for funding, there is no strategic overview of the sector, which might promote more collaborations, mergers and acquisitions. In the commercial sector, these beasts of necessity often provide the only means of survival.

Knell's solution to this problem is that organisations should learn 'the art of dying'. Those that survive need to reorganise or merge and focus on their strategic mission rather than on struggling to survive. The sector needs to engage in an open and honest debate about the future of arts funding and design effective business models for the 21st century. Arts organisations must stop being defensive and become more flexible, better networked and more commercial in their models and practice (Knell, 2005). More efficient models could include sharing back-office functions and production facilities, for example, with savings being used to free up artists to do what they do best.

But these transformations will not happen overnight:

> This strategic shift requires radical intent. It requires leaders of arts organisations to commit to radically different conceptions of how they might operate, and to accept that one of their primary leadership responsibilities is to make their organisations more adaptive. As in other sectors, this means embracing a vision of organisations as more mobile and fluid and less tied to an unshared fixed cost base. This demands partnering with others in more imaginative ways, whether with the private sector or through emerging public interest company type vehicles, and embracing new operational models which are more dependent on networking and collaboration.

(Knell, 2005: 8)

Some of the emerging models discussed above have responded to this call to arms – Artsadmin has been providing producing and administrative support for artists and arts organisations since 1979, freeing them from the burden of budgets and red tape to create the best work they can; and in the past few years, flagship national companies like the National Theatre of Scotland and National Theatre Wales have rejected the static, building-based model in favour of a collaborative, mobile, fluid and even online approach. This model has succeeded in reducing their fixed cost base (there are no expensive venues to design, construct and maintain) and in bringing theatre to the people through imaginative partnerships and artistic collaborations. Models such as these have finally found a way to add value to both the organisation and the audience.

Adding value

At the beginning of the chapter, we noted that the overriding aim of a good business model is to maximise value. We also discussed how in the arts and entertainment industry, value can be a subjective concept that is often hard to define and concluded that the only objective way to measure value is therefore to measure it against an organisation's mission statement. A business model should provide the link between an organisation's mission and the value it aims to create. For as Magretta (2002: 92) points out: 'Because a business model tells a good story, it can be used to get everyone in the organization aligned around the kind of value the company wants to create'. In this section, we are going to consider how and where value can be created in the arts and entertainment industry.

In the wider world of commerce, the way an organisation configures its resources and activities to create value and competitive advantage is often illustrated via a framework known as a value chain. Value chains are usually applied to manufacturing based organisations and therefore focus predominantly on commercial and product-based activities such as procurement, logistics and operations. But there have been attempts to apply the framework to the arts and entertainment industry, as illustrated in Figure 2.1.

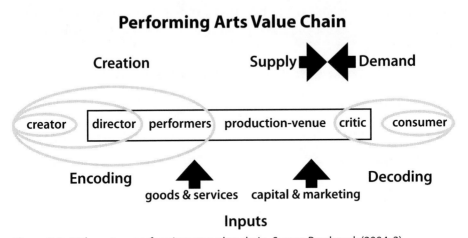

Figure 2.1: 20th century performing arts value chain. *Source*: Brecknock (2004: 2)

This simple framework illustrates the supply chain or creative process for the performing arts sector. It presents a traditional approach, where the work of art emanates from the 'creator' (e.g. playwright or composer), is 'encoded' (shaped and nuanced) by the director through the performers and produced by the venue or company, before being 'decoded' (interpreted and judged) by the critic and consumed by the audience.

The main purpose of the value chain is to pinpoint where value is being created or lost, and this works in one of two ways. First, an organisation can add value by excelling in any of the processes described above. So, for example, it could rest on the laurels of an excellent composer or blow the audience away through stunning production values (an amazing set, for example). Second, it can add value in a holistic way by excelling at the process itself. This will involve excellent communication between different teams (creative, production and marketing, for example) and the implementation of appropriate systems and structures so that the entire process works like a well-oiled machine. This can only be achieved through training, strong leadership and passionate, experienced staff.

However, considering the discussion in the previous chapter about the changing relationship between producers and audiences, cracks start to emerge in the value chain depicted above. For example, writers, composers and choreographers no longer always create a piece of art in isolation: they may work with or be influenced by audiences or other social groups; or the work might be devised by a collaborative group of artists, including the performers themselves. Furthermore, audiences no longer 'consume' the performing arts in isolation: they may engage with the creative team and process by attending rehearsals or post-show discussions; and they may share and shape their views via social media. Taking these changes into account, the 21st century performing arts value chain might actually look something closer to the one illustrated in Figure 2.2 .

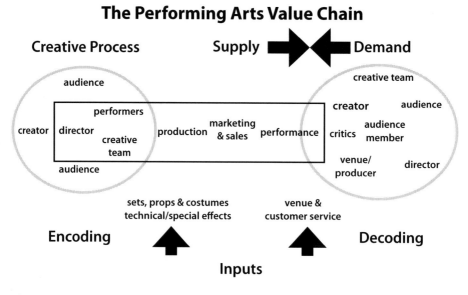

Figure 2.2: 21st century performing arts value chain

Figure 2.2 illustrates a new value chain for the performing arts. It represents a messier, more complex system of encoding and decoding by reflecting the more collaborative creative process adopted by many modern arts organisations and the more democratic, interconnected consumption experience engaged in by modern producers, critics and audiences. Most significantly, this creative process has become more of a network of dialogues – between critics and audiences (via blogs, for example); between producers and audiences (via post-show events and Twitter, maybe); between critics, creators and creative teams; and between audience members themselves. The modern performing arts organisation can add value at each stage of the chain by supporting, facilitating and enhancing these processes; and, as discussed, they can excel by designing a business model that masters the value chain itself.

But the value chain is only part of a larger entity known as 'the value network', which has been defined as 'the set of inter-organisational links and relationships that are necessary to create a product or service' (Johnson *et al.*, 2009: 77). In the performing arts sector, this might include the design agency which produces the print, the set builders, or even the actors and venue itself. For a touring company, the value network is particularly important, as touring shows are heavily reliant on the size, reputation, marketing, sales and customer service of the venues they tour to.

Case study: Watershed

Watershed is a cross-art-form producer, which shares, develops and showcases exemplary cultural ideas and talent. Curating ideas, spaces and talent, Watershed enables artistic visions and creative collaborations to flourish. Watershed is rooted in Bristol but places no boundaries on its imagination or desire to connect with artists and audiences in the wider world.

In 1998, Watershed was a traditional arts centre with two cinema screens, a photography gallery, an education department and a café/bar. In 1999, Watershed hooked up to high speed broadband for the first time. This was initially just an experiment to see what it could achieve by embracing new technology. This experiment soon made Watershed realise that its world was about to change, and since this digital road to Damascus, technology has pushed Watershed into spaces it wouldn't normally have entered.

As technology is always changing, it is constantly pushing Watershed to innovate. For example, Watershed realised that many projects required a great deal of new material to be produced and shown outside the creative programme. This was continually creating new relationships and the staff team soon realised that they had to engage with these new relationships, get to know the people behind them and determine their relationship to Watershed. This new, closer relationship with the audience soon led the staff to ask themselves the following questions:

- Who are we?
- What is Watershed?
- What does Watershed mean and stand for?
- What does 'media centre' mean?
- What does 'art' mean?

According to Watershed's Managing Director, Dick Penny: 'Mixing it all up is important, but just as the soup becomes richer, an organisation's role in it becomes increasingly complex' (Penny, 2009: 49). In Watershed's case, this led to the realisation that its building (converted in 1982) was no longer fit for purpose. Watershed decided that although it had built its reputation on film and photography exhibition, they now needed to drop photography to focus on the moving image and digital work, which reflected 'the inevitability of its growing importance' (Penny, 2009: 50). Watershed wasn't just refurbished, but significantly changed. In the process, it also learned to be more open and honest in its communications with audiences and its other stakeholders.

Its refurbishment and new identity pushed Watershed to become a more joined-up organisation, and it quickly realised that everything had to be dedicated towards creating a learning environment. In Dick's own words:

> We understood that we were not just making and selling products, but offering an experience. As part of the capital project the public space in the building was flooded with free wireless, which transformed the spaces. Suddenly the social space became an active space where people did business, where people were not consuming, but getting active.

(Penny, 2009: 51)

Over the last decade, Watershed has transformed itself from a traditional arts centre which specialised in film and photography exhibitions to an interconnected creative space in which audiences feel a sense of ownership. Watershed's audience has transformed from a passive group of consumers to an active group of engagers and its core consumer product has morphed into a genuine experience. In a nutshell, Watershed has handed over ownership of its building to its audiences in the true sense of co-creation.

As a learning organisation, Watershed acknowledges that it has not reached the end of its journey, and its team is constantly asking itself how it can keep

Image by Toby Farrow, courtesy of Watershed

renewing and developing its relationships. Watershed has realised on its journey that the organisation is all about providing spaces where 'things can happen'. This means physical spaces, intellectual spaces and virtual spaces. Watershed believes that the arts' main role is to bring people together to create fresh conversations and encourage new thinking; and the important word here is *people*: technology is a great enabler, but human beings are people who like to get excited (Penny, 2009).

Conclusion

In this chapter, we have seen how the traditional business models of arts and entertainment organisations are evolving and, in some cases, transforming. This is largely due to changing relationships between audiences or consumers and producers. But it is also influenced by rapid developments in technology.

We noted at the beginning of the chapter that effective business models should maximise value, and by critiquing and updating existing models of the value chain, we have explored how arts and entertainment organisations are able to achieve this in the 21st century world of fast and cheap technology, active engagement and the hunger for genuine experiences. By focusing in depth on two different sectors of the arts and entertainment industry, namely music and the performing arts, we have also analysed how effective business models can add tangible value to the entire marketing mix. At the same time, we have seen how some sectors of the industry (like music) have been revolutionised, while others (like the performing arts) have largely remained intact.

The case study on Watershed illustrated how on some occasions, a business model can be turned on its head. Watershed's journey highlights the courage it takes to become a genuine learning and listening organisation, which is brave enough to relinquish creative control and open up its spaces to its audiences.

References

Brecknock, R. (2004) 'Creative capital: creative industries in the creative city', report prepared for Brecknock Consulting, www.brecknockconsulting.com.au.

Byrnes, W.J. (2009) *Management and the Arts*, 4th edn, Oxford: Elsevier.

Connolly, M. and Krueger, A.B. (2006) 'Rockonomics: the economics of popular music', *Handbook on the Economics of Art and Culture*, **1**, 667–719.

Falk, J.H. and Sheppard, B. (2006) *Thriving in the Knowledge Age: New Business Models for Museums and Other Cultural Institutions*, Oxford: Rowman and Littlefield Publishers.

Johnson, G., Scholes, K. and Whittington, R. (2009) *Fundamentals of Strategy*, Harlow: Financial Times Prentice Hall.

Knell, J. (2005) 'The art of dying', available from http://www.scribd.com/doc/23974643/Art-of-Dying-John-Knell-2005

Magretta, J. (2002) 'Why business models matter', *Harvard Business Review*, **80** (5), 86–92.

Penny, D. (2009) 'Imagine an arts sector which works collaboratively to deliver excellence and engage the public', in: *Proceedings of the Arts Marketing Association Conference*, 21–23 July 2009, London: Arts Marketing Association, pp. 48–53.

Rayport, J.F. and Sviokla, J.J. (1995) 'Exploiting the virtual value chain', *Harvard Business Review*, **73** (6), 75–85.

Further reading and research

Fox, M. (2004) 'E-commerce business models for the music industry', *Popular Music and Society*, **2**, 201–220.

Vaccaro, V.L. and Cohn, D.Y. (2004) 'The evolution of business models and marketing strategies in the music industry', *International Journal on Media Management*, **6** (1 & 2), 46–58.

Websites of featured organisations

http://www.artsadmin.co.uk

http://www.nationaltheatrescotland.com

http://nationaltheatrewales.org

http://www.roh.org.uk

http://www.watershed.co.uk

3 The Funding Agenda: Social relations and the politics of cultural production

James Oliver

At best, a policy focus on individualism might be defended as being consistent with libertarian ideals of individual freedom, autonomy and self-determination; at worst, it can be seen as leading to an exploitative, materialistic and uncaring society.

(Throsby, 2001: 138)

The crucial development in the recent period has been the ideological de-legitimization of state intervention and public-sector arts and media. They persist but with an uncertain and poorly defended rationale. Even where they persist, however, their operations are reconfigured increasingly by market reasoning so that publicly funded organizations must behave like private businesses, hereby further undercutting their own legitimacy.

(McGuigan, 2004: 59)

The key words, to repeat, are complex, ambivalent and contested.

(Hesmondhalgh, 2007: 17)

Figure 3.1: Promotional shot for Polyglot's production *Muckheap*

Image by Gavin D. Andrew, courtesy of Polyglot Theatre

Introduction

Are the arts, so to speak, on the 'muckheap' of public spending? From the point of view of an arts activist, or any advocate of public spending on the arts, particularly in times of austerity, it can certainly appear that arts funding is lobbed out of the window at the first opportunity. At best, it appears that many in the arts sector are expected to feed off the scraps of funding from the residue of public spending. There is a certain 'sink or swim' attitude that prevails, where the environment of the liquid (or not so liquid) marketplace is deemed the ultimate arbiter of value.

However, and despite the protestations of some who may espouse a more Darwinian economic model, making art (whatever the quality) and making money (or should that be making a profit?) are not always going to be in the same trajectory. Sure, at one extreme, some commercial contexts of the creative arts and entertainment industry make some people very rich (and can often employ very many people), but that does not mean that productions will turn a profit or that companies will not go out of business, even if they make millionaires and stars out of individuals. The point being, a market-driven privatisation of individual talent, skills and product can have negative effects for the wider ecology of a company or sector.

For the everyday arts company or practitioner, the economics is much smaller in scale than that of the celebrity industry; nevertheless, sustainability is as key a concern. Sustainability is the watchword, then, which is why systematic business models are keenly sought out within the sector (see www.mission-modelsmoney.org.uk). The point of this chapter, though, is not to provide such a model but to point out that such models are themselves subject to more systemic economic and political conditions, and crucially, social relations. Traditionally, public funds have been a key issue, not just in broadening the scope and range of access and participation (including the training of artists), but also of sector sustainability, under the broad rubric of public good. And therein lies the conundrum: what does 'public good' actually come to mean?

Public good has basically become a rationalised question of value rather than responsibility (we will come back to this point); and, particularly, it has become a question of use value, frequently reduced to economic value and impact. This understanding of public good has been a challenge for public spending on the arts, or at least has helped to keep the status of the arts low (or lower) in a hierarchy of public spending commitments. As the McGuigan quotation at the beginning of the chapter suggests, in terms of government intervention, the relative economic success story of the creative industries (at the commodity extreme of the arts and creativity sector) has also helped to undermine public spending on the arts. In these conditions, populist and normative economic discourse does not readily distinguish between the contexts of labour and space-intensive art with low or zero profits (such as theatre) and the high economic turnover and profits available from cultural 'products' that are highly reproducible through technology (cf. Benjamin, 2008), and through the exploitation of intellectual property (such as music, film, software and even books), particularly in the digital age of interaction.

So, if your understanding of the arts is of a sector primarily concerned with producing content that can be turned into a commodity (a sellable product), then economic value is possibly all that really matters to you; cultural value is secondary. In these conditions, the space for diversity in creative and artistic expression (expressions of human potential and imagination) is reduced. The real danger here is that social and cultural references become more self-referential, and empathies across diversity become narrower. Is this a desirable outcome in terms of public good? This becomes an instrumental argument for the arts, where if the conditions for diversity are removed, an economy and society becomes more homogeneous and self-referential, and then, the very conditions for creativity, the intrinsic worth of the arts, become stifled.

But this is not to suggest that there is no room for improvisation or adaptation in the arts sector, or that there can be no arts sector without public funding. To take a situational analysis (see Chapter 6), it is much more dialectical than that. A key factor in a situational analysis is that conditions are situated, socially embedded and relational (and therefore dialectical). It is important to take as full an appreciation of the context of political, economic and cultural conditions (or situation) as possible; particularly across normative dualisms or dichotomies such as public versus private value, instrumental versus intrinsic value, and, for that matter, economic versus cultural value. In sum, all of this informs our negotiation of public good and value, because these values are embedded in the social relations which reproduce them and which then inform our practice of, and engagement with, debates and processes of funding.

The question becomes: 'What is sustainable in terms of promoting creativity and developing arts practice?' As noted above, if the politico-economic conditions limit the sharing of creative and cultural experiences, becoming narrower and more self-referential, then there is a relational decrease in the public space for cultural expression. For sustainability, then, the debate and terms of engagement cannot just be about economics in the narrow sense of metric value. There needs to be a commitment to sustainable funding of the arts and cultural sector that does not ultimately devalue the very conditions for creativity that we seek to nourish and express ourselves with, or seek solace or entertainment through. How that ultimately happens will depend on the prevailing conditions and debates in a given society, so we should be careful of being too polarised in our perceptions and opinions, or in seeking one-size fits all answers (such as the 'the market') or practices (such as activism or advocacy). These are all driven by human interest, and in some cases, ideology, and are no less or more flexible than each other but dependent on forms of governance and embedded in social relations.

In order to prevent the reproduction of inequalities and power dynamics, it is not enough to just consider and analyse the context of our conditions (or situation); we need to creatively engage with it, even adapt for change. As noted, some of this discussion resonates with the discussion in Chapter 6, to the extent that it is an introduction to a 'situational' question of 'value', and a similar, broadly 'political economy' and critical perspective (cf. Hesmondhalgh, 2007). But, to briefly refer to the writing of an influential cultural economist, in terms of what we should not be trying to do (and to assert what this chapter is not):

> Although it may be tempting to economists within the confines of a fully articulated economic model, to claim that the economic value of a cultural good gives a complete account of both its economic and its cultural worth, thereby making a separate measure of cultural value redundant, it has to be remembered that the economic model itself is limited in its reach and specific in its coverage.
>
> (Throsby, 2001: 1659)

In short, this chapter is a provocation to consider more political questions of how the arts are positioned and embedded in society, which they are, and no less so than economic 'realities' are. In emphasising the value of this exhortation, epistemologically, there will obviously be limitations to what this chapter can achieve; nevertheless, a brief historical overview follows below, along with some discussion of the policy dimension. Further reading is recommended at the end of the chapter, particularly in relation to cultural policy, the creative industries and the economics of the arts sector.

Public spending and cultural policy

As David Hesmondhalgh (2007: 83) describes, for the 'advanced' capitalist economies of Europe, North America and Australasia, the period from the 1950s to the early 1970s was one of 'steady economic growth'. But then there was the Long Downturn: 'The era of slowed or reduced growth in the global economy, following the supposed Golden Age of growth in the post Second World War period. The Long Downturn is usually taken to have begun in 1973 and ended, (perhaps temporarily) in the mid-1990s' (Hesmondhalgh, 2007: 312).

It is fair to suggest that this era ushered in what is now described as a neo-liberal era, as distinct from the industrial capitalist era, particularly in the West. But the period also had globalising consequences, particularly through the internationalising of unregulated markets and the emphasis on pure economic value. And, not inconsequentially, the attendant oil crisis of 1973 at the start of the Long Downturn refocused the geo-political attention of the West in a manner that still influences the public spending of the state today (not least through military spending). As neo-liberal politics took hold, particularly through the Thatcher and Regan administrations – but also continued with parties that were ostensibly of the Left, with social democratic leanings, such as the Labour Party in the UK – the public sector became increasingly 'managerial' in practice, ushering in an audit culture and bottom-line agenda; all in the name of efficiency and transparency. With such efficiency drives comes the ubiquitous opportunity to cut costs – as opposed to enhancing or expanding public services and their delivery. In a managerial culture, the opportunity for career civil servants and politicians to get ahead is practically irresistible. Furthermore, when there are enormous strategic international alliances and commitments made to the global-military complex, there is also enormous pressure to appear to be spending what 'little' money there is wisely; so it is not a good idea for careerists to get caught up in complex debates that they may care little for, such as the value of art in society versus the value of a community hospital or local school.

Nevertheless, it is fair to say that public spending has become so tightly administered that any suggestion that the arts live off public handouts is to not take the public funding process or the arts very seriously. I have been cautious up to this point not to use the word 'subsidy', which is how public funding for the arts, with all good intention, is often argued for. For example, economists use the term 'cost disease' in the arts, also known as Baumol's Law (see Towse, 2010: 10–12), to describe the problem of rising production costs over time. If such costs are passed on to the consumer then there is the risk of reduced participation (and profit), or even an 'artistic deficit'. Part of the whole point of Baumol's Law is based on the fairly standard social welfare argument in economics: that is, the utilitarian argument of justifying state intervention in terms of the greatest good for the greatest number. So an economic case for subsidy of the arts is made. Nevertheless, subsidy is a subtly pejorative term along the lines of the insidious suggestion that public spending is subsidising the public who pay taxes (although this is increasingly how governments imagine public spending, to surprisingly little protest).

So, there is a more complex ecology at play if we are willing to reformulate our thinking towards sustainability and not short-term savings or gains. Effectively, the current ecology between the arts and public funding is along the lines of the public sector seeks to make short-term savings (based on fixed budget cycles) and it offers the arts short-term gains through limited project-based funding (often aligned with government priorities). With that comes an insecurity that is not compatible with the sustainable practices or outcomes, whether financial, social or artistic, championed by influential practitioners and commentators such as McMaster (2008). This lack of sustainability needs to be recognised and understood within its context – it is embedded in social relations and therefore requires a situational perspective and analysis (see Chapter 6).

To return to the neo-liberal paradigm shift, cultural policy has clearly not been immune, particularly in relation to the increasingly heavy emphasis in our 'knowledge society' on the ubiquitous rhetoric of creativity:

> [T]he sheer pervasiveness of creativity discourse as a liquid synonym for dynamism, growth, talent formation and national renewal is quite remarkable. … In economic and political terms, our funding and our public validation come from being seen to meet increasingly refined performance indicators. … There is, furthermore, increasing official emphasis on how we might help public agencies, commerce, business and industry, and the 'third sector' of voluntary and charitable bodies, to operate knowledgeably in democratic society. … this is a necessity-driven, demand-led model.
>
> (Schlesinger, 2009)

This rise to prominence of the creative industries model in defining much of the approach to cultural policy is based on wealth and job creation – the normative value of an economic approach – incorporating the commodification of cultural products, particularly through intellectual property and copyright, and deploying technological reproduction and interaction, increasingly digital and new media. The consequence of such developments has been to brand as 'creative' and 'innovative' such organisations or individuals that can exploit the market consumer. This should encourage reflection on the way we might see arts funding in relation to society, its social conditions and relations.

The arts are not unique here in terms of public spending: the same de-funding is happening in the higher education sector, possibly because both sectors have been positioned as commodities within the 'knowledge economy'. Here they have a shared experience of fewer opportunities for job security and an increased emphasis on outputs that can be measured, so there is a project and performance-based form of funding (applied to research activity in the case of education, which, like the arts, is often expected to be 'applied' and aligned with government priorities). In the knowledge economy, if you want a secure teaching post, it will depend on whether students will pay your wages. So in practice, courses and opportunities for public engagement will disappear, and through market principles, cultural knowledge and experience will narrow – as discussed above for the arts. But it is not that difficult an equation: if public spending reduces (to reduce public debt) then public engagement will be limited, and probably elitist – i.e. for those who can afford to take part in civil society, including the arts and education. This almost sounds undemocratic.

Whatever public money goes into the arts is therefore fought very hard over in a competitive environment and often comes with substantial non-artistic commitments to be met and measured. This has been particularly true in the UK, where there has been a strong tradition of public funding that has withered to such an extent that much public spending is now tied to instrumental crossovers with wider public policy. However, this is not always a negative thing in that public spending has reduced across all sectors, and it is no bad thing that the arts have been brought into more and more policy contexts. So, in effect, arts money goes towards enhancing the social and cultural dimensions of schools, hospitals, communities and public spaces, and therefore towards artists' visions and wages. In recent times in the UK, there was a relative boon for the arts due to successive New Labour governments (1997–2010) and their distinct policy programmes focusing on social inclusion and urban and community regeneration projects that afforded a wide use of the arts and cultural engagements, albeit as an instrumental focus for the arts to earn their crust if they wanted public funds. But in the face of a change of government and the global financial crisis, we are thrust further into a period of neo-liberal governance, complete with its efficiency drives and spending cuts that focus on making the arts pay their way.

In this seemingly interminable process of perennial cuts in public spending, what would happen if there were no public funding of the arts at all? Is this even possible? And if money talks, what is it telling us, and what does that really mean?

Friction and cultural production

Is it possible that there is no such thing as public funding of the arts? Adapting Raymond Williams (1981), David Hesmondhalgh (2007: 9) refers to the contemporary era as the 'complex professional era of cultural production' and he explains that he uses the term as a 'heuristic device to describe the whole era of cultural production from the 1950s onward, but in fact it refers to a mix of different forms' (ibid.: 55). His point is that there is increasing complexity in the mode of cultural production, and modes of production dominant in previous eras are not completely displaced by new modes – they can remain as part of the socio-economic dynamic, as it were, and are able to adapt in certain ways, or conditions persist that enable them to. The previous dominant eras referred to (see Hesmondhalgh, 2007: 53–55; Williams, 1981: 38–56) are:

♦ th epatronage and artisanal era, where artists were retained by elites, and skilled craftspeople sold goods directly to buyers, dominant from the Middle Ages to the early 19th century;

♦ the market professional era, where artistic works became increasingly for public sale and organised by 'the market' and often sold through distributors or 'productive intermediaries', i.e. publishers, dominant from the 19th century;

♦ the complex professional era, where increasing numbers of people are employed through cultural companies (which could tangentially include the establishment of arts councils and the arm's-length principle in the UK). This period is characterised by the shift towards new technology and the rise of advertising since the 1950s, and effectively describes the era of the cultural and creative industries.

With a prevailing practice and ideology of public sector spending cuts across much of Europe, North America and Australasia in order to curb national, public debt (despite the advice of luminaries such as Joseph Stiglitz, Nobel Prize winner and former Chief Economist of the World Bank), the arts are, for the foreseeable future, facing extremely uncertain times. They have arguably never been in such a precarious position. Whilst some organisations and programmes will inevitably cease to exist, I am not so sure that the so-called 'consumer' will disappear: the public will still spend money on the arts, whether there is public funding of the arts or not. Above, I noted that public good has basically become a rationalised question of economic value rather than responsibility. Part of what this means is that responsibility is disaggregated (and abrogated) by government and shifted to the individual in society – the taxpayer, the consumer, the citizen, all at once – to obtain public services or goods as modelled on the demand-led economy of the market. This is part of the 'complex professional era' in which democracy, public services and tax-paying are also implicated.

I am not sure when I first purchased a lottery ticket, but I can remember with great clarity the general public interest and media attention (and not a little razzamatazz) when the National Lottery first began in the UK in 1995. Since that time, the Lottery has accumulated some £25 billion for its Good Cause fund. These monies are gathered into the National Lottery Distribution Fund (NLDF) and the Olympic Lottery Distribution Fund (OLDF), administered by the Department of Culture, Media and Sport (DCMS), who then pass on the monies to independent National Lottery Distribution Bodies (NLDBs). If nothing else, the acronyms certainly hint at the level of managerialism that now influences public governance and bureaucracy. Nevertheless, in effect the lottery functions as an indirect tax, where on top of state taxes that its players already pay on their incomes and rising value added tax, the usefulness of the 'game' is rationalised by its potential of providing direct individual benefits of extreme wealth (that is not directly taxable). But the odds are stacked even more extremely against an individual player winning a top prize.

However, probably everyone in the UK has in some way derived some benefit, perhaps small and indirect, from the redistribution of National Lottery funds, and this is through its Good Causes mechanism. This is so because amongst the NLDBs mentioned above are in fact the various UK arts councils and other community, heritage and sports bodies. This form of privatised tax collection is just one mode of cultural production that has subtly emerged in the UK (for example, the London Olympics will be part funded by the Lottery, as well as the millions of tax pounds already committed). More recently, the coalition government in the UK is currently emphasising further individual respon-sibility by promoting philanthropy (or old school patronage) for the arts. By themselves, none of these things are inherently wrong; but in practice, rich people get tax breaks for donating to the cultural production that they value and wish to support (and reproduce), whilst poorer people get to pay tax, buy a lottery ticket and keep their fingers crossed that the benefits of the Lottery might filter down to their community.

The anthropologist Anna Tsing writes of the importance of understanding exploitation and creative labour as simultaneous; and she refers to the concept of 'historical experience' to describe the 'subjective labor [sic] of the marginal-ized and displaced, which fuels narratives of capital and nation yet falls beyond these narratives' scope of explanation' (Tsing, 2005: 270). Or, in other words, the suggested self-evident 'truth' of the value of the nation and/or free-market, and therefore their inevitability in terms of power across social relations, can be quite inadequate in terms of accounting for the sometimes miserable conse-quences of such social relations where inequities in the lived experience of marginalised or displaced individuals emerge, including in relation to social and cultural practices, aspirations and community sustainability.

You may well be wondering what Tsing's ethnography (on the forests of Indonesia) has to do with the funding of the arts. But her concept of 'friction' is very useful for cutting through the dichotomies and dualisms that we can be prone to fall into and reproduce, and instead to emphasise the social dialectic or dialogue. Simply put, if arts funding is a question of cultural policy, it is also symbiotic with the nation and the market, and embedded in social relations; this has been the thrust of the discussion so far. Therefore, I introduce the concept of 'friction' not to emphasise an inhibiting or hidden force within social structures, such as political or economic; nor to ennoble ideological clashes as if diametrically oppositional and exclusive (e.g. society and the individual); but as a reflection on the mutuality and generative interface inherent in social relations, within societies and economies.

What is implied is that the cultural, political and economic are embedded in the social, and further inform social relations, and that these are not by any means determined, fixed or absolute. In brief, another way of contextualising this would be that because of social diversity, mobility and contact, the market and its emphasis on consumption is not inherently disposed towards equity and diversity, any more than public funding with an emphasis on social welfare and inclusion will guarantee an audience for the arts or than the arts will not exclude or stigmatise. In other words again, both the market and public policy (inter alia) are the products and reproducers of social relations, and, therefore, cultural, political and economic relations. So, in the context of the arts, the generative or creative friction of social relations that situate an arts organisation or artist in terms of their practice and at a broader community context, informs the artistic and financial success of an artist or arts organisation, rather than it being abjectly subject to a set formula of public or private funding. Nevertheless, this is not to dissociate public policy from negatively affecting the arts (as we have already addressed above).

Furthermore, at a macro level, there needs to be a settlement that gives space to a creative friction of social relations, including the balance between private and public good, resting in a mission of social and cultural sustainability that is not centred on belligerent rhetoric on the pros or cons of economic subsidy (the word itself being inappropriate). This discussion, then, emphasises the importance and relevance of a situational perspective on funding, emphasising the relevance of social relations, in as holistic, relational and reflexive a manner as possible (notwithstanding whatever contextual constraints will inevitably apply). This perspective is not devised to exclude others (indeed it fundamentally should not, hence the value in the metaphor of friction), when narrower, technical solutions and quick-fix toolkits are often the order of the day in the business world, including making an arts business or practice sustainable.

As Schlesinger (2009) points out: 'whether advocating creative cities, cultural clusters, bohemian and industrial quarters, skills development, quotas, tax breaks, global branding or niche marketing – the recipes (and the cooks – aka the consultants) abound to help governments and nations in their quest for global economic success'.

I have no pretension to being one of the cooks; nevertheless, I do not suggest that in the everyday practice of the arts, people should ignore more banal issues of economic or technical relevance, such as how to pay bills, develop audiences or actually produce creative content and experiences. This has been more of a reflexive 'call-to-arms' to recognise the underlying creative friction in cultural production, and, crucially, to centre this in the recognition that even the economic is embedded in social relations:

> Neo-liberalism has been in the ascendancy, the assumption being that market mechanisms are the superior means for allocating resources, producing and circulating cultural products, giving the consumer what he or she is said to want. However, customers are also citizens, some of whom may not be entirely satisfied with the prevailing state of affairs.
>
> (McGuigan, 2004: 59)

Case study: Polyglot Theatre

There has been a rise in market-oriented approaches to funding the arts across the globe (particularly through the promotion of the creative industries paradigm), but there is still some commitment to public funding of the arts, for example within the UK, Australia, Canada and in much of Europe, albeit in ever-decreasing sums. For the vast majority of artists and organisations, within the performing and visual arts in particular, while there is this expectation to try and make money (if not a profit), there is also a need to demonstrate public good in order to obtain public funds in the absence of any likely commercial success. Increasingly, as this funding is also based on a project-by-project model, core-funding becomes ever scarcer and risk-averse in a culture of spending cuts. Effectively there is a constant threat of not generating money or of losing a funding stream, including core-funding; in the case of gaining or losing funding, then, an arts organisation has to relate to the situation at hand. This is not due to a passive and inert context of social relations and cultural production but to the inherent creative friction of that situational context (and relational, social dialectic) which is 'complex, ambivalent and contested', to refer back to the Hesmondhalgh quotation at the start of the chapter. So outcomes are not fixed and determined as if in some positive or negative causal manner.

In concluding this chapter, we will now consider the recent experience of an arts organisation within the context of conditions described above. Established in 1978, Polyglot Theatre (previously Polyglot Puppet Theatre) is a small to medium sized arts company with over 30 years of experience in making interactive theatre for and with children. Despite being a dynamic and successful theatre company, Polyglot were set to lose a significant element of their funding (approx 20 per cent of their total income) by the end of 2008, when they would no longer receive the core funding they previously had from their national arts council in Australia. Merely two years later, their Artistic Director and Executive Producer were classified amongst ArtsHub's top ten arts leaders in Australia, largely in recognition of how they had reacted to the situation they had found themselves in.

To use the situational concepts we have introduced in this chapter: Polyglot creatively harnessed the friction evident from their loss of core funding, rearticulating their social relations to alter the economic conditions of their arts practice and cultural production. What happened next has been documented as follows:

> Executive Producer, Simon Abrahams and Artistic Director, Sue Giles set themselves a funding target, built a database, looked to the actual and potential donors they could reach and got all their staff and especially their board involved. Through personalised and active ongoing contact they transformed donations from $1,160 in 2008 to over $80,000 in 2009, far exceeding their original target. The program they developed known as the Ambassadors' Circle, has raised the company's profile, given the company new momentum and well known Melbourne philanthropist Betty Amseden OAM has become its patron.
>
> (Mackrell, 2010)

In addition to this, Polyglot was awarded an Australian Business Arts Foundation (AbaF) award in 2010 for the Ambassadors' Circle giving programme mentioned above (see www.abaf.org.au). They have also increased their turnover dramatically, with projected figures that in a matter of two years represent virtually a 100 per cent increase on their total income from where they were when they lost their core funding. The figures themselves are not the key issue here. First, this clearly displays aspects of adapting a business model for the situation, with a mixed economy approach to income, so there are clear signs of innovation and entrepreneurial action (see Chapter 2).

Figure 3.2 demonstrates the diversity of the company's income streams. But as the quotation above implies, and most importantly (as this is where the economic is embedded), there has been considerable emphasis on human engagement and social relations. This is also demonstrated in Figure 3.3, where the majority of expenditure is shown to be on people, relative to 8 per cent for production and venue costs combined. Of course, this is a very positive story, and that is partly the reason for telling it.

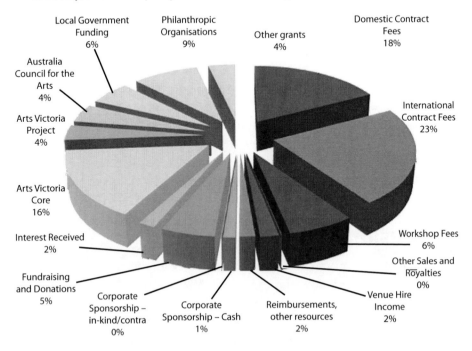

Figure 3.2: Detailed breakdown of Polyglot Theatre's income for 2010

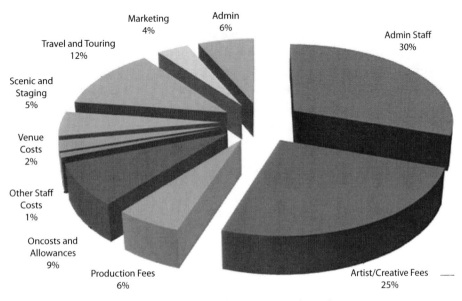

Figure 3.3: Detailed breakdown of Polyglot Theatre's expenditure for 2010

There is perhaps a black and defensive humour at play in the arts when plati-tudes abound that times of austerity are good for the arts, and that in such times creativity flourishes and the best work is produced. Perhaps this is true, but it is also misdirected – it is not because of austerity per se, as in a lack of funds, that creativity abounds. For example, Polyglot increased their income in the aftermath of losing core funding. Whether it is tight financial times or oppressive politics and policies, such examples serve as contexts or situa-tions to highlight social friction over the conditions of social relations. This situational perspective highlights the crucial and creative friction of social relations that inform cultural production and reproduce social relations, in a feedback loop, if you like. We need to engage with and invest in these rela-tions, and in different situations there will be different outcomes – economic, political and cultural; all being embedded in the social. In a sense, Polyglot was thrown on the muckheap but landed somewhere much more organic.

Conclusion

This chapter has been a discussion on the context of funding and the arts, which has directed consideration to the importance of the terms of the debate as much as the content. In particular, it has emphasised a contextual focus on the over-lapping issue of cultural policy – its production and consequences in relation to funding – as a starting point for stimulating critical engagement with broader social relations and practices that inform cultural production (and reproduce social relations).

This is where the value of friction we discussed above comes into play – where the complexity, ambivalence and contested nature of the production of culture and its social relations (in which the economic is always embedded) is potentially a very creative and innovative space of open engagement. In these terms, the 'state of affairs' should not be read backwards as if the end point is somehow self-evident or known, inevitable, or in some way imagined to be complete. In other words, even in the face of desperate situations, social and cultural adaptation is possible as political and economic contexts change and new situations emerge.

References

Benjamin, W. (2008) *The Work of Art in the Age of its Technological Reproducibility and Other Writings on Media*, Cambridge, MA: Belknap Press of Harvard University Press.

Hesmondhalgh, D. (2007) *The Cultural Industries*, 2nd edn, London: Sage.

Mackrell, F. (2010) 'ArtsHub's top Australian arts leaders'. Available from: http://www.artshub.com.au/au/news-article/opinions/arts/artshubs-top-australian-arts-leaders-183057, accessed 10 January 2011.

McGuigan, J. (2004) *Rethinking Cultural Policy*, Maidenhead: Open University Press.

McMaster, B. (2008) 'Supporting excellence in the arts: from measurement to judgement', research report for DCMS. Available from: http://www.culture.gov.uk/images/publications/supportingexcellenceinthearts.pdf

Schlesinger, P. (2009) 'The politics of media and cultural policy', MEDIA@LSE Electronic Working Papers, 17. Available from: http://www2.lse.ac.uk/media@lse/research/mediaWorkingPapers/ewpNumber17.aspx, accessed 8 January 2011.

Throsby, D. (2001) *Economics and Culture*, Cambridge/New York: Cambridge University Press.

Throsby, D. (2010) *The Economics of Cultural Policy*, Cambridge/New York: Cambridge University Press.

Towse, R. (2010) *A Textbook of Cultural Economics*, Cambridge/New York: Cambridge University Press.

Tsing, A. (2005) *Friction: An Ethnography of Global Connection*, Princeton, NJ: Princeton University Press.

Williams, R. (1981) *Culture*, London: Fontana.

Further reading and research

For in-depth historical analysis of the development of the cultural industries and of cultural policy see Hesmondhalgh (2007) and McGuigan (2004); for an overview of cultural economics see Throsby (2001, 2010) and Towse (2010).

Online resources

www.artscouncil.org.uk/publications

www.missionmodelsmoney.org.uk

www.polyglottheatre.com

www.abaf.org.au

www.artshub.com.au

4 Branding the Arts and Entertainment

Daragh O'Reilly

Introduction

Given the extraordinary changes in the global business environment within the past ten years, the pressures on arts and entertainment organisations to adapt are enormous. For example, as we saw in Chapter 2, the digital revolution has brought radical changes to many businesses in the creative and cultural industries, creating significant opportunities and threats for producers. The issues raised by this turbulent environment include intellectual property protection, user-led innovation, new routes to market for producers, celebrity culture, the power of online audience or fan communities, as well as multi-channel and multi-platform marketing – and the growth in the use of branding discourse within the arts and entertainment sector.

This chapter explores the idea of arts and entertainment brands and branding in the context of the sector's turbulent operating environment. Within this context, it continues to investigate the changing relationships between arts and entertainment consumers and producers. To talk of branding in relation to the arts (though less so entertainment) runs the risk of being accused of applying neo-liberal ideology to the sacred, and of daubing the altar of culture with the filthy marks of lucre. However, branding discourse has already penetrated the world of arts and entertainment. Arguably, a better line of resistance is to point to the culturalist idea of brands as signs. When speaking of culture in relation to the arts and entertainment, we are therefore on home territory and able to mobilise a range of constructs and arguments which help to frame a critical view of branding in this area. This chapter attempts this very line of resistance.

The tide of 'brandspeak'

The word 'brand' is now commonplace in popular, journalistic, business, entertainment, everyday and even political parlance, and it is increasingly being applied to the arts and entertainment industry. Branding is said by its proponents to be important for artists, entertainers, provider organisations, media, intermediaries and agents, not forgetting consumers. Brand consultants argue that having a 'strong brand' is necessary if an arts or entertainment organisation wishes to attract and retain the best talent and the best audiences.

But in so far as 'brand-speak' frames its referents as brands, it brings with it connotations of commerciality which may not always be welcome in an arts or entertainment context. Is it appropriate, for example, to use branding terminology to talk about artistic and creative offerings? Is it right to talk of Shakespeare as 'the UK's leading drama brand'? There is an inherent tension in using branding concepts to talk about the more artistic end of the arts and entertainment spectrum in particular. While those on the more commercial side of arts and entertainment (e.g. marketers) may be comfortable talking about art brands and entertainment brands, others (e.g. writers, directors, musicians and choreographers) may, on grounds of artistic integrity or psychological congruence, feel a strong resistance to their work being treated as a 'brand'.

This resistance can no doubt partly be traced back to the long-running tensions between commerce and art which have been so frequently written about. For the sake of argument, I take the King Canute view, namely that there is little point in trying to stop the tide of brandspeak. Instead, by querying the 'nature' of brands from a culturalist point of view, I argue for a much more complex analysis of 'brand' meanings than mainstream branding discourse provides, and offer a series of analytical frameworks which seek to take full account of the production, circulation and consumption of arts and entertainment meanings (or brands).

What is a brand? The mainstream view

From the mainstream commercial perspective, a brand is a range of things, including: a mark of ownership; a differentiating device; something which communicates capability; a symbolic device which enables consumers to express something about themselves; a means by which companies reduce the risk of purchase for consumers; and a kind of symbolic asset. From a strategic marketing point of view, branding is the practice of positioning the offering (functionally, competitively, and culturally), and brand identities are built through integrated marketing communications. Any communicative practice or behaviour contributes to brand-building or brand positioning, including advertising, personal selling, public relations, merchandising, sponsorship, point-of-sale materials, and consumer word-of-mouth. A wide range of terms has been developed to enable branding discourse to have a more diverse application. Key terms include 'brand identity' (the meaning of a brand as projected by an organisation) and 'brand image' (the meaning which is received or made by a consumer or other stakeholder). Other important terms are 'brand equity', 'brand vision', 'brand proposition', 'brand community', 'brand values' and 'brand heritage'. These compound nouns enable branding to incorporate many different aspects of business, such as psychology (image), sociality (community), history (heritage) and capital (equity).

According to mainstream branding thinking, everything is a brand. Therefore, you are a brand, I am a brand, and so are the Angel of the North, BBC News, the Glastonbury Festival, John Rambo, J.K. Rowling and *Pirates of the Caribbean*. Mainstream brand scholars and practitioners assert that the brand is not just the logo;, it is everything which the company or brand owner does, says or owns. In other words, in order to understand the brand of a commercial organisation, one needs to understand its positioning, pricing, promotional communications, product design, people, processes, physical assets and its organisational culture – i.e. the totality of what it stands for, its brand identity. The implications of this are that we cannot know what a company's brand is, what it stands for, what mark it wishes to make in the world, unless we analyse the meaning of all of those constituent parts and somehow calculate their sum.

But, if everything is a brand, branding theory in the arts and entertainment sector needs to be sufficiently flexible to account for a very wide range of elements: thing-brands, people-brands, place-brands, story-brands, event-brands, film-brands, character-brands and so on. Unfortunately, it isn't. People, places, stories, events, films, characters and things are quite different entities. A theory which was originally designed to talk only about things (products) is not so easily adapted to talk about people, places, films and events. Witness for example the ongoing unresolved debate in the place branding literature about how to brand major urban areas, or the absence of a theory on film or music brands. Furthermore, every stakeholder or member of the public has potentially a different viewpoint and image of brand identity. The analytical task of grasping the meanings of a brand is, therefore, a complex one.

Types of arts and entertainment brands

Applying mainstream branding logic, wherein everything is a brand, then the arts and entertainment industry is awash with an extraordinary variety of brands, including artist brands (e.g. Beyoncé Knowles, Stephen King, Nigel Kennedy, Kenneth Branagh, Stephen Fry); arts organisation brands (New Adventures, Tate); content provider/media brands (BBC, Sky, CNN, MySpace, YouTube, MTV); producer/director brands (David Lynch, Jane Campion); intermediary brands (Rick Rubin); event brands (the SXSW, Sundance, and Edinburgh Festivals; the Turner Prize, the Oscars); venue brands (Bayreuth, Globe Theatre, Disneyland), character brands (Harry Potter, Buzz Lightyear, Doctor Who, James Bond) and object brands (the Mona Lisa and Tracey Emin's *Bed*).

Hogwarts Castle at The Wizarding World of Harry Potter, Islands of Adventure Theme Park, Orlando, Florida, USA.

Source: Wikimedia Commons, credit: Michelle Moss

Using the vocabulary of mainstream branding, it is possible to talk about, for example, Damien Hirst's 'brand equity', Madonna's 'brand DNA', the Tate's 'brand values', William Blake's 'brand proposition', Simon Cowell's 'brand vision', Covent Garden's 'brand heritage', the Glyndebourne 'brand community', or Diaghilev's 'brand identity'. It is also conceivable that one could frame

Shakespeare as a 'key brand asset' for the Globe Theatre, the BBC as a 'leading media brand', and the chief executive of any arts organisation as a 'brand advocate' for their 'brand offering'.

Problems applying mainstream branding terms to arts and entertainment brands

If linking brand terminology to the arts and entertainment jars a little in some of these examples, it is arguably because of underlying tensions between the values of brand discourse and those of some art discourses. After all, branding is normally used to help industrialists and grocery multiples sell butter, toilet rolls, and beauty products. It is perhaps a bit much to expect that they can be unproblematically applied to the arts and entertainment sector. People interested in a holistic understanding of arts and entertainment brands need to look at more than just the commercial aspects; those interested only in the business aspects of branding in this industry are in danger of missing the wider cultural dimension. However, it must be acknowledged that the use of brand terminology may be less problematic in more commercial areas of arts and entertainment. For example, one might speak about EMI's or Tristar's 'brand portfolio' or 'brand architecture' without raising too many eyebrows, because these can be more easily seen as commercial organisations.

There are several problems with mainstream branding terminology if applied to the arts. First, to say that something or someone *is* a brand is a discursive move rather than a definitive statement about reality. It means the speaker is choosing to frame his or her account of something by means of branding discourse. By framing something or someone as a brand, the speaker invokes a particular way of speaking, a discursive repertoire, or a lens, which focuses on certain features of a phenomenon and pushes others out of focus.

Second, calling a person, or a piece of art, a 'brand' is regarded by some consumers and commentators as an unhelpful or distorting commodification or commercialisation of elements which should not be for sale. Given that branding discourse has largely been generated by capitalist practitioners and business school academics, it is not surprising that the word 'brand' has acquired strong connotations of commerciality. Because of its commercial provenance, brandspeak is a very blunt instrument in the cultural arena.

Third, branding was originally developed around fast moving consumer goods (FMCG), not arts and entertainment offerings. Despite what some commentators may say, selling breakfast cereals is, generally speaking, not quite the same as selling art. The arts and entertainment industry has far more to offer than FMCG in terms of the symbolic richness of its core offerings and potential experiences.

Fourth, branding discourse is not as good as other discourses – for example film studies, popular music studies, cultural studies – at explaining the possible significance of complex arts and entertainment offerings, which include characters, narratives, artistic conventions, traditions and genres. Much work has been done in cultural studies and other disciplines – popular music and film studies, to take just two examples – which is mostly ignored by mainstream branding and marketing theory.

Finally, brandspeak tends to ignore or tune out political or ideological content, whereas artists and entertainers often address and even celebrate these issues. The relative lack within branding discourse of a discussion about ideology is a major blind spot – a weakness, therefore, in its ability to develop holistic accounts of arts and entertainment offerings.

Challenging mainstream branding ideas

There are two reasons for subjecting branding in the arts and entertainment sectors to cultural critique: first, because brands are cultural entities; and second, because the arts and entertainment industry is built on cultural offerings with rich symbolic content. Marketers tend to regard brands as 'devices', which reveals a managerial, instrumental approach to branding. Media scholars call brands 'media objects' or 'immaterial capital' (Arvidsson, 2006). The first of these metaphors, media objects, makes brands seem like tangible things, which they are not, although they may contain some tangible elements. The second metaphor, immaterial capital, employs a financial perspective within which to frame brands. This sits comfortably alongside other brand terminology which is financially coloured, such as brand assets and brand equity, and also helps to point to the role of capital.

Arguably, brands are more helpfully understood as *meanings* and therefore proper to the domain of cultural studies, from which an alternative view of brands can be developed. This approach treats brands as signs or meanings, and branding as a signifying, or meaning-making, practice. What we mean when we talk about brands is therefore *signs*. Taking this culturalist approach to branding helps to clarify some of the confusion which frequently attends brand discourse.

From a culturalist point of view, then, brands may be read as signs which are exchanged, or *meanings* which are constructed, through the ongoing dialogue and social interaction between and amongst producers, consumers and other stakeholders. Contrary to the notion that brands have a DNA, a kind of central essence and scientific truth, from a socio-cultural point of view, they can be read as socially constructed and negotiated. Commercial branding can after all be viewed as one example of the human tendency to make signs. It is not only major corporations who make signs and meaning: people, audiences, fans, and consumers make signs and meanings all the time, and they do so in particular *contexts*, which must be taken into account in any analysis. As Schroeder and Salzer-Mörling (2005: 1) contend: 'brand culture provides a third leg for brand theory – in conjunction with brand identity and brand image, brand culture provides the necessary cultural, historical and political grounding to understanding branding context'.

I suggest that it is possible, as a matter of discursive choice, to talk of branding in the context of film, radio, comics, music, literature, fine art, dance, sculpture, television and theatre, but only if we also ask ourselves the following questions:

1. In whose interest is branding discourse or terminology being mobilised?

2. Who is speaking to whom through this branding discourse?

3. What are the ideological implications of branding discourse for ways of thinking and talking about these art forms?

If mainstream brand commentators wish to talk about the symbolic positioning or cultural dimensions of brands in a cultural industry like arts and entertainment, then they need to acknowledge and accept that the arts and entertainment context has an artistic, ideological and political dimension.

For the purposes of this chapter, I make a distinction between **b®ands** (essentially commercial products, services or organisations which make no bones about being commercial) and **brands**, which are the less commercial, more cultural offerings. This distinction is not one found in the academic literature, merely a shorthand device for distinguishing between commercial/mainstream (b®and) and artistic/independent (brand) in the following discussion.

A culturalist view of branding

In order to develop a culturalist view of branding, I will draw upon two key constructs: first, the circuit of culture (du Gay *et al.*, 1996); and second, the notion of text. Du Gay *et al.* developed the framework known as 'the circuit of culture', using the case of the Sony Walkman as an illustration. They aimed to show how culture was produced and consumed around consumer goods. The circuit of culture includes five primary processes, namely production, consumption, regulation, representation and identity (although it has to be said that 'identity' is not a word that conveys the notion of process). If one wishes to apply the circuit of culture framework to arts and entertainment brands, then it is necessary to see how meaning is produced, consumed and regulated around arts and entertainment offerings, what representations are made by and about those offerings, and what identities are projected in the process.

A text, on the other hand, is a set of signifiers arranged according to certain codes. This could be the notes in a jazz tune, the textures of a sculpture, the gestures of a dance performance, the colours and forms of a painting, or the words on the page of a crime novel. Hesmondhalgh (2007) has suggested that it makes sense to think of offerings in the cultural and creative industries as texts. This construct privileges the cultural and symbolic character of offerings in arts and entertainment. Indeed all products are always already cultural, in terms of their production process, their properties and their consumption. The text metaphor is widely used in marketing and consumption studies, but very seldom in branding theory.

The Producer–Consumer Circuit

Using the circuit of culture framework as a source of inspiration, the framework in Figure 4.1 The Producer–Consumer Circuit – has been developed to show how brand meanings are constructed amongst two of the primary players in any branding situation: producers and consumers. Note that this is a simplified framework, including a generic producer and a generic consumer. In the real world, there are many more stakeholders in arts and entertainment projects, for example the media, cultural intermediaries and so on, all of which have

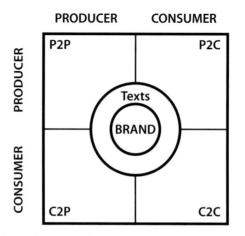

Figure 4.1: The Producer–Consumer Circuit

an influence on the brand, and all of which are involved in creating texts. This greater level of complexity is dealt with later in this chapter.

This simplified model focuses only on the relationship between the producer and the consumer, ignoring other players for the sake of illustration. The P2P quadrant represents the production culture aspect of the circuit, the interaction between those on the production side of the exchange – for example, a rehearsal for a theatre or dance performance, a band on a tour bus or in a recording studio, a writer talking with her editor, and so on. It is these interactions, these meaningful discussions, which shape the eventual offering, the brand. This is also meant to include back-office, off-stage and behind-the-scenes activities of an artistic or commercial kind.

The bottom right-hand quadrant (C2C) represents the consumption culture in the circuit. It covers consumer-to-consumer or fan-to-fan interaction, including meeting in a pub before a gig, discussing a performance at the interval, attending fan conventions, taking part in online discussion forums, a critic writing for prospective audience members, and so on. This is an important site where consumers, fans or audiences make sense of their response to the art and/or artist by sharing opinions and impressions, thus helping to create the meaning of the brand, its reputation.

The top right-hand quadrant (P2C) represents occasions where producers are communicating with consumers. This could be a dance company performing on stage, an opera company's director doing a radio interview, an actor appearing on a talk show, a provider putting up billboards for a Broadway show, or a drummer writing the history of a band.

Finally, in the bottom left-hand quadrant (C2P) is action or talk initiated by fans and directed at the artist. This could include feedback on the artist's website, applause, singing along, booing, shouting 'Encore!', sending fan letters, throwing bottles at the stage and so on.

The top right and bottom left quadrants together (P2C and C2P) are those areas in which production and consumption are articulated, joined together, or connected. All of the activities in these four quadrants produce texts – including sounds, images, movements, gestures, and talk – and these texts, when performed in real time, construct or shape the brand's meanings. When all of these quadrants are put together as part of an analytical study, a holistic sense of the arts or entertainment brand emerges.

Art, brands, commerce

In the arts and entertainment industry, a broad (and overly simple) distinction is often drawn between more mainstream or commercial products on the one side and more independent or artistic offerings on the other, i.e. b®ands and brands. An issue which should be of concern to all artists, whether they believe in art for art's sake or art for money's sake, is the economic survival and success of the project. Consequently, there is usually some discussion of whether an offering has commercial appeal or is primarily of artistic interest with little likelihood of significant financial success. Figure 4.2 attempts to frame this issue.

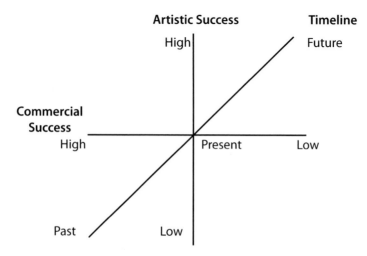

Figure 4.2: The Art–Commerce Issue in Arts and Entertainment

In Figure 4.2 there are three axes: artistic success, commercial success and a timeline. These can be important considerations when discussing an arts or entertainment brand. Commercial success is relatively easily measured by standard measures such as sales volume or value and also by return on investment. Artistic success is more difficult to measure, because this may be argued to depend on short-term critical acclaim or long-term historical reputation, as well as on who precisely is making the judgement and what they consider to be artistic. The time period under consideration is important, as it is sometimes a long time before artistic success emerges at all.

Figure 4.3 opens up another aspect of these issues by placing art and entertainment as contrasting poles on one axis, and by separating mainstream from independent art and entertainment on the other. We must of course acknowledge here the problem with such a marked dichotomy between art and entertainment. The agreed meanings of 'mainstream' and 'independent' may vary over time, so we must be clear about the context and focus of the branding analysis. A work of art which did not entertain, in the sense of giving some kind of pleasure, would be unlikely to endure, being too solemn for all but the highest minds; similarly, entertainment without some dimension of artistry or craft is difficult to imagine. The contrast between mainstream and independent is one which is often used to differentiate between more commercialised offerings and those which purport to have an artistic integrity unsullied by dirty cash.

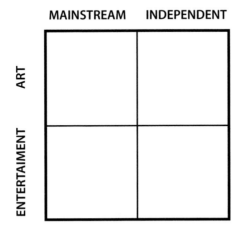

Figure 4.3: Mainstream and Independent Arts and Entertainment

For example, *The X-Factor*, the UK television talent-spotting programme, could be considered as a mainstream entertainment brand (bottom left-hand quadrant), because it is shown on a major commercial television channel, the show achieves high viewing figures, and it is aimed at securing chart success for the winner and others. So also could the James Bond films, because they are product placement vehicles aimed at a young, mainstream audience. Independent art is a term that could be applied to resistant art movements, art-house films, some indie music, some contemporary dance troupes, and so on. Independent entertainment brands could be represented by alternative comedians, although again it is important to be clear about the meaning of alternative. Finally, Damien Hirst could be considered as mainstream art, depending, for example, on what is considered to be art by whom, which particular piece one is thinking of and what view one takes of originality.

The meanings of arts and entertainment offerings are complex

The cultural meanings of arts and entertainment brands can be very complex, and it is beyond the resources of mainstream branding theory to account for them. Figure 4.4 illustrates how a rock band layers its texts to create an intricate interleaving of meanings. To understand a cultural offering fully, we need to understand all these meanings and appreciate their complex interrelationships.

Layer 1	Layer 2	Layer 3	*Market Community Partners Creative News*	Layer 4	Layer 5
				Web site	**Gigs**
				Newsletters	Stage design
			News	Tour	Lighting
		Merchandise		Record News	Instruments
				News Archive	Equipment
Songs	**Cover art/**	T-shirts		Talk	Sound mix
Music	**Sleeve notes**	Sweatshirts	*Creative*		Movement
Lyrics	Artwork	Hoodies		Lyrics	Setlist
Sounds	Text	Hats		Music	Musical
	Lyrics			Art	performance
Visual	Logo	**Musical**			
Images	Photographs	**Product**		Side Projects	**Personal**
Artwork		Vinyl			**Appearance**
Photographs		CD	*Market Community Partners*	Noticeboards	Jewellery
		Concert DVD		Links	Tattoos
		Music DVD		Contact	Piercings
					Clothing
				The Shop	**Merch Booth**
					Musical Product
					Merchandise

Figure 4.4: Layering of Texts

Figure 4.4 shows how the different layers of text and meaning are built up in a band. Starting with the left-hand side of the diagram, the music, sounds and lyrics are then put together with artwork. These elements find their way onto album covers, musical product and merchandise. The website is a key platform for the carrying and presentation of texts (see for example Madonna's video wall). The many texts and their interrelationships (or intertextuality) support the range of complex meanings which an art or entertainment offering can provide.

A contextual framework for arts and entertainment brands

Figure 4.5 is another framework designed to help with the analysis of art brands. It points to the importance of cultural context, of diverse stakeholders, and of the format of the arts or entertainment offering for the understanding of an arts or entertainment brand. If branding, in mainstream discourse, is supposed to be partly about symbolic positioning, then the symbolic meaning of the arts or entertainment brand must be understood in its full symbolic significance.

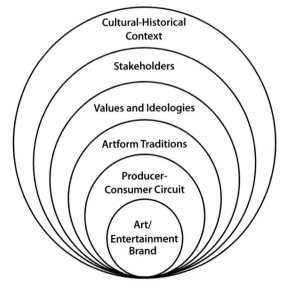

Figure 4.5: Contextual Framework for Arts and Entertainment Brands

The first step in the analysis of an arts or entertainment brand is to understand its cultural-historical context, whether it's English 1960s pop, or 1990s Japanese animation. The analyst then needs to consider who the stakeholders are – producers, consumers, intermediaries, regulators and so on – and understand the nature of their interaction. Through an analysis of the work and the conditions of its production and reception, we can identify the values and ideologies which appear to be in play. The nature of the art form, be it indie music or contemporary ballet, for example, is likely to impose some genre conventions and practices which will help to understand the meanings of the work. The Producer–Consumer Circuit (see Figure 4.1) will help to identify key texts in the interaction between producer and consumer, from which, finally, the principal meanings of the cultural brand can be elicited.

A cultural brands framework

Finally, Figure 4.6 illustrates a cultural brands framework, which is designed to facilitate the cultural analysis of arts and entertainment brands.

At the top left of the diagram, the words 'Cultural context' indicate that all cultural brands should ideally be analysed in the specific context under discussion, whether 1960s Brazilian popular music or Korean new wave films being marketed in China today. The four ellipses on the left-hand side of the diagram are elements adapted from du Gay *et al.*'s circuit of culture. They indicate that meanings are produced, consumed, articulated and regulated in a circuit.

Production involves the encoding of discursive resources (ideas, images, words, sounds) into texts which are communicated and consumed, or decoded for meanings. All texts are about something, i.e. they have *referents*. What the framework proposes is that to be fully understood, cultural brands require the following kind of analysis: Where do artists get their materials (resources)? How do they put them together and present them to audiences? And in what context and under whose scrutiny? These are similar questions that the value chain approach might pose (see Figure 2.2 in Chapter 2).

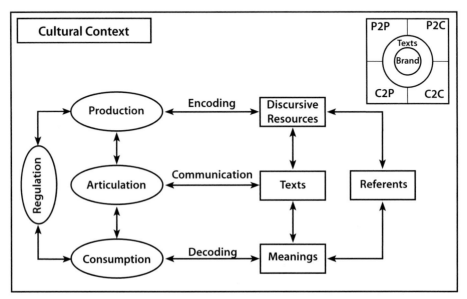

Figure 4.6: Cultural Brands Framework

This section contains two case studies: the James Bond franchise and New Model Army (NMA). The James Bond example is obviously a b®and from the world of commercial film; the NMA example is a cultural brand from the world of independent popular music. The examples have been chosen to illustrate contrasting approaches to branding as they might apply to the arts and entertainment sector.

Case study 1: Film B®ands: The James Bond franchise

In a film project, the different elements of branding can be complex. For example, the producer, director, screenwriter and stars may be regarded as brands in their own right. The male actors who play Bond are usually already celebrities, or certainly become so if their performance is successful. Their status as celebrities means that their images circulate in the global media, making them familiar to many millions of people. The film may include product or service brands, whose presence in the film has been sponsored by commercial brands. The musical score may include songs or tunes which are marketed separately, composed by musicians who are distinctive brands in their own right and sung by well-known artists. Finally, the film itself may be regarded as a product brand in a studio's portfolio or back catalogue.

The James Bond franchise is the longest-running and most successful cultural franchise in film history. Viewing this film series as a commercial property (a b®and), we can see that it is saturated with brands and brand connections. Most of its lead actors have become stars, or celebrity brands; Eon Productions may be regarded as a studio brand; and the Bond films have established themselves as vehicles for significant amounts of product placement capable of reaching large audiences internationally. For example, the most recent film, *Quantum of Solace* (2008) had products placed by Omega, Aston Martin, Sony, Ocean Sky and Ford. Brands are placed according to certain modalities, i.e. they can be seen, spoken about or used in the plot, which requires that they be woven into the production design and screenplay, creating a kind of branded entertainment (Hudson and Hudson, 2006). Sponsoring brands use the films to develop their own co-ordinated marketing campaigns and stories. In fact, an important focus of the pre-launch publicity for the latest Bond movie was the issue of which brands had secured placement in the films. The stars explicitly or implicitly endorse the brands placed in the movies. The Bond films have also generated significant amounts of merchandise, such as toys, video games and books, as well as a touring exhibition. At the same time, the Bond films are cultural texts which carry narratives about an archetypal hero-warrior-magician, who is a spy for the British government. The novels and films may therefore be read for ideological content as well as being showcases for commercial brands.

Daniel Craig (*Quantum of Solace*, New York City premiere, 11 November 2008)
Source: Wikimedia Commons, credit: NY Trotter

Case study 2: Popular music brands: New Model Army

New Model Army (NMA) is a Bradford-based independent rock band which celebrated its 30th anniversary in 2010. The band has released 14 studio and six live albums and is led by original frontman, Justin Sullivan. The band would not wish itself to be called a b©and, nor would this appeal to the fans. This is not what it is about, nor what its fans are looking for from it. To treat NMA solely as a commercial, profit-oriented organisation would be completely to ignore what it stands for and would therefore fail as an analytical approach. However, the word 'brand' is being used in this instance in the culturalist sense explained above. In other words, an analysis of NMA as a brand becomes an analysis of an artistic project which generates a wide range of meanings.

How has this band lasted so long in such a tough business? It was certainly not by virtue of a commercial branding effort. NMA was signed to a couple of record labels for a while, but for most of its life it has operated independently of the musical mainstream. It operates its own record label and recording studio, and uses alternative channels of distribution. Its ethos is broadly left-wing and anti-commercial. The band exists because of its members' sustained interest in music and creative practices over many years, because of the loyalty of its fans, and because of its ability to attract new generations of fans. Its vision is about making music rather than money. The core part of its offering comprises its music and lyrics, together with the band artwork or visual aesthetic.

Of course the band members need to make a living and are therefore engaged with the business side of music. Shows have to be booked with venue promoters; band members have to get a living wage; record production has to be paid for; and records have to be sold. The website needs to be maintained, and touring, recording and sales/promotion and distribution costs need to be met. NMA makes money by charging admission to live gigs and by selling recordings and merchandise. But the band is primarily about its members pursuing their creative musical project. The fact that they do this authentically and have done so for three decades gives them a lasting credibility and appeal to their fans.

To understand the meaning(s) of NMA, we need to understand its name and its historical roots, its political stance, lyrics and artwork, including album covers, paintings, stage design, performances, interviews, reviews, and all of the other texts which are generated between and amongst the band and its fans. The combination of all of these 'texts' provides a rich set of meanings which act as resources for fans in their day-to-day lives.

Concert Photo of New Model Army – Berlin, Kesselhaus, 8 November 2009
Source: Wikimedia Commons, credit: Thomas Huntke

There is space here for only a brief and selective account of the band's identity. Let us take the name 'New Model Army' as a starting point. There is always a story or stories around why bands choose particular names. Back in 1980, when it was founded, NMA was a left-wing band which wanted to distance itself from the dominant Tory ethos and neo-fascist groups. One way to achieve this was to draw upon a tradition of left-wing dissent that had existed in England for hundreds of years, and could claim a legitimate English political heritage as well as a stance of powerful counter-establishment critique. The band's choice of name fell upon the 'New Model Army', which was the name of the anti-monarchist army in the English Civil War. The historical New Model Army was on the parliamentarian, anti-monarchist or republican side. Its military significance was that it was the first professional army in English history, and its political significance was that it was the nearest thing to a revolution that England has ever experienced.

But NMA's historical connections run deeper than the name. There are similarities between NMA and the 17th century ranters, diggers and levellers with their ideologies of protest and resistance in times of division and strife. In fact, in the early 1980s, Justin Sullivan referred to himself for a time as 'Slade the Leveller'. For at least part of their repertoire, NMA come from broadly the same place politically as anarcho-punk group Chumbawamba, and The Levellers. It is worth mentioning also NMA's 'cover version' of the English Romantic poet Shelley's poem *Song to the Men of England*, which is also in this political vein: 'Men of England, wherefore plough/For the Lords who laid you low?/ Wherefore weave with toil and care/The rich robes your tyrants wear?' (Shelley, [1818] 2009).

In interview, Sullivan has asserted that the choice of the band's name was not specifically politically motivated. However, from a marketing point of view, the choice of name is a highly significant choice. First, an 'army' suggests militancy, and NMA have certainly been militant over the years, from the 1980s, when they took stances on issues such as the Falklands War, through the 1984 miners' strike, the anti-roads protest, and, more recently, the Iraq War.

Whereas marketing theory seeks to foster *exchange* relationships, an important part of the ethos of NMA and its fans is the notion of *sharing* and togetherness around the common or shared wealth provided by the musical project. The link to 17th century politics introduces another idea, namely that of the original Commonwealth, or democratic government for the common good. A key element in building the band's relationships with fans was the notion that both are in a community known as the 'Family'. In this way, the band opposed the kind of Thatcherite thinking which holds that 'there is no such thing as society' and created its own social ties around its musical project, helping to sustain and nurture it successfully for three decades.

Apart from these ideas of political protest and community, there are many other meanings which could be explored in the NMA texts – for example, the references to mythology and spirituality in the band's artwork; the band's touring art and artefacts exhibition; the individual band members' side projects; the love of nature and many other themes in the nearly 200 recorded songs; the band's connections with other people in the music business; and the controversies which have attended its work over the years. Without a clear and full understanding of these things, an analysis of the band's meaning is simply not complete, and any claim to have understood its (cultural) 'brand' or meanings must fail.

Conclusion

In this chapter, we have addressed the issue of how branding discourse may or may not be applied in the arts and entertainment industry. My argument has been that it is wrong to apply commercial branding terminology to arts and entertainment brands without carefully considering the cultural context, the social interaction between all the stakeholders, what meanings are generated and understood around the specific artistic or entertainment project, what art-generic conventions apply, and what ideologies and values inform production and consumption practices in the project in question.

'Brand' is simply a narrow, commercially-toned word for what should more correctly be understood as a sign. In the cultural and creative industries, and in the arts and entertainment industry above all, it is the culture, the art, the entertainment practices and their signs (meanings) which must be respected and analysed in cultural terms. If this analytical work is carried out, then generally speaking, the commercial meanings are relativised and made less central and salient, the market is backgrounded, and the most important thing, namely the art or entertainment, retains its central importance. Although some marketing and branding commentators seem to believe that branding *is* culture, there are strong grounds for arguing instead that commerce, including commercial branding, is simply one small part of human culture.

References

Arvidsson, A. (2006) *Brands: Meaning and Value in Media Culture*, London: Routledge.

Du Gay, P., Hall, S., Janes, L. and Mackay, H. (1996) *Doing Cultural Studies: The Story of the Sony Walkman*, London: Sage.

Hesmondhalgh, D. (2007) *The Cultural Industries*, 2nd edn, London: Sage.

Hudson, S. and Hudson, D. (2006) 'Branded entertainment: a new advertising technique or product placement in disguise?', *Journal of Marketing Management*, 2006, **22**, 489–504.

Schroeder, J.E. and Salzer-Mörling, M. (2005) *Brand Culture*, London: Routledge.

Shelley, P. (2009) *Percy Bysshe Shelley: The Major Works*, Oxford: Oxford University Press.

Further reading and research

Aaker, D. (2010) *Building Strong Brands*, New York: Pocket Books.

Arvidsson, A. (2006) *Brands: Meaning and Value in Media Culture*, London: Routledge.

Clifton, R. (2009) *Brands and Branding*, London: Economist Books.

Lash, S. and Lury, C. (2007) *Global Culture Industry: The Mediation of Things*, Cambridge: Polity Press.

Lury, C. (2004) *Brands: The Logos of the Global Economy*, London: Routledge.

5 Intellectual Property in the Digital Age

David Bollier

Introduction

Once a backwater of law that elicited little interest beyond arts and entertainment industries and their lawyers, over the past generation, copyright law has become a major arena of social and political conflict. Many clashes amount to tactical skirmishes among companies for competitive advantage – a long and familiar dynamic in copyright law. But much of the turmoil revolves around a deeper issue: what legal principles and social norms should be used to promote new creativity, especially when the Internet and other digital technologies are involved? Many Internet users, academics, software programmers, artists and citizens criticise the expansion of copyright law and its enforcement as an obnoxious limitation on their basic freedoms. Content industries, for their part (with significant exceptions among large Internet-based companies like Google) tend to regard expansive copyright protection and enforcement as indispensable for sustaining creativity itself.

This chapter describes the profound shifts that copyright law has undergone over the past 20 years as digital technologies have disrupted mass media markets and changed people's stake in copyright law. As we saw in Chapter 2, the 20th century business models for media industries treated people as passive audiences, whose chief role was to 'consume' works made by professionals and sold in the marketplace. This changed with the arrival of the Internet. Telecommunications and digital technologies have enabled ordinary people to become prolific creators in their own right. The 'people formerly known as the audience', in Jay Rosen's memorable phrase (Rosen, 2006), have become bloggers, musicians, remix artists, video producers, website curators, hackers, academic collaborators, and much else. Ordinary people can generate, copy, modify and share works with a global public without having to deal with commercial content intermediaries such as publishers, record labels or studios.

The rise of this new 'sharing economy' outside the marketplace – in which self-organised communities can generate and manage their own 'commons' of content – poses profound challenges to a system of production based on exclusive ownership and control. A commons is a self-organising social system in which a defined community of people manage the access, use and allocation of resources sustainably without money, legal contracts, and other features of markets. Commons-based platforms such as Wikipedia, social networking and open source software divert people's time and attention from commercial platforms, resulting in smaller audiences and lower advertising rates. They also provide new cultural spaces in which amateurs can create qualitatively different new sorts of content that may or may not be marketable, but nonetheless attract considerable web traffic and thus compete with commercial media and content producers.

This chapter will explore the key drivers of the sweeping transformations in market structures, technology and social practice. It will also examine some of the new 'open business models' that are challenging traditional, centralised market structures for the arts and entertainment. Special attention will be paid to the dynamics of new *non-market* structures for creating and enjoying music, video, books, web content and other creativity and information.

Copyright Law

The new models of content production and distribution have engendered intense political and legal conflict. While this strife manifests itself in many areas of law – antitrust, telecommunications regulation, privacy, consumer protection, and more – copyright law is a primary venue in which this drama is playing out.

Despite the new pressures from digital media, copyright law is not destined to undergo a radical transformation any time soon. Existing business models of various arts and entertainment industries remain highly dependent upon copyright protection, and so incumbent businesses tend to resist open platforms and innovative business models that might render their existing investments less valuable. Thus for years, the record industry insisted upon encrypting its music and bitterly fought any form of digital distribution that might undercut its lucrative compact-disc market franchise. So, too, book publishers have historically resisted developing 'e-books' – digitised forms of conventional books –

for fear that the digital versions would be more easily 'pirated' and cannibalise sales of physical books. In defending their existing business models against disruptive challenges, media industries frequently rely upon their ownership of copyrights of works. Copyright is not always used for defensive purposes, however; it has important economic functions within proper limits, especially in allowing distributors (studios, publishers, record labels) the chance to recoup their investments in creative works.

So, while copyright law is not going to disappear any time soon, at the same time, the social sharing and copying unleashed by the Internet and digital technologies are not likely to disappear either. User-generated content and personal networking are becoming culturally popular, giving rise to new business models that rely upon 'open platforms' accessible to anyone. This latest generation of interactive web creativity and culture is often known as 'Web 2.0'.

In an attempt to ease tensions between industry and consumers, the then UK's Chancellor of the Exchequer, Gordon Brown, commissioned an independent review of intellectual property law in 2005. The resulting report, known as the Gowers Review, essentially affirmed the current state of copyright law, while calling for stronger enforcement action and proposing some concessions to consumers and the public. For example, the report recommended 'balanced and flexible rights' to reduce business costs and foster greater market competition (HM Treasury, 2006: 4). But it also called for an expansion of the public's 'fair dealing' rights, which allow people to legally excerpt 'reasonable' amounts of copyright works for non-commercial research, journalism, criticism and private and incidental uses (HM Treasury, 2006: 61–62).

Despite such searches for a stable equilibrium that might reconcile the conflicting demands of copyright-based industries and the public, copyright law will remain an arena of intense political, legal and cultural contestation for the foreseeable future. The most salient points of contention involve industry's use of encrypted controls on DVDs and CDs using 'digital rights management' (DRM); the privacy rights that Internet users may enjoy; the scope of people's 'fair dealing' rights; the legality of Google's project to digitise out-of-print books in the public domain and works whose copyright owners cannot be found (known as 'orphan works'); and the severity of punishments for Internet users found guilty of violating copyrights.

For the moment, we are caught in a messy interregnum between two different media ages – centralised mass media and distributed networked media – with only fitful, transitory accommodations between the two. Only time is likely to resolve or mitigate the current impasse, as large numbers of people choose which modes of creative production and use they find most efficient, entertaining, valuable and socially satisfying.

A brief history of copyright

The first copyright law, the Statute of Anne, was enacted in the United Kingdom in 1709. It gave authors an exclusive property right to print, reprint and sell their books for 14 years. After that, the author could renew copyright protection for another 14 years. The Statute of Anne made it illegal to make or sell copies without permission of the copyright holder.

The law was a major advance in challenging the monopoly of the Stationers' Company, a trade guild of printers that enjoyed a monopoly on book production. The Statute of Anne diminished this monopoly by vesting rights in authors. The rationale behind this shift was that an author ought to be able to protect the fruits of his labour and originality. In practice, despite this recognition of authors' rights and the prospect of greater market competition, book publishers fared fairly well: they typically purchased copyrights from authors, and so had the dominant economic stake in protecting copyrighted works.

These days, copyright law is generally seen as a bargain between authors and publishers on the one hand, and the general public on the other. The public, via the legislature, grants limited monopoly rights to authors and publishers so that they will have the incentive to creative and distribute original works. In return, the public enjoys certain benefits: not just the availability of new works for purchase, but the fair-dealing right to excerpt copyrighted works for private, non-commercial purposes. The public also enjoys free, unfettered access to the 'public domain' of works after the term of copyright protection in a work has expired. This is an important point: the terms of copyright protection are limited so that works may 'enter the public domain' and be freely re-usable, and thus benefit future authors and creators.

Many authors and content industries like to portray copyright as a natural right that pre-exists governments. But at least in Commonwealth countries and the United States, copyright has functioned as a utilitarian policy mechanism, not as a moral or natural right. Its primary purpose is not to reward authors; it is to advance public knowledge, education and culture.

The evolution of copyright law since the 1700s has been marked by piecemeal adaptations as new technologies arose or as different industries succeeded in securing expansions of copyright protection for themselves. For example, the performance of dramatic works became eligible for copyright protection in

Great Britain in 1833, a right extended to musical works in 1842. Parliaments subsequently authorised copyright protection for engravings, paintings, drawings, photographs and sound recordings.

The terms of copyright protection, later expanded to a fixed 28-year term, now extend to 50 or 70 years, depending upon a variety of legal variables. To ensure the recognition of copyright laws internationally, the Berne Convention for the Protection of Literary and Artistic Works was adopted in 1886.

Growing tensions between copyright law and the 'sharing economy'

A paradox lies coiled within the philosophical core of copyright law: it seeks to promote the creation and distribution of works by artificially restricting access to them, through a state-granted monopoly to authors.

The copyright regime served its intended purposes fairly well when creative works were embedded on vinyl disks, celluloid film or codex of paper. Borrowing or sharing tended to occur within fixed geographic areas, and did not significantly undermine market sales. However, with the arrival of digital technologies (and especially the Internet, which make copying and sharing easy and inexpensive), the balance of traditional copyright law has been harder to sustain. The monopoly rights conferred by copyright have also come at a steeper price to culture. Instead of necessarily expanding knowledge or stimulating competition, copyright law in the digital age has in many instances served to artificially limit the circulation of valuable creative works.

Steward Brand put his finger on this paradox back in 1984 when he famously declared: 'On the one hand, information wants to be expensive because it's so valuable. The right information in the right place just changes your life. On the other hand, information wants to be free, because the cost of getting it out is getting lower and lower all the time. So you have these two fighting against each other' (Brand and Herron, 1985: 49).

The astonishing growth of the Internet has only intensified the force of this paradox. As digital technologies help create new markets, content owners are more intent on controlling and profiting from the newly invented 'downstream' uses of their products. In the 1980s, for example, Hollywood studios fiercely fought the introduction of the videocassette recorder as a mortal threat, a battle that they lost in the US Supreme Court. The videocassette went on to become a major ancillary source of revenue for film studios.

Nonetheless, content industries continue to try to control ancillary markets as much as possible, to the extent of trying to control the potential uses that people may make of copyrighted products. Film studios and record labels use 'geographic coding' on DVDs and CDs, for example, to prohibit their usage on electronic equipment on other continents, and thus prohibit their re-sale elsewhere. Digital rights management is a similar attempt to prevent users from copying works or using them in unauthorised ways.

Besides such technological locks, film and record industries in particular have sought to expand their control over DVDs and CDs by seeking broader public policy protections and stiffer legal sanctions. In the United States, for example, Congress enacted the Copyright Term Extension Act of 1998 to retroactively extend the terms for copyrighted works by 20 years. The law essentially locked up tens of thousands of works from the 1920s and 1930s – most notably Disney's Mickey Mouse character – that were due to enter the public domain. The term extension represented a giveaway to major copyright industries and authors' estates because a retroactive extension of copyright protection could not possibly incentivise a roster of deceased authors (Robert Frost, Walt Disney, George Gershwin, etc.) to create new works. Film studios responded that they would have no incentive to preserve old films and other copyrighted works without the additional 20 years of copyright protection.

Another major US copyright law enacted in 1998, the Digital Millennium Copyright Act, has been emulated by many countries. The law gives copyright holders the unilateral right to lock up digital content and so pre-empt fair dealing/fair use rights such as excerpting, reverse engineering and user modifications not authorised by the seller. Content industries see the law as a vital way to protect their intellectual property in an era of cheap and easy copying. Critics regard the law as a serious hindrance to consumer rights, innovation, competition and cultural freedom.

Other laws in the 1990s gave companies broader protections under trademark law, limiting how people may use trademarked products and logos. Companies argue that they need to protect the value of trademarks on which they have spent considerable money on marketing; critics retort that trademark laws now attempt to suppress parody and dissent, effectively controlling the public meanings of trademarks.

Internationally, content industries have stepped up their efforts to win stricter enforcement powers to prosecute the unauthorised copying of copyrighted works. Content industries condemn large-scale, unauthorised copying for commercial purposes as 'piracy', noting that it is often implicated in organised criminal activity. However, content industries have also labelled as 'piracy' certain types of private copying, music remixes and video mashups that aggrieved individuals insist should be treated as fair dealing. Thus the term 'piracy' itself has become a controversial term. In the UK, there have been periodic calls for a legal 'public right to copy' and the right to 'format shift' works for personal use, but to date none has been formally adopted.

The 'Great Value Shift'

Much of the political and social struggle over the terms of copyright law can be traced to the disruptions caused by the Internet and the economic logic of 'open platforms' accessible to anyone via the World Wide Web. Essentially, the Internet provides an infrastructure that enables distributed innovation and sharing to occur at a much lower cost than that of conventional mass media. Television and radio broadcasting, for example, require large amounts of centralized capital, corporate management and professional control (see Chapter 9). Their business models depend upon distributing a limited spectrum of content choices to large, fairly undifferentiated audiences. 'Sellers' are seen as the prime source of expertise, innovation and production. They mostly determine what choices will be offered, and they tend to have greater market power and cultural influence than large masses of unorganised consumers.

The Internet has disrupted the centralised mass media apparatus by enabling disaggregated individuals to come together to create, collaborate and curate their own content. Whether through blogs, listservs, collaborative archives, wikis, social networking sites, or online gaming communities, Internet users have been able to control their own creative and cultural production, much of which is generated and distributed entirely outside the marketplace (with no cash transactions, legal contracts or corporate structures).

This new paradigm of creation has been called 'the commons' by a number of commentators such as Professors Lawrence Lessig, Yochai Benkler and James Boyle. 'What we are seeing now', wrote Benkler, in his landmark book, *The Wealth of Networks*, 'is the emergence of more effective collective action practices that are decentralized but do not rely on either the price system or a managerial structure for coordination' (Benkler, 2006: 60). Benkler's preferred term is 'commons-based peer production' (Benkler, 2006: 59–90). By that, he means systems that are collaborative and non-proprietary, and based on 'sharing resources and outputs among widely distributed, loosely connected individuals who cooperate with each other' (Benkler, 2006: 60).

Essentially, peer production on open networks enables people to self-organise themselves into communities, and to devise their own rules for granting access, use and control of resources. The resources can take many forms – the software code that hackers share, the remix songs or video mashups of web artists, user contributions to a web archive on a specific topic, or the collection of leaked documents hosted by Wikileaks. Commons-based peer production can be seen in the mass collaboration of Wikipedia and open source software projects such as GNU Linux, the computer operating system. It can also be seen in many scientific disciplines that use wikis to amass pools of shared data, and in academic disciplines which publish their articles in open-access journals that can be shared, at no cost to readers, in perpetuity. Commons-based peer production is evident in NASA's Clickworkers Project, which has recruited thousands of online volunteers to classify the craters of Mars, and in projects which use volunteer proofreaders to read through book texts for typographical errors.

Such informal social relationships, working in the unregimented, free space of open platforms, are beginning to change economic production and culture. Instead of needing markets and money to animate people to create valuable information, social friendships and cooperation on a mass scale can be coordinated to produce significant economic (and social) value.

Bollier (2009: 122–144) calls this deep structural change in how valuable things are created online 'the Great Value Shift'. On open networks, the value of strict proprietary control over works diminishes, altering the value of traditional copyrights. Allowing people to have open access and use of a work on the Internet can prove to be more valuable than outright 'ownership' (exclusion) in the traditional sense.

The copyright scholar Siva Vaidhyanathan has quipped that 'the only thing worse than being sampled on the Internet is not being sampled' (Norman Lear Center, 2005: 142). His point is that 'value' in the Internet context increasingly comes from being socially accessible and circulated, and not from being closely held as private property. This shift has far-reaching implications for business strategy and organisational behaviour, and thus for the very definition of wealth.

On the Internet, wealth is not just financial, nor is it necessarily privately held. It is often 'socially created value' that is shared, evolving and non-monetised. It hovers in the air, so to speak, accessible to everyone. Thus the value of a creative work *grows* as software code is collaboratively developed by online communities (enhancing its utility and eliminating bugs); as songs and videos are remixed and shared on the Internet (stimulating public exposure and sales); and as academic books and articles are more easily discovered online and cited (enhancing their authors' reputations and the circulation of their ideas).

Needless to say, copyright-based industries are often confused and threatened by these commons-based models of cultural value. These new models represent a fundamental shift in the structures of 'cultural production' and a departure from the logic of traditional justifications for private ownership. Yet the Great Value Shift is an inexorable force in creative industries. It is one reason why the music industry, after years of resistance, finally capitulated and removed digital rights management from most of its online music. Consumers were rejecting DRM-protected music, and sales were plummeting. As the social circulation of CDs and digital music slowed, so did the consumer market for the music (the record industry continued to see piracy as the chief culprit, however). Only now are record companies starting to explore new forms of digital distribution of music, even as independent musicians experiment with innovative business models (see Chapter 2) and law scholars propose policy solutions such as compulsory licensing schemes to remunerate artists.

Creative Commons licences and new business models

Perhaps the most significant impact of the Great Value Shift has been the development of new forms of legal online sharing through Creative Commons (CC) licences, and new types of business models that exploit 'open platforms' on the Internet. The CC licences have given consumers/users/amateurs much greater control over their own creativity. They regard works as things to be shared, and not necessarily as market *products*.

A popular tool for expressing this attitude towards culture is the Creative Commons licence. These are a series of free, public licences that let copyright holders make their videos, music, designs and writing freely available without advance permission or payment. The licences were expressly designed to let creators bypass the strict controls of copyright law and enable new pools of content to be shared, copied and re-used. Especially since the advent of Web 2.0 software in 2002, the Creative Commons licences have enabled the creation of new types of information commons for photographs, songs, remix music, video mashups, academic literature and much else. Many scientific disciplines are using the CC licences to sidestep commercial publishers and start their own open access journals. More than 5000 open access scholarly and scientific journals are now published, making their articles available for free online in perpetuity.

Free culture has become so popular over the past decade that more than 50 countries around the world and several large-scale legal jurisdictions (such as Scotland and Puerto Rico) have adapted the Creative Commons licences. Another nine are in the process of adapting the licences and more than 150 million works are now estimated to be available under Creative Commons licences.

While CC licences encourage people to share their works on web-based commons such as Wikipedia, the Internet Archive and open access journals, digital sharing also occurs on corporate-hosted *open platforms* such as Facebook and Flickr, which invite people to contribute and share their own content (so-called 'user-generated content'). Unlike online commons, however, these platforms are managed to serve the commercial interests of companies and their investors, and may or may not give users full control of their works. Some open platforms, such as the iPhone, select which applications may run on the platform; others require users to consent to 'terms of service' contracts that dictate their legal rights on the site.

A new breed of Internet-oriented companies is developing new business models to take maximum advantage of open platforms on the Internet. They realise that a reliance on open source software, freely available content and an ethic of transparency are more likely to capture consumer attention and loyalty, and therefore leverage the social dynamics of life on the Internet. By contrast, companies that rely upon 'closed' business models that seek to manage consumers' behaviour and impose strict copyright controls are seen as less attractive to consumers and are thus becoming less competitive.

A classic instance of the power of open business models is the Mindstorms robotic kit produced by the Danish toymaker Lego. The kits let young people build a variety of customised robots out of a huge assortment of plastic Lego pieces, programmable software, sensors and motors. When some early users of the kits began to reverse-engineer the robotic 'brain' of the system, the company initially considered suing them. Then it realised that their inquisitive customer base represented, in effect, a large and robust research and development team that could actually improve the product over time.

So Lego decided to insert a 'right to hack' provision into the Mindstorms software licence, giving hobbyists explicit permission to invent whatever new robotic innovations they wanted. The best of these innovations are incorporated into the product, which makes them more attractive to customers and improves sales. By treating their customers as part of the creative ecosystem, Lego learned how to transcend the conflicts that often occur between copyright holders and users. Their new, less controlling business model works to the benefit of both the company and its customers.

A leading scholar of user-driven innovation is Eric von Hippel (2006) of MIT, whose book, *Democratizing Innovation*, describes dozens of 'innovation communities' that work closely with manufacturers. Von Hippel contends that customers – especially the most active, enthusiastic customers – are rich sources of innovation who can clearly benefit industry. He notes that the sports drink, Gatorade, the sports bra, and circular irrigation systems were all initially invented by individuals, not companies. As the Internet makes user-driven innovation more feasible and accessible, von Hippel argues that competitive companies must learn to develop more open, interactive relationships with their user communities.

The politics of owning and sharing culture

Despite the appeal of open business models, incumbent industries have been more interested in resisting than adopting innovative production and distribution models. Much of this has to do with their large, fixed investments in existing ways of doing business, which cannot be inexpensively modified or abandoned. Business scholar Clayton Christiansen (2003) calls this problem 'the innovator's dilemma' – the difficult choice facing businesses that have a lucrative, established commercial franchise that might be undermined or cannibalised by embracing new technologies or business strategies.

Incumbent industries have therefore tended to resist new technologies and business models through lawsuits, by lobbying for broader copyright protections and via public relations campaigns. The film, recorded music and publishing industries have undertaken numerous campaigns over the past 20 years to encrypt copyrighted content, mandate technological controls to restrict copying, and persuade legislatures and international bodies to mandate stronger copyright protections and penalties.

More recently, industries with large inventories of copyrighted works have worked in collaboration with national governments to forge a trade agreement to 'internationalise' their policy goals. Recently, a key vehicle for such aspirations has been the Anti-Counterfeiting Trade Agreement. Negotiated in secret over the course of two years, the agreement deals not just with trademark counterfeiting, but in fact with many copyright issues. It reportedly seeks to expand surveillance of online activities and authorise personal searches of electronic equipment. One apparent provision would require Internet service providers to monitor copyright violations and to cut off Internet service to subscribers with three episodes of alleged infringement.

Civil society has frequently greeted many of the copyright industry's proposed policies and initiatives with derision, protest and civil disobedience. Hackers and computer programmers have often been at the forefront of such protests, particularly when the rights to reverse-engineer, modify or re-use software have been involved. The Free Software Foundation and Software Freedom Law Center have been two leading advocates for limits on the scope of copyright protection and the right to share and re-use software. Public Knowledge and the Electronic Frontier Foundation are leading policy advocates and litigants for copyright reform in the United States and internationally. In the United Kingdom, digital activists have often addressed issues of freedom of expression, privacy, innovation and consumer rights through the Open Rights Group.

International copyright activism has become far more organised in recent years. Advocates in Sweden formed the Pirate Party in 2006, which soon inspired the formation of national Pirate Parties in more than 20 nations, now represented by an umbrella organization, Pirate Parties International. The Pirate Party in Sweden is now the country's third-largest party; following the 2009 elections, it won two seats in the European Parliament. Other significant advocacy for changes in EU copyright policies are being advanced by the Free Culture Forum, an international body of free software, free culture and Internet-oriented citizen groups that meets annually in Barcelona.

Case study: Should fashion be 'ready to share'?

While the music and film industries fiercely protect their copyrights, limiting any sharing and re-use of their works, the fashion industry, driven by similar market interests, readily accepts the idea of derivation and appropriation as a creative tool. To be sure, the fashion industry aggressively protects its brand names and logos, utilising trademarks and licensing agreements to assure a steady flow of consumer revenues. However in most cases, the actual creative design of garments is not owned by anyone. The couturier dress worn by a Hollywood starlet on the red carpet can be immediately 'knocked-off', as the fashion world puts it, and legally appear days later on department store racks.

Copying is the norm in fashion. The renowned fashion designer Miuccia Prada was once rummaging through the Paris shop of vintage clothes dealer Didier Ludot when she espied a coat with a silk faille and a rosebud print, which had originally been designed by Balenciaga (according to her friend, Mauela Pavesi). Prada loved the design so much that she copied it *exactly* and sold it as her own. Ralph Lauren once made an exact copy of a tuxedo that had been designed by Yves Saint Laurent. Designer Nicholas Ghesquiere, a Balenciaga designer, copied a vest that had been designed by Kaisik Yoon for his 1973 collection. Fashionistas note how Adolfo built his fashion business on an interpretation of a Coco Chanel suit; that Tom Ford's work was clearly derivative of Halston's designs; and that Alexander McQueen closely copied Vivienne Westwood.

New York Times reporter Guy Trebay (2002) has noted that Gallagher Paper Collectibles, a Manhattan shop with a vast collection of fashion magazines going back a hundred years, is a favourite haunt for contemporary fashion designers and their assistants: 'We get them all, Hedi Slimane, Karl Lagerfeld, Marc Jacobs big time, John Varvatos, Narciso Rodriguez, the Calvin assistants, the Gucci assistants, Dolce & Gabbana, Anna Suit – you name it!' said Michael Gallagher, the store's proprietor. 'They all come here for inspiration …' Mr Gallagher added. 'At least that's what we call it!'

Film studios and major record labels consider it self-evident that creativity must be strictly controlled through copyright law, lest it be 'stolen' and creators forced out of business. It is a significant point: creators, especially individual artists, need effective, reliable ways to be paid for their work, and copyright offers one important vehicle. But the fashion industry has shown that despite scant copyright protections, fashion businesses are still willing to invest enormous sums of money in each new season's creative cycle – and reap substantial profits year after year. Derivative creativity, recombination, imitation, revival of old styles and outright knockoffs are the norm. Few denounce, let alone sue, the appropriator for 'creative theft': they are too busy trying to stay ahead of the competition through sheer power of their design and marketing prowess.

Occasionally someone may protest about a 'rip-off' and obtain murmurs of sympathy. And quite rightly, the counterfeiting of brand-name products is condemned as theft. However in general, certainly as a legal matter, creative derivation is an accepted premise of fashion. Indeed, the industry's growth and prosperity has been built upon the famous maxim of Isaac Newton: 'If I have seen further, it is by standing on the shoulders of giants' (Quote DB, n.d.).

The legendary designer Coco Chanel understood this reality. She once said: 'Fashion is not something that exists in dresses only; fashion is something in the air. It's the wind that blows in the new fashion; you feel it coming, you smell it … in the sky, in the street; fashion has to do with ideas, the way we live, what is happening' (Evan Carmichael, 2010). There are obvious parallels between the legal status of creativity in fashion and on the Internet, especially in free and open source software and viral memes and videos on the Internet.

References

Benkler, Y. (2006) *The Wealth of Networks: How Social Production Transforms Markets and Freedom*, New Haven, CT: Yale University Press.

Bollier, D. (2009) *Viral Spiral: How the Commoners Built a Digital Republic of their Own*, New York: New Press.

Brand, S. and Herron, M. (1985) '1984 AD', *Whole Earth Review*, May.

Christensen, C. (2003) *The Innovator's Dilemma: The Revolutionary Book that Will Change the Way you do Business*, New York: Harper.

Evan Carmichael (2010) 'Coco Chanel quotes', evancarmichael.com. Available from http://www.evancarmichael.com/Famous-Entrepreneurs/631/Coco-Chanel-Quotes.html, accessed 10 July 2010.

HM Treasury (2006) Gowers Review of Intellectual Property, Norwich: HMSO. Available from http://webarchive.nationalarchives.gov.uk/+/http://www.hm-treasury.gov.uk/d/pbr06_gowers_report_755.pdf, accessed 2 August 2010.

Norman Lear Center (2005) 'Ready to Share: Fashion and the ownership of creativity', Conference proceedings, edited by D. Bollier and L. Racine, Los Angeles, Norman Lear Center. Available from http://www.learcenter.org/pdf/RTStranscript.pdf, accessed 28 July 2010.

Quote DB (n.d.) Isaac Newton, quotedb.com. Available from http://www.quotedb.com/quotes/3102, accessed 22 June 2010.

Rosen, J. (2006) 'The people formerly known as the audience', Pressthink. Available from http://journalism.nyu.edu/pubzone/weblogs/pressthink/2006/06/27/ppl_frmr.html, accessed 27 July 2010.

Trebay, G. (2002) 'Imitation is the mother of invention', *New York Times*, 7 July. Available from https://www.nytimes.com/2002/07/07/weekinreview/ideas-trends-fashion-replay-imitation-is-the-mother-of-invention.html?ex=1279684800&en=61a3311e6b3ab479&ei=5070, accessed 28 July 2010.

Von Hippel, E. (2006) *Democratizing Innovation*, Cambridge, MA: MIT Press. (PDF file available from http://web.mit.edu/evhippel/www/democl.htm).

Further reading and research

Bollier, D. (2005) *Brand Name Bullies: The Quest to Own and Control Culture*, New York: John Wiley.

Boyle, J. (2008) *The Public Domain: Enclosing the Commons of the Mind*, New Haven, CT: Yale University Press.

Brand, S. (1988) *The Media Lab: Inventing the Future at MIT*, New York: Penguin.

Fisher, W. (2004) *Promises to Keep: Technology, Law and the Future of Entertainment*, Stanford, CA: Stanford University Press.

Knopper, S. (2009) *Appetite for Self-Destruction: The Spectacular Crash of the Record Industry in the Digital Age*, New York: Free Press.

Lessig, L. (2008) *Remix: Making Art and Commerce Thrive in the Hybrid Economy*, New York, Penguin.

Patry, W. (2009) *Moral Panics and the Copyright Wars*, Oxford: Oxford University Press.

Penalver, E.M. and Katyal, S. (2010) *Property Outlaws: How Squatters, Pirates and Protesters Improve the Law of Ownership*, New Haven, CT: Yale University Press.

Vaidhyanathan, S. (2001) *Copyright and Copywrongs: The Rise of Intellectual Property and how it Threatens Creativity*, New York: New York University Press.

Online resources

http://www.mpaa.com

http://www.riaa.com

http://www.creativecommons.org

http://www.electronicfrontierfoundations.org

http://www.publicknowledge.org

http://www.openknowledgefoundation.org

http://www.openrightsgroups.org

6 Assessing the Value of the Arts

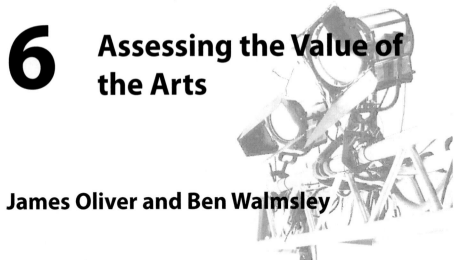

James Oliver and Ben Walmsley

Introduction

> Every art contributes to the greatest art of all, the art of living
>
> (Bertolt Brecht, 1964)

This chapter presents a general introduction to the contemporary concern of public value in relation to the arts, and particularly how this relates to the concept of social impact – an issue that has dominated the public funding agenda for the arts in the UK and beyond since the 1990s. What follows is an analysis of how the public value of the arts has been framed and assessed in recent times, and how this reflects adaptations to changes in the political climate.

This analysis will be illustrated through a brief historical and conceptual overview of attempts to capture public value, followed by a review and critical evaluation of some models and frameworks that have attempted to capture the benefits of the arts. The challenges of assessing and measuring value will then be further discussed through a case study on the National Theatre of Scotland's production, *Black Watch*, to demonstrate the reductive nature of traditional models and point towards the need for developing more nuanced and reflexive approaches to assessing value, informed (and preferably led) by the practice of the art in question. We can call this a 'situational' approach to research.

The chapter therefore argues for approaches informed by these principles. Drawing parallels with themes from Performance Studies, it suggests that greater account needs to be given to *context* and the conditions of the context, including its social formation and relations, which requires reflexivity and ethnographic analysis. The chapter concludes by reflecting on the dialectical conditions of value (as both instrumental *and* intrinsic), particularly emphasising the spatial dimension of practice, which emphasises that the arts are not just situated in a temporal context of ideological shifts, but are active players in the making of value as a practice of cultural production. This spatial dimension is brought into being as a practice of social relations through articulations of inter-subjective values, thereby broadening the dialogue on the subject of public value and considering the productive value of the arts as a wider practice of living.

Benefits or value?

'[I]nstrumentalism' should not be just be seen as a recent and unwelcome encroachment of politics in the aesthetic sphere. It should, perhaps, be seen more as a mode of understanding, which, far from being peripheral, has actually been central to the long, intellectual tradition that we have traced. ... The arts have been a tool to enforce and express power in social relations for as long as the arts themselves have been around.

(Belfiore and Bennett, 2008: 190, 194)

If you take a scan through an industry magazine such as *Arts Professional* (www.artsprofessional.co.uk), you will frequently find commentary or reportage on what the arts are good for (health, justice, social inclusion, and sometimes just sheer output or even making money). This is understandable in an industry magazine. But it is also representative of a defensive stance of advocacy imposed on the arts by tough (and increasingly tougher) funding regimes. Advocacy, then, is frequently about benefits and is actually a value judgement, depending on the value system by which we measure what is a 'good' outcome.

The point here is that the arts are very rarely measured in terms of anything other than a so-called 'instrumental' outcome (such as alignment with broader public policy aims including making money, which is often the most valued outcome). In their book *The Social Impact of the Arts*, Belfiore and Bennet (2008) present a robust scholarly argument on the intellectual history of the theme at large here. They conclude that there is something of a false dichotomy in the either/or debate on the instrumental and intrinsic value of the arts, and that instrumental arguments have always been made for the arts (citing Plato's *Republic* as one of the first). The broad inference is that instrumental and intrinsic values are mutually informing and reflective of socio-cultural relations over time.

More importantly, Belfiore and Bennet recognise the error of a dualism that only serves to reinforce the structures that perpetuate it (i.e. if you value one concept over the other and seek to demonstrate that by exclusive examples, then the dualism is reinforced and the structures that validate it are merely reproduced). Instead, the instrumental versus intrinsic debate needs to be understood in terms of a relational and situational dialectic, to lay bare the structures that seek to contain (and potentially limit and exclude) the contingent and negotiated processes and experiences of social relations and cultural production.

What is generally at stake, then, is the efficacy of measurement in the context of a hierarchy of knowledge (qualitative knowledge being lower down the food chain than quantitative knowledge). On this point, there has been much research conducted in relation to cultural policy and its overlaps into other policy areas (Galloway *et al.*, 2006; Galloway, 2009). A broad conclusion of this research is that there are problems quantifying the effects of the arts at the level of social impact. Nevertheless, it has also been noted that this is largely due to a 'dominant rationalist–modernist paradigm' (Sanderson, 2000: 439) and a related 'dominant successionist model of causation' (Galloway, 2009: 127).

Here's the underlying problem: the arts are rarely afforded benchmark status in their own right, but are subject to the benchmarks of other disciplines and practices. In plainer terms, cultural value in terms of public value is subject to the cultural values in society at large (including the ordering of knowledge). This is a problem for all socio-cultural practices and processes that are to an extent reliant on public funding, the vagaries of cultural policy and the subjective gaze of evaluation – unlike other human practices, such as science, that are internally calibrated by metrics and therefore measured for validity in their own terms.

Our approach to value here therefore argues for stronger, practice-based models of value within the arts, and consequently a stronger foundation of and reference to practice-based and practice-led research. In a sense, it is about engaging with our own roles and values concerning the arts in society. A key argument is that we must approach value *reflexively* and that this must inform our methodologies of analysis (either as artists or cultural producers) in order to overcome reductive dualisms or dichotomies that are the mainstay of entrenched debates on value. In doing so, we contend that the central dualism in the cultural field, the so-called intrinsic and instrumental divide, is artificial and should instead be understood as part of the spatial (or situational) dialogic of practice and production, incorporating the dialectic of social relations and structures (including public policy).

Historical and conceptual framing

The arts are increasingly positioned within what is now being referred to as a creative economy. This is revealing of the overriding economic gaze of government; and in recent years, there has been an increased policy emphasis on the creative industries, largely driven by forms of creativity explored through technological innovation, screen industries and new media production (and, crucially, reproduction) as a commercial model for cultural activity. This philosophy has led to a reductive emphasis on consumption over the broader artistic focus on experience.

This works well for many players in the so-called creative economy. According to Government figures, the creative industries accounted for 7.3 per cent of the UK's GDP in 2007 (DCMS, 2008) and 5.6 per cent of its 'Gross Value Added' in 2008 (DCMS, 2011). However, this measurement shift to metrics in the form of economic rationalism also demonstrates a paradox (and gap) where the perceived market value of particular creative practices is elevated as the key performance indicator in terms of public value for the arts and culture more broadly. This is, of course, problematic where public funding is crucial in terms of access to or participation in artistic events and of them ever even happening in the first place.

Public funding of the arts is always subject to the shadow of doubt and public debate, which is a good thing, and this is where the first ideological markers can be laid bare – where people can test whether they are more inclined towards the economic rationalist view that only the 'fittest' of the arts (as in fit-for-purpose) should survive. This question should lead people to consider what the fundamental purpose of the arts really is, which should in turn make them consider what their public value is and how that is most appropriately accounted for. The answers to these questions may appear simple to some, but for many people, they become increasingly complex.

Superficially, public value can be perceived to be about the politics of 'value for money' and why money should or should not be allocated in a particular arena. But the economics of culture is not specifically what this chapter will be looking at – see Hesmondhalgh (2007) and Throsby (2001) for a thorough analysis of this. In the context of the dialectic regarding intrinsic and instrumental value, public value becomes part of a broader political economy where economics should be regarded as embedded in the social and therefore imbued with social foundations as much as implications (Polanyi, 2001).

The arts in the UK were ostensibly 'protected' by royal charter through the original founding of the Arts Council of Great Britain in 1946 (now dissolved into national agencies) on the back of what might be termed an Arnoldian view of culture (in reference to Matthew Arnold, the 19th century poet and cultural critic). This was effectively predicated on the view that the (high) arts are edifying, if not transformative, for both the individual and society; and, importantly, that they should be afforded autonomy, or 'arm's length' govern-ance. The premise of that charter is now challenged because the edifying or transformative power is no longer assumed, at least not in all instances, and certainly not across all art forms; and the arts, where implicated in cultural policy, are conceived as being in service of the state's interests, as determined through increasing economic rationalism and risk aversion strategies as a means of calculating and inculcating levels of trust and promoting public value.

Of course, this is all very normative language within so-called progressive democratic societies, and is certainly intended to appear as such. The key substantive task remains how to measure or evaluate policy achievements. One way is to set the parameters of public engagement. In terms of policy, this has been advanced through developments such as 'evidence-based policy making' in the public sector, which offered a boon for research practitioners across the academic and consulting fields as well as for arts projects. But this policy direction also led the arts into the value framework of the pre-deter-mined outcomes of government agendas. Hence the arts, particularly since 1997 under the New Labour governments, have been obligated and contracted to fulfil many social policy or health policy objectives of government, where so-called softer outcomes are desirable and achievable towards building social capital, promoting social cohesion, developing community wellbeing, etc. Of course, the community arts and arts-in-health practitioners had always been doing such work – for an interesting overview of this area see White (2009). So in terms of public value, there was enough evidence available to justify funding similar projects in the wider arts community. But there has been little commit-ment to exploring the value of such arts practice beyond the limited terms of 'proving' impact.

In short, we live in an increasingly global political world, which models itself on corporate business and managerial practices. This is related to other develop-ments in public policy relating to notions of open government, accountability, efficiency, and crucially, it seems, public value. Administration skills are not only highly valued but are evaluated through Public Service Agreements with defined targets and Key Performance Indicators that become the gold standard of public value for bureaucrats and politicians alike. As indicated above, it is not only a public value based on conceptions of economic growth, but one based on minimising risk and maximising trust; and with such process comes a trickle-down of this modelling of value into everyday governance practices and its distribution throughout workforces – including the almost ubiquitous 'outcome-focused evaluations' that attend any publicly funded project or organisation, including in the arts. This is not to devalue evaluation or outcomes per se, which can play an important role in terms of maintaining and developing good arts practice. But evaluation that is based on the needs or expectations of the paymaster does not necessarily adequately reflect the performance of an artist or arts organisation in terms of their own practice, needs and expectations (let's say creativity). In terms of public value, there is an over-evaluation of the arts in terms of impact outcomes and an under-researching in terms of practice leading the terms of discussion and analysis on value and impact.

Modelling value

At this point, it is appropriate to introduce the key concern and concept in this discussion, which is also a very practical or practice-based issue, a form of praxis (whether in terms of the arts, research or governance) known as reflexivity. Reflexivity is more then the mere reflection on, or documentation of, who we are and what we do, whether as individuals or as a collective. Rather, it is a form of critical analysis of *context* (including the subjective) to inform action. Particularly, it relates to an acknowledgement of the conditions (social, cultural, economic and political) of the contexts we are operating in, including our own role in producing, reproducing or even obviating those conditions.

In terms of public value, reflexivity is about not taking the so-called objective or subjective measures of value for granted, of imagining one or the other to be real or true, but in seeking out greater objectivity, recognising that it can only be approached from various inter-subjectivities (including institutional) with a central reference point being practice, its conditions and situation. A consequence of this praxis should be to challenge a predetermined value that is imagined as the real goal or achievement, and thereby challenge a conception of value based on a single or linear reality of practice and its productions. In other words, value is emergent, not fixed and given; but as a dialectic of practice and its productions (the spaces of social relations), it is always under negotiation and in-the-making, and contingent on the multiple experiences and expressions of inter-subjectivity.

In terms of thinking of this spatially, particularly in terms of informing a 'situational' approach as intimated in the introduction, we are following on here from Doreen Massey (2005), who broadly describes space as the product of social relations, as multiple in its formations and negotiations, and as always in the making. This imagining of space can also be applied to everyday human practices of living, including arts practice and the public value it may have; and, as stated above in the introduction, greater account needs to be given to context and the conditions of the context, including its social formation and relations, which demands a reflexive and ethnographic approach.

This approach is broadly aligned with what Richard Schechner (2007) refers to as the 'broad spectrum' approach to performance studies, by drawing on the initial conception of everyday life as performative. The arts formulate part of that performativity and, in cultural terms at least, this approach has something to add to conceptions of public value: 'Because of the inclusionary spirit of Performance Studies (and the theoretical concerns with what inclusion presumes), the field is particularly attuned to issues of place, personhood, cultural citizenship, and equity' (Kirshenblatt-Gimblett, 2007: 51). Under this 'broad spectrum' approach, anthropological and ethnographic perspectives on arts practice are crucial because of the central focus of reflexivity in ethnographic practice: in what is effectively a spatial and situational practice, context will be included and made visible. It is also interesting here to reflect on what Brecht contended was the reflexive point of Epic Theatre – which he saw as not about lulling people into a false situation of consciousness or reality (an emotional 'suspension of disbelief'), but rather as an opportunity to provoke people into action with what is not real or linear by creating multiple inter-subjectivities.

Figure 6.1: Audiences engaged in a National Theatre of Scotland production
Image by Dominic Ibbotson, courtesy of National Theatre of Scotland.

In the context of assessing the value of the arts, then, reflexivity is about theorising practice as spatial and situational; and as Appadurai (1996: 182) reminds us, ethnography is 'isomorphic with the very knowledge it seeks to discover and document, as both the ethnographic project and the social projects it seeks to describe have the production of locality as their governing ethos'. We will illustrate the benefits of a reflexive, ethnographic approach to understanding the value of the arts in a case study of National Theatre of Scotland's *Black Watch*. But first, we will trace the more traditional benefits-based approaches to capturing artistic value.

Benefits models and frameworks

In the past decade, there has been a revival of interest in the intrinsic, as opposed to instrumental, benefits of the arts, and this has led to a rebalancing in the critical debate on impact. But the nuanced concept of value discussed above, based on a reflexive, ethnographic approach, has consistently been eclipsed by a more rudimentary and even quantitative focus on benefits. To illustrate the thinking behind this benefits approach, we will now compare and contrast three key models that have emerged in the literature over the past few years: McCarthy *et al.*'s (2004) benefits framework; Brown's (2006) benefits map; and White and Hede's (2008) schema of impacts and enablers.

McCarthy *et al.*'s (2004) *Gifts of the Muse* marked an attempt to reframe the debate on the benefits of the arts. It strove to achieve this by reviewing the totality of arts-related benefits, illustrating the relationship between private and public benefits and dichotomising them into intrinsic and instrumental benefits. The resulting framework is depicted in Figure 6.2.

Figure 6.2: Framework for Understanding the Benefits of the Arts
Source: McCarthy *et al.* (2004)

This framework raised a few eyebrows amongst academics and practitioners when it was first published and it has certainly succeeded in refocusing the impact debate, if only by posing some pertinent questions. The benefits illustrated here all represent claims that have been made for the arts over the years and we can all probably relate to some of the private, intrinsic benefits such as 'pleasure' and 'captivation'. But the public and instrumental benefits identified in the framework are harder to conceptualise, possibly because they are longer-term and far removed in space and time from the immediate context of the artwork or performance. There are also some high claims here that are almost impossible to evidence: for example, does seeing a good production of *Macbeth* really improve students' test scores and expand their capacity for empathy? Complex psychological concepts like empathy illustrate the need for a more nuanced, reflexive and ethnographic approach to conceiving value.

McCarthy *et al.* (2004: xvi) contextualise public value in the following terms:

> Intrinsic benefits accrue to the public sphere when works of art convey what whole communities of people yearn to express. Examples of what can produce these benefits are art that commemorates events significant to a nation's history or a community's identity, art that provides a voice to communities the culture at large has largely ignored, and art that critiques the culture for the express purpose of changing people's views.

In the fields of sociology and leisure studies, there is an increasing interest in the importance of the arts in enhancing community and social engagement. Nicholson and Pearce (2001: 460) list 'enhanced socialization' as a benefit of cultural events and at the heart of this philosophy is Borgmann's notion of 'focal practices – those pursuits which bring an engagement of mind and body and a centring power – and the way in which such practices create shared meaning and communities of celebration' (Arai and Pedlar, 2003: 185). There is a clear link here with anthropologist Victor Turner's (1969) concept of 'communitas' and with Ehrenreich's (2007) notion of 'effervescence'. To this extent, McCarthy *et al.*'s framework represents the literature relatively well, acknowledging intrinsic public benefits which are often overlooked within more instrumental language of policy.

A key insight of this framework is that it presents a balanced map of both intrinsic and instrumental benefits and attempts to demonstrate the relationship (or 'spill-over') between private and public benefits. But it ignores the complex interrelationships between these benefits and disregards the growing body of literature on aesthetic growth, wellbeing, self-fulfilment and transformation. By placing private and public, and intrinsic and instrumental benefits in a transecting opposition, the framework simplifies the debate and arguably reinforces the dichotomies it is aiming to destroy.

However, as Brown (2006) points out, the authors' intention was to spark a policy debate rather than to provide a comprehensive toolkit for practitioners. With this in mind, he proposes an extended version of the framework, aimed at providing a kaleidoscopic 'architecture of value' to visually articulate the arts experience (Brown, 2006: 19). This value architecture is displayed in Figure 6.3. It maps a range of arts benefits by value cluster and Brown divides these clusters as follows: imprint of the arts experience; personal development; human interaction; communal meaning; and economic and social benefits. As we can see, he broadens the framework out from one of opposition to one of interaction, which succeeds in highlighting the connections, complexities and interrelationships of the various different benefits.

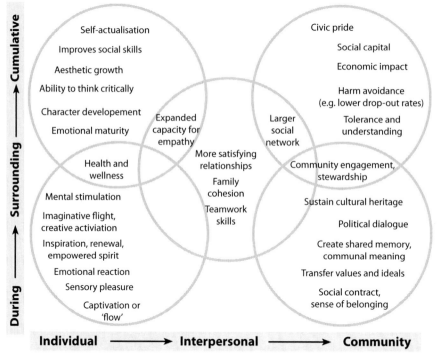

Figure 6.3: Map of arts benefits by value cluster
Source: Brown (2006: 21).

This enhanced model rectifies some of its predecessor's omissions, including aesthetic growth, self-actualisation and wellbeing. It also includes 'interpersonal needs', which Getz (1991: 85) defines as 'expressions of community and national identity'. However, as before, the separation of some of these benefits is somewhat arbitrary, with cultural heritage, for example, in a different sphere from civic pride; and although there is an indication of the direction of 'benefits transfer', from the individual to the community and from the instantaneous to the cumulative, there is again a limited focus on process or context. This weakness is acknowledged by Brown (2006: 20), who himself advocates further research into the connections between benefits and enablers: 'Many factors affect the creation of value, and a next step would be to gain a better understanding of the full range of factors and to connect them with specific benefits.'

Brown and Novak's (2007) subsequent research into the intrinsic impacts of live performances attempted to address this weakness and culminated in the delineation of a three-stage process, namely:

$$\text{Anticipation} \longrightarrow \text{Captivation} \longrightarrow \text{Intrinsic Impacts.}$$

Their survey of 19 artistic performances in 2006 aimed to provide a toolkit with which to *measure* intrinsic impact and concluded that captivation was the most reliable determinant of satisfaction and therefore represented the very 'lynchpin of impact' idealised in 'the state of consciousness described by Csikszentmihlyi's as "Flow"' (Brown and Novak, 2007: 11). To the delight of performers, producers, programmers, ethnographers and sometimes even audiences themselves, this privileged state of consciousness is often visibly manifest in the spectator: 'Through their facial expressions, body language and audible reactions, audiences communicate impact as it is happening. There is no mistaking the silence of rapture during a concert, the moments of shared emotion in a theater [sic] when the plot takes a dramatic twist or the post-performance buzz in the lobby. All are reliable evidence of intrinsic impact' (Brown and Novak, 2007: 5). Brown and Novak are touching on something of profound importance here: namely the role of context and the ethnographer in understanding and capturing or articulating value, particularly as a situational experience.

White and Hede also pick up Brown's challenge to explore the relationship between benefits and enablers, defining an enabler as 'a factor that facilitates the occurrence of impact' (White and Hede, 2008: 27). Their model, replicated in Figure 6.4 , illustrates the various dimensions of the impact of art.

Unlike the previous two examples, this model combines individual and collective impact, depicting the blurred lines between the personal and social benefits of the arts. The inner circles again reflect the main themes from the literature – wellbeing, social bonding, aesthetic growth, vision and empathy. But whereas the previous models illustrated the direction of the benefits' interconnectedness, White and Hede's 'circumplex' portrays impact as a ripple effect, emanating outwards from the core artistic experience. This is an interesting development and provides us with a fresh, more situational perspective, but it again fails to reveal the process or context through which value is created in the first place.

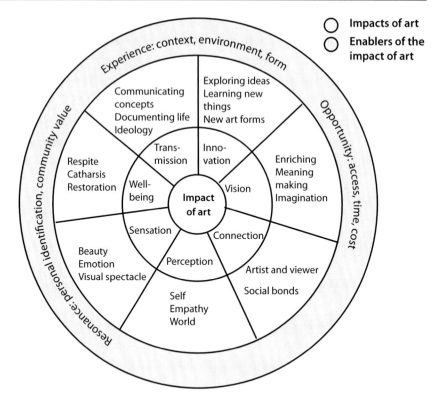

Figure 6.4: Circumplex of preliminary impacts and enablers of the impact of art
Source: White and Hede (2008: 27)

However, the introduction of the realm of enablers is a big strength here, reflecting significant elements of the literature absent from the previous frameworks. The notion of self-congruence, for example, is reflected in the resonance enabler, which proposes personal identification and the value placed on the art form by the community as significant indicators of impact. The opportunity enabler reflects the marketing impact – the relationship between the consumer and the artistic product in terms of price, location and distribution. The experience realm covers the three areas of context, environment and form, and thus incorporates Brown and Novak's (2007) anticipation or 'readiness to receive' construct as well as the physical and social packaging (the augmented product) and the presentation of the core artistic product itself. Arguably the most significant addition provided by this model is the inclusion of the concept of catharsis.

Catharsis is a complex concept, whose precise interpretation has triggered centuries of critical debate. The dominant view of catharsis has been the purgation theory, which holds that tragic drama can arouse emotions of pity and fear in an audience, which it then quells or purges in the resolution. Falassi's

(1987: 4–6) typologies of ritual fit with this interpretation, identifying the rite of purification as 'a cleansing, or chasing away of evil'. But there remains strong opposition to the purgation theory. According to Golden (1973: 473), there are three main schools of thought in the opposition camp: those who see catharsis as a 'moral purification'; those who perceive it as a 'structural purification in which the development of the plot purifies the tragic deed of its moral pollution'; and a third group who recognise the concept as 'a form of intellectual clarification in which the concepts of pity and fear are clarified by the artistic representation of them'. There is no room here to extend this critical review of catharsis, but its inclusion in White and Hede's model succeeds in establishing a link between classical and modern performance theory.

This brief survey of benefits models has shown particular areas of convergence on the theory of impact, with key concepts such as individual pleasure and wellbeing and the creation of social bonds represented in all three models. As discussed, each model has its strengths and weaknesses and each poses some pertinent questions. But by focusing on benefits and impacts, rather than on the less tangible concept of value, all these models are guilty of reducing the arts experience from an inter-subjective, situational, relational and ever-emerging process to a two-dimensional series of outputs, whose values are predetermined and externally imposed. They thereby risk reproducing the dualisms they may well be trying to counter, such as the intrinsic/instrumental or objective/subjective. By reducing complex benefits to measurable outputs, these frameworks reflect the metric approach to policy in a market-driven economy; but they inevitably fail to fully represent the complexity of art form and practice as situational and relational – i.e. as social and spatial contexts that variously contain the dialectic or embeddedness of process and product and of experience and value, as both intrinsic and instrumental. This shortfall highlights the need to move beyond bounded or outcome based theories and models of value, and to take more ethnographic and reflexive account of arts practice as situational forms which comprise it or to assess them on their own terms and in their own vernacular. This call is expanded in the following analysis of *Black Watch*.

Case study: National Theatre of Scotland's *Black Watch*

Black Watch recounts the story, from the soldiers' perspective, of the deployment of Scotland's Black Watch regiment at Camp Dogwood during the Iraq War. The play premiered at Edinburgh Fringe Festival in August 2006 to uniformly rave reviews and has since played to audiences all over the world, with performances at London's Barbican Centre, the Sydney Festival, the New Zealand International Arts Festival, Toronto's Luminato Festival and several runs in New York.

In terms of critical acclaim, *Black Watch* has won a Herald Angel, a Scotsman Fringe First, a List Best Theatre Writing Award, a Stage Award for Best Ensemble, the South Bank Show Award for Theatre, a Writers' Guild of Great Britain Award and four Critics Awards for Theatre in Scotland. *Time Out New York* featured the play in its best plays of 2007 and *New York Magazine* gave it the accolade of Theatrical Event of the Year. This last award is perhaps the most telling, because *Black Watch* is indeed more of an event than a traditional play. Combining documentary drama with political theatre, stylised movement, bagpipes, film, surround sound, and military songs and laments, the play engages with its audience on a range of levels and provides them with a multi-sensory experience, not only of what it's like to fight a modern war but also of what influences people to join an army – a reflexive and situational analysis of war.

National Theatre of Scotland's Artistic Director, Vicky Featherstone summarises the play's global success as follows:

> *Black Watch* has been described in the press as a cultural landmark of the twenty-first century (*Sunday Herald*, March 2007). A lofty claim indeed, but it is only once in a lifetime that a piece of theatre is created which celebrates the vibrancy and possibility of the art form with every second of its performance, which explodes something we are collectively struggling to understand – in this case the Iraq War – and provides a visceral resonance which permeates universally.

(Burke, 2007: xv)

Given its global success and the almost unanimously positive response from its audiences, it is fair to conclude that *Black Watch* has had a significant impact. But how can we even begin to capture and assess the value of this impact? In economic terms, this may be relatively easy because this can be measured in terms of box office income and net profit (although as a highly subsidised piece of theatre which was never designed to tour, it took the play almost two years to break even). But even this crude analysis fails to capture the wider economic impact and valuation of the play (the value of cultural tourism, for example).

In terms of 'value for money', it is fair to say that the Scottish Government's investment has paid off – not only by raising the international profile of Scotland's flagship new national company but also by touring the Scottish brand (along with the Scottish National Party's anti-war message, of course) abroad. This recognition was acknowledged in 2007 with the Government's unprecedented invitation to National Theatre of Scotland to open the parliamentary session with a gala performance of *Black Watch*.

If we apply McCarthy *et al.*'s framework to *Black Watch*, we can identify clear links between the theory and the audience response. In terms of intrinsic benefits, audience members consistently reported feelings of pleasure and captivation, employing adjectives such as 'magnificent', 'fantastic', 'moving' and 'intense', while critics found it 'thrilling', 'spectacular' and 'compelling' (National Theatre of Scotland, 2009). Many spectators spontaneously communicated their increased understanding of and empathy with the soldiers, whether physically (by laughing and crying) or verbally: '[The play] humanized people who sometimes are not understood in society' (David Loyn, quoted in Artworks Scotland, 2007). There was also strong evidence of a creation of social bonds: 'Burke's play [represents] a massive step forward in our understanding and recognition of a vital part in our national story, and – potentially – of the relationship between Scottish theatre and the widest possible popular audience, both at home, and far beyond our shores' (McMillan, 2007). McMillan's review expresses the collective empathy and cognitive growth unleashed by the play and demonstrates the ability of theatre to engage audiences far beyond the immediate theatre space itself. Her review also touches on the much more complex area of communal meaning.

In terms of McCarthy *et al.*'s intrinsic public benefits, *Black Watch* commemorated a significant event in Scotland's (and indeed the world's) history, providing a voice to the ordinary soldier and changing people's views by critiquing the whole premise and operation of the Iraq War. As the psychotherapist Shapiro (1998: 100) points out, 'the stories of our lives, told by our most talented writers … help us enrich our resources for living and healing'. Anecdotal evidence has revealed the therapeutic benefits of *Black Watch* to a host of soldiers past and present, particularly in regards to post-traumatic stress disorder; indeed the BBC documentary on the play concludes with the girlfriend of David Ironside, one of the soldiers interviewed by the playwright, declaring: 'I hope it brings a closure to it for him' (Artworks Scotland, 2007).

There is no scope here to delve into the educational benefits of the play – suffice to say that the play has already been adopted onto Scottish drama syllabuses. But in terms of social capital, the cumulative benefits of creating new communal meaning and social bonds have perhaps left a lasting legacy. Brown (2006: 20) defines social capital as 'the trust, mutual understanding, and shared values that bind human networks into communities'. By tackling such a timely and explosive social issue in such a politically neutral and empathetic way, *Black Watch* has certainly succeeded in fostering a sense of mutual understanding of its subject matter amongst an international audience of largely non-traditional theatre-goers.

Regarding enablers, there is also a close fit with White and Hede's model. Feedback from the play's audiences revealed a strong element of personal and social resonance, both generally among the war-weary spectators and specifically among the strong military component of the audience. In terms of catharsis, there is certainly an abundance of pity and fear in *Black Watch*. Audience members often spoke of being 'touched' and 'moved' and of the 'pulsating', 'visceral' brutality of their experience (National Theatre of Scotland, 2009).

So benefits models can clearly provide a framework and vocabulary to articulate some key aspects of value. But they fail to provide the whole picture because, as discussed earlier, they reduce the complexity of the audience experience and shoehorn it into predetermined outcomes. White and Hede's experience enablers of context and environment illustrate this point perfectly, and they take us back to our previous discussion on ethnography and reflexivity. For how can we properly capture and assess the holistic value of plays like *Black Watch* if we don't understand the context and the environment of the play? And how can we understand the context and environment of the play unless we are *there*, immersed in the physical environment and witnessing the value emerge? If we consider reflexivity as a critical analysis of context concerned with inter-subjectivity, then the only way to reach a reflexive assessment of a play's value is through an ethnography which embeds us in the context of the play. For if we don't *experience* what the actors and audiences do, how else can we appreciate the creative process and assess the myriad layers of value it creates?

In relation to *Black Watch*, a situational, ethnographic approach might have captured the value of the stories generated in the initial research process; it might have described the authenticity of the rehearsal process, during which the cast were ordered to march around Glasgow by a serving Sergeant Major; and it might have depicted the sense of anticipation on the first preview of the play as the audience took their seats in two opposing banks and noted their tears as they rose as one to applaud at the end.

Conclusion

In this chapter, we have addressed the relevance of the concept of 'value' in the arts sector and critically analysed traditional ways of assessing it. This is of particular relevance to contemporary concerns with the impact of the arts on society (both economic and social), and particularly where public funding or interest is identified. The point has not been to define or measure 'value' but to emphasise the situational and relational context of attempts to capture it. In part, this recognises that 'value' is formed from a social and cultural imaginary that emphasises an economy or balance sheet of dualisms (e.g. insert the word 'value' after any of these words: positive and negative, traditional and modern, product and process, intrinsic and instrumental).

The rationale, therefore, has been to subvert dualistic and didactic statements such as 'the arts are of intrinsic *or* instrumental benefit'. Rather, value is deemed to be practice-based, performed and experienced in situational, relational and ethnographic contexts. Broadening access to the arts, whether through audience development, co-creation or participatory projects, can therefore only broaden our knowledge of the conditions and articulations of cultural value.

In brief, 'value' needs to be considered both intrinsically *and* instrumentally, and spatially as well as socially: value is a consequence of, and embedded in, social relations (which include cultural, economic and political dimensions); value can be understood and interpreted in multiple ways in any given context or time (directly related to the previous point of social relations); and value is contingent, negotiable and always in formation. 'Value' is therefore a dialectic of these conditions and should be understood as such, particularly when questions of impact are being considered.

References

Appadurai, A. (1996) *Modernity at Large: Cultural Dimensions of Globalization*, Minneapolis/London: University of Minnesota Press.

Arai, S. and Pedlar, A. (2003) 'Moving beyond individualism in leisure theory: a critical analysis of concepts of community and social engagement', *Leisure Studies*, **22** (3), 185–202.

Artworks Scotland (2007) *Black Watch – A Soldier's Story*, directed by I. Scollay, BBC Scotland [Documentary: DVD].

Belfiore, E. and Bennett, O. (2008) *The Social Impact of the Arts: An Intellectual History*, Basingstoke: Palgrave Macmillan.

Brecht, B. (1964) *Brecht on Theatre: The Development of an Aesthetic*, New York: Methuen.

Brown, A. (2006) 'An architecture of value', *Grantmakers in the Arts Reader*, **17** (1), 18–25.

Brown, A.S. and Novak, J.L. (2007) 'Assessing the intrinsic impacts of a live performance'. San Francisco: WolfBrown, http://wolfbrown.com.

Burke, G. (2007) *Black Watch*, London: Faber and Faber.

DCMS (Department of Culture, Media and Sport) (2008) 'Creative Britain: New talents for the new economy', London: DCMS.

DCMS (Department of Culture, Media and Sport) (2011) 'What we do', London, DCMS. Available from http://www.culture.gov.uk/what_we_do/creative_industries, accessed 4 January 2011.

Ehrenreich, B. (2007) *Dancing in the Streets: A History of Collective Joy*, London: Granta.

Falassi, A. (1987) *Time out of Time: Essays on the Festival*, Albuquerque: University of New Mexico Press.

Galloway, S. (2009) 'Theory-based evaluation and the social impact of the arts', *Cultural Trends*, **18** (2), 125–148.

Galloway, S., Birkin, N., Hamilton, C., Bell, D. and Petticrew, M. (2006) 'Quality of life and wellbeing: measuring the benefits of culture and sport – a literature review', research reprot prepared for the Scottish Government, Edinburgh.

Getz, D. (1991) *Festivals, Special Events, and Tourism*, New York: Van Nostrand Reinhold.

Golden, L. (1973) 'The purgation theory of catharsis', *Journal of Aesthetics and Art Criticism*, **31** (4), 473–491.

Hesmondhalgh, D. (2007) *The Cultural Industries*, 2nd edn, Los Angeles/London: Sage.

Kirshenblatt-Gimblett, B. (2007) 'Performance studies', in H. Bial (ed.) *The Performance Studies Reader*, 2nd edn, London/New York: Routledge, pp. 43–55.

Massey, D.B. (2005) *For Space*, London: Sage.

McCarthy, K.F., Ondaatje, E.H., Zakaras, L. and Brooks, A. (2004) *Gifts of the Muse: Reframing the Debate about the Benefits of the Arts*, Santa Monica, CA: RAND.

McMillan, J. (2007) 'Reaping war's bitter harvest', *The Scotsman*, 7 August 2006.

National Theatre of Scotland (2009) 'Black Watch – audience reactions video', Glasgow, National Theatre of Scotland. Available from http://www.nationaltheatrescotland.com/content/default.asp?page=s222, accessed 1 July 2009.

Nicholson, R.E. and Pearce, D.G. (2001) 'Why do people attend events? A comparative analysis of visitor motivations at four south island events', *Journal of Travel Research*, **39** (4), 449–460.

Polanyi, K. (2001) *The Great Transformation: The Political and Economic Origins of our Time*, 2nd Beacon Paperback edn, Boston, MA: Beacon Press.

Sanderson, I. (2000) 'Evaluation in complex policy systems', *Evaluation*, **6**, 433–454.

Schechner, R. (2007) 'Performance studies: the broad spectrum approach', in H. Bial (ed.) *The Performance Studies Reader*, 2nd edn, London/New York: Routledge. pp. 7–9.

Shapiro, E.R. (1998) 'The healing power of culture stories: what writers can teach psychotherapists', *Cultural Diversity and Mental Health*, **4** (2), 91–101.

Throsby, C.D. (2001) *Economics and Culture*, Cambridge/New York: Cambridge University Press.

Turner, V.W. (1969) *The Ritual Process Structure and Anti-structure*, London: Routledge and Kegan Paul.

White, M. (2009) *Arts Development in Community Health: A Social Tonic*, Oxford: Radcliffe.

White, T.R. and Hede, A.-M. (2008) 'Using narrative inquiry to explore the impact of art on individuals', *Journal of Arts Management, Law and Society*, **38** (1), 19–35.

Further reading and research

Galloway, S., Birkin, N., Hamilton, C., Bell, D. and Petticrew, M. (2006) 'Quality of life and wellbeing: measuring the benefits of culture and sport – a literature review', research report prepared for the Scottish Government, Edinburgh.

O'Reilly, K. (2005) *Ethnographic Methods*, London/New York: Routledge.

Pitts, S.E. (2005) 'What makes an audience? Investigating the roles and experiences of listeners at a chamber music festival', *Music and Letters*, **86** (2), 257–269.

Rojek, C. (2000) *Leisure and Culture*, Basingstoke: Macmillan.

Thyne, M. (2001) 'The importance of values research for nonprofit organisations: the motivation-based values of museum visitors', *International Journal of Nonprofit and Voluntary Sector Marketing*, **6** (2), 116–130.

Turner, V. (1982) *From Ritual to Theatre: The Human Seriousness of Play*, New York: PAJ.

Unger, L.S. and Kernan, J.B. (1983) 'On the meaning of leisure: an investigation of some determinants of the subjective experience', *Journal of Consumer Research*, **9** (4), 381–392.

7 The 21st Century Venue

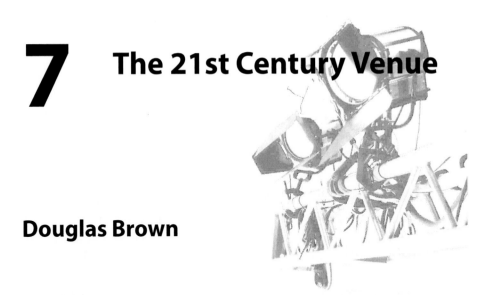

Douglas Brown

Introduction

A fundamental ingredient of presenting quality arts and entertainment experiences to contemporary audiences is the imaginative design, management and use of the places in which they happen: the venues. This chapter will continue to explore the changing relationship between audiences, producers and presenters of live arts and entertainment by looking at the design and use of physical spaces.

Whether we are talking about a large arena, a formal theatre space, a temporary performing space or a mobile cinema, many of the issues facing producers and managers are similar. This chapter will explore a number of issues affecting the design and use of spaces – large and small, formal and informal – and the current trends in venue design and management for presenting entertainment and the arts.

In the course of the chapter, we will consider topics such as the history of venue design and the justifications for different venues and building processes, as well as design issues including inclusivity, sustainability, flexibility and the use of technology. Trends including the move towards intimacy and transparency will be looked at in the context of how these issues relate to key values, such as equality, community, innovation and empowerment of the individual.

Public provision

Different countries offer alternative examples of the provision of performing arts and entertainment venues, depending on who controls and manages the buildings and how they are funded. Venues can be owned and managed by local governments, private trusts, voluntary bodies, universities and commercial enterprises. The public funding used to sustain and support buildings varies widely. The models and debates range from contributing full public funding and control to offering no public support whatsoever, which compels venues to run as commercial entities. In reality, most models fit somewhere in the middle of this spectrum (Strong, 2010).

Justification for public spending on buildings relies upon the following arguments. First is the **cultural** argument that having a performing arts venue protects and promotes cultural heritage, offering a place for the presentation of valued art forms, as well as preserving historic performance venues as important examples of architectural heritage. This perspective regards the buildings themselves as instruments to understand past cultural activities. Second are **economic** arguments, focused on economic impact reports, which promote the notion that venues can boost a local economy and bring money into its region, offering employment opportunities and stimulating business activity, both within and around the venue. Third is a **prestige** argument, that a venue can reinforce local identity, attract national and international attention and become an iconic symbol for the place itself, boosting cultural tourism. The most notable international example here is the Sydney Opera House, but more contemporary examples include London's O2 Arena, the Sage in Gateshead and the Wales Millennium Centre in Cardiff. Fourth is the **wellbeing** argument that people's quality of life is improved by venues offering complementary activities to work and home responsibilities, which enrich people's social and leisure time. Fifth, the argument that a venue can assist in the formation or rebuilding of a community or revitalising of a locality is about **regeneration**, which occurs by attracting visitors and stimulating tourism. Finally is the **educational** standpoint that venues offer learning and development opportunities by championing cultural engagement and encouraging active participation (Appleton, 1997).

Barriers to attendance

However, good design of public performing spaces must also address the challenges of increasing attendance and attracting new audiences. The planning and design must focus on combating the public's natural anxiety about crossing the threshold of an unfamiliar building, such as those that offer educational, sporting and other leisure activities. Buildings perceived to be arts and entertainment venues find it particularly difficult to attract tentative new audience members: numerous audience development studies have concluded that ticket prices are not the main barrier to attendance, but rather that audiences are inhibited by *physical access factors* such as location, public transport and parking difficulties, and *psychological factors* such as feeling socially uncomfortable in new situations and interacting with unknown groups (Kay *et al.*, 2008). It follows therefore that arts and entertainment venues should strive to limit all these perceived and actual barriers in order to maximise attendance and increase their public support.

Building processes

As we will see, buildings designed for performance and entertainment are functionally complex and often have a large number of diverse constituencies or stakeholders to satisfy. The building itself may also be used for aesthetic expression or to create a dynamic visual statement both inside and out. As such, people who either plan and design a new, or refurbish an existing, building need to balance the time, the cost and the quality of the process carefully.

A successful (re-)design process is guided by the following key principles: a clear vision, being informed, an excellent team, design quality, sustainability, accessibility, realistic finances, communication and consultation (Strong, 2010). A clearly defined vision should inform all aspects of the process. This will enable the design and management team to assess the needs of the various stakeholders on an ongoing basis and be clear about what the venue is actually going to deliver. This in turn involves identifying the driving factors and forces behind the building or refurbishment of a venue and deciding how they should be managed. Increasingly, it involves planning the space for flexible and maximum use, including a strategic view of incorporating partner organisations in order to encourage and stimulate the local 'creative ecology'. Planning managers need to be conversant with and fully informed of the latest developments and issues in venue design by visiting similar buildings, attending and observing events there, and talking to their managers.

Recruiting and developing an excellent design team involves a robust selection process to choose a range of designers, engineers, specialists, cost consultants and project managers with expertise in promoting strong, positive relationships and clear communication. Ultimately, it is good quality design that will attract people into a venue, overcoming the natural reluctance that potential audiences have of crossing the threshold of a building they are unfamiliar with. As we have seen, just getting people through the door is one of the major barriers to participation in the arts experience and a performance venue must therefore have 'an attractive shop window' and a 'welcoming shop layout'.

Good design also gives venues environmental sustainability, and as green concerns are progressively more prevalent in building legislation worldwide, strict attention must be paid to building materials, systems, maintenance and the building lifecycle. These should incorporate measures to reduce energy consumption, minimise the use of resources such as building materials and water, reduce the release of pollutants, maximise the use of recycled materials and promote sustainable travel choices. Attention to accessibility issues results in venues that are comfortable and easy to navigate, both physically and conceptually, for all users, without separating them unnecessarily into disabled and able-bodied visitors.

Regarding communication and consultation, for an architect, the process will begin with a brief from the commissioning team, which will take into account the process described above, along with the drivers, issues and values that inform it. The architect's job is to interpret these elements, often adding his or her own ideas, and transform them into a tangible, practical space that people will want to visit.

Changes in audience behaviour

A hundred years ago, home entertainment was live. It was centred on the piano in the parlour, the playing of instruments, and singing, dancing, reading and personal performance. However, while this home entertainment was live, it was only shared with a small and intimate group. Similarly, theatres built in the 19th and early 20th centuries sought to emphasise the divisions between, and physically separate, the various audience groups attending. This can be seen and experienced in the designs of the older, un-refurbished theatres we still attend today across the UK, and especially in London's West End. These theatres still have segregated entrances, foyer spaces and bars. In the auditoria themselves, this translates into clearly delineated levels and spaces (Carlson, 1989). In this way, audiences are made well aware of how much they have paid for their seats and which parts of the theatre they can access, and this directly affects their experiences, influencing how well they can see, hear and enjoy a performance.

The 20th century witnessed unparalleled technical developments in recording equipment and broadcasting that culminated in greater possibilities and variety for home entertainment. As discussed in the following chapter, we now live in an era where the easy option is to stay at home and enjoy a quality experience of watching a programme or film, or listen to music, alone or in a small domestic group. So our home entertainment is now often high quality, but passive, and it fails to satisfy our urge for social interaction and communication (Hammond, 2006). Despite the visual and technical sophistication of modern home entertainment, we still 'go out' for the dynamic experience of a live performance and to share the experience with others, as part of an audience. As we saw in Chapter 6, this is one of the key benefits of the arts and entertainment experience. The challenge for today's producers is to continue to draw people out of their homes by offering a quality social element that heightens their experience. So, along with a quality presentation, heightening the 'buzz' and making people feel included and welcomed into the place of performance is vital.

Imagine the challenges

Preferably, when we invite friends home to watch a favourite film or television programme, we seek to create the ideal environment – the right time, space and setting – in which to enjoy it. The controllable environmental factors take on an extra importance when we seek to share our enthusiasm for this favourite film or programme with them. We ask ourselves: Can they see clearly and hear well? Are they comfortable? Are there any distractions? Are they safe? What would they like to eat or drink?

Imagine the increasing challenges in trying to create a perfect space for sharing a favourite programme with two friends, or 20 friends, and then 200, 2000 or 20,000 people. The challenges of arranging the perfect setting in pursuit of complementing the performance or presentation by managing the whole environment in which to share or witness it are heightened with increasing audience numbers. But although the technicalities and issues become increasingly complex, the essential elements remain the same, and these are the elements which venue architects, designers and managers of public performance spaces seek to manage, prioritise and balance in order to create the optimum shared, memorable experience for a live public performance (Appleton, 1997).

Drivers, issues and values

Venues that have been planned and built during the past decade intend to draw new audiences into, and entice existing audiences back to, exciting, dynamic spaces. They aim to offer a stimulating experience that includes appropriate levels of comfort, access, intimacy, spectacle, safety, flexibility and opportunities for additional income generating activities such as corporate hospitality. They also need to incorporate, and indeed anticipate, the latest technological advances, while proving that they are efficient and environmentally sustainable projects. Across the UK and Europe, we can see these challenges being tackled in new and refurbished public performance spaces, with opera houses, arts centres, museums, art galleries, concert halls, theatres and cinemas being built and altered to reflect the ever shifting values of our time.

As we have discussed, the values of the past favoured the separation of groups and social classes, whereas now we expect a more inclusive and democratic approach to our spaces. We need the physical flexibility to be able to adapt and change our spaces in order to present a wide variety of styles and types of performance. And while audiences often crave both to 'lose themselves in a crowd' and 'experience a spectacle' (Hatlen, 1972), they also demand an intimacy that must be delivered by the design of the particular space or the appropriate use of technology. As discussed in Chapter 1, producers are increasingly trying to 'open up' the creative process to audiences and offer them an insight into how productions are created and put together. Venues such as Curve in Leicester are built specifically to offer such a glimpse (see www.curveonline.co.uk).

Current issues and values reflected in buildings

As a competent venue manager (and indeed as an aware audience member), it is important to identify the factors and recognise the drivers that are forming 21st century venues and their management. It is possible to identify within all venues the compliance with legislation and guidelines, most tangibly recognised with elements of access and adherence to the Disability Discrimination Act with lifts, doors, ramps and wheelchair spaces, plus adequate toilets and fire exits. Also present, but more difficult to spot, is adherence to the green agenda in the form of sustainability issues including heating, lighting, ventilation, water usage and overall carbon efficiency of the building. It is also, however, important to take note of other factors, including those in Table 7.1.

The factors are some of the major current social, economic and psychological drivers that a venue designer must take into account.

Table 7.1: Issues, Trends and Values Matrix

Issues and Trends	Design Solutions	Examples	Illustrations and Sources
Inclusivity	Consulting audiences in the design process	The Egg Theatre in Bath The Unicorn Theatre in London	www.theatreroyal.org.uk/the-egg www.unicorntheatre.com
Flexibility	Differing configurations of the audience, technical features and acoustical arrangements	The Brighton Dome Concert Hall Curve, Leicester	www.brightondome.org www.curveonline.co.uk
Technology	Using the latest technology to design a cutting-edge venue and improve the audience experience	Curve, Leicester The refurbished Royal Festival Hall in London	www.curveonline.co.uk www.southbankcentre.co.uk
Removing segregation/facilitating audience mix	Redesign of Victorian and Edwardian foyers, bars and circulation spaces	Refurbishment of the London Coliseum	www.eno.org
Intimacy	Reducing capacity and rearranging the seating	The new Royal Shakespeare Theatre in Stratford-upon-Avon	www.rsc.org.uk
Transparency and demystification of the creative process	Blurring the boundaries between the audience and the production spaces	Curve, Leicester The planned refurbishment of the National Theatre, London	www.curveonline.co.uk www.nationaltheatre.org.uk
Regeneration	Transformation of disused industrial spaces into new performance spaces	The new Elbe Philharmonic Hall in Hamburg, Germany	www.elbphilharmonie.de
Democratisation, inclusion and benefits for all	Multi-use design, welcoming facade and purpose-built education spaces	The Wales Millennium Centre in Cardiff The Lowry in Salford, Greater Manchester	www.wmc.org.uk www.thelowry.com
Desire for iconic buildings, promotion of civic pride and the need for spectacular experiences	Eye-catching venues that become a symbol of a city or place	The Sage in Newcastle/Gateshead The Elbe Philharmonic Hall in Hamburg	www.thesagegateshead.org www.elbphilharmonie.de
Access	Temporary and travelling venues that are pioneering and alluring	Kneehigh Theatre's 'Asylum' tent The Screen Machine in Scotland The Mini Opera Space in Munich	www.kneehigh.co.uk www.screenmachine.co.uk www.bayerische.staatsoper.de
Innovation and creating unique experiences	Use of found spaces, site sensitive performances and 'fringe' festival spaces	Artichoke Numerous venues at the Edinburgh Festival Fringe	www.artichoke.uk.com www.edfringe.com

Key spaces

Architects of public performing spaces have always faced the multiple challenge of joining together three main physical spaces that address three vastly different, yet equally important, functions. The first is the 'foyer space', a socially interactive space where audiences can gather, meet and greet. This should be a space that heightens the excitement and anticipation of the event. In practical terms, it needs to be accessible to audiences and offer essential services like toilets and refreshments. This is, overall, the place of anticipation, a space to heighten the 'buzz'. Also, it should offer extra services such as a cloakroom, shop, crèche, first aid facilities, display and exhibition space and, of course, clear access and signage to the auditorium (Appleton, 1997). Also, as part of and in addition to the foyer space, are particular concerns surrounding the support facilities. These include the public entrance, which must satisfy audiences' needs regarding public transport, parking and access. It needs also to include the box office as the primary point of sale and contact and should ideally offer augmented products, such as bars and restaurants, a shop, education rooms, plus flexible spaces for functions and special events.

How well these facilities are arranged and managed can increase the income that a venue can generate and add to audiences' overall comfort and convenience. Their prominence and arrangement will clearly signal the priorities of the venue design and management. That these areas and services have gained in size and importance shows a shift in social values towards actively promoting inclusion, openness, public access, comfort and community; and in times of decreasing public funding, this trend also highlights the necessity for venues to generate more of their own earned income.

The second space is the functional area, the stage, platform or playing area. This is a place for presentation, interaction with the audience and, in the case of theatre, also potentially the space for transformation. It is essentially an industrial space that contains the technical equipment and flexibility to create and change an on-stage picture. In the best of these spaces, the stage picture can be transformed from all directions: actors and scenery can enter from left and right, front and back; from the top (via the stage flying systems and the fly-tower); and from below (via trap doors and machinery in the stage floor). This dynamic ability to transform a spatial picture so completely is unique to theatre stages (Hatlen, 1972). It is in this space that we can experience the fusion of the values of innovation, creativity, beauty and spectacle, combined with the practical application of science and technology.

The third and most challenging space for architects and designers to create is the most important space for the distinctive audience experience: the auditorium. The core challenge here is to design a space which, in order to maximise venue and producer income, 'packs in' as many people as possible. This must be done as comfortably as possible, so that each member of the audience can see and hear well and has an optimum experience of what is happening on the stage. This is a place of concentration on the performers or events occurring on stage, the place of communication. It is also the space where the architects and designers must aim to achieve a proper balance of technology, comfort, scale, clear sightlines to the performance area and clarity of sound. Ultimately, it is the quality of the auditorium space in creating the connection between the audience members and the performers that will offer a meaningful experience for the audience and generate success for the venue.

The architecture and design of auditorium spaces of theatres in the 20th century has been most influenced by successful cinema design, which aimed to meet ever-increasing audience demand for greater comfort, extra services, ease of booking, travelling to and navigating the venue, and the overall quality of the experience. The theatre experience should be one where the audience is aware of sharing the live experience with others as part of a collective. To offer just one example of how this is achieved, think of the contrasting design of seating in theatres and contemporary cinemas. In live performance venues it is usual to be able to see the head and shoulders of those in front, have staggered seating, sloping seats rather than steps, limited legroom so people need to squeeze past, shared armrests and curved rows. Each element of the venue design can be carefully planned to unconsciously stimulate group behaviour, heightening the live experience, making it unique, and uniting a 'crowd' into an 'audience'. A different design can separate that crowd into behaving as individual spectators, depending on the planned experience – think of wide rows in modern cinema complexes with individual armrests complete with holders for drinks and popcorn.

But even when the space for performance is temporary, 'found' or 'site specific' – and even when a street performer creates an improvised live performance experience – the three main ingredients need to be carefully planned and considered: the time and space for anticipation, presentation and communication. So the challenges and complexity of bringing all of these various functional spaces together by an architect and designer are becoming clear. The most astute audience members are aware of, and the best venue managers take note of, the following principles that underpin the finest of these buildings, namely integrating audiences, maximising ease of use, and creating a stimulating ambiance and a sense of occasion.

Historic approaches and technical history

Performance spaces have always embraced and incorporated the latest technological advances in lighting, sound, projection and imaging in order to enhance performances. These advances began to take a modern shape that we would recognise about 200 years ago, beginning with advances in stage lighting. It was in 1816 that the Chestnut Street Theatre in Philadelphia became the first theatre in the world to light its stage area with gas. Until then, candles, oil burners and the filtering of daylight were used to light stages and auditoria; and, although they incorporated rudimentary mechanical elements in order to control the colour, density and direction of light, the flexibility and indeed brightness were limited.

Gas systems brought new possibilities to performance including new systems of controlling brightness, direction, colour changes, movement and special effects. In 1815 the Lyceum Theatre in London may have been the first to incorporate gas lighting into the auditorium, allowing the auditorium to be dimmed and the stage focus to be intensified. Gas lighting was used for exterior lighting at Covent Garden also in 1815 and when, in 1822, the opera house in Paris introduced gas lighting throughout the whole theatre, other theatres were quick to follow (Brockett, 1987).

Experiments continued and, while there were still serious drawbacks to using gas, such as heat, smell, fumes and the ever-present danger of fire, the advantages were that the stage could be as brightly lit as desired, the light focused more effectively and control boards, or 'gas tables', could manipulate the elements from a central control point. In Paris, in the 1840s, the first rudimentary spotlight, or 'limelight', was created by mixing the gas flow with hydrogen and oxygen, heating a cylinder of quicklime until it glowed (Brockett, 1987). In 1879, Edison invented the incandescent lamp and, as it greatly reduced the risk of fires, it was quickly adopted into theatres. In 1881, the Savoy Theatre in London was the first to be lit throughout by electricity, and by 1900 almost all English theatres were the same (Brockett, 1987).

Meanwhile, in Germany, theatre practitioners were busy inventing new ways of shifting three-dimensional settings, including rolling platforms, elevator stages and, in 1896, the first effective revolving stage.

Incorporating the latest science and technology into their buildings and productions, modern venues continue to use the most advanced lighting, sound, projection and screen technology in order to maximise intimacy and spectacle, subtlety and excitement, comfort and variety, and to use their resources efficiently and sustainably. While developments continue to be made in lighting, sound, projection and digital technology, the current major developments lie in computer control systems, which run the lighting, sound, flying systems and dynamic stage equipment. There have also been key advances recently in acoustical engineering, which means that the sound modelling of venues can be created, tested and altered before a building is even built. This technology can prevent venues being constructed with inadequate key functions and can also help to correct mistakes of the past, as in the recent refurbishment of the Royal Festival Hall in London's South Bank Centre, which had suffered from poor acoustics since it was built in 1951 until the improvements made in 2009.

However, 'designers and architects must remember that no matter how sophisticated technologies become, human contact lies at the heart of live performance' (Pilbrow, 2002). For it is the human element that remains at the core of the artistic experience, and no matter how sophisticated technologies become, human contact and the sense of occasion will remain the essence of live performance.

Case studies

As discussed earlier, there are many key challenges facing performing arts venues. These fundamentally involve where and how to create, arrange and manage the 'perfect setting' for a live performance. However, the different solutions available to meet these challenges mean that the tangible outcomes, the venues themselves, can be quite different. This is because of the varied histories of producing companies, the agendas of the main funders and stakeholders, the current social drivers, the ever-changing external social, political and economic environments and the vision and artistic objectives of companies and producers themselves. These factors mean that each venue is unique and every venue is therefore worth exploring in depth to uncover the circumstances, challenges and solutions that have led to their final form. The final result, like any piece of art, will reflect the external environment – the times in which it was created – as well as the vision, aims, budget and talents of all those involved in its formation.

This section will analyse three different types of venue building projects: creating a brand new building; redeveloping a historical venue; and designing temporary or touring spaces.

Case study 1: Curve, a new building

In 2003, Leicester, located in the East Midlands of England, with a population of just under 300,000 and a further 400,000 living in the surrounding area, was a culturally diverse city, with large and varied communities of South Asian origin. But it was a city in decline. One district of the city, St George's, boasted high quality architecture and was designated as a conservation area. But 80 per cent of its buildings were vacant or under-used. In order to stimulate the regeneration of the area, plans were made to create a 'cultural quarter' which would contain a new theatre with two auditoria. However, the main funders, Leicester City Council, were concerned that this theatre could be perceived as too elitist for many of the local population and were keen for Leicester's multi-cultural ethos to be reflected and to see the conventional barriers between theatres and audiences broken down.

In actuality, the renowned architect who was appointed to design the new building, Rafael Viñoly, sought not just to find an architectural solution to issues of inclusion, transparency and access, but also to break down barriers that can arise when various groups and departments are working within the same building – actors, production staff and administrators; those on-stage, back-stage and in the offices. What he eventually created was a whole building that can be used as a fully flexible performance space.

The theatre was built by a partnership of Leicester City Council, Arts Council England (with funds from The National Lottery), East Midlands Development

Curve, Leicester. Image by David Brook, courtesy of Curve.

Agency and Leicester Shire Economic Partnership, with the project part-financed by the European Union Regional Development Fund, in partnership with Leicester Theatre Trust and in association with Phoenix Arts. Leicester's Curve, as it is now known, cost £61 million to construct and is run by the Leicester Theatre Trust, an independent charitable organisation. It opened on 11 November 2008 with a celebratory opening show called 'Lift Off', a promenade production which showcased the potential of the new space.

Iconic and eye-catching from the outside, the transparent nature of the architecture, using glass, clever lighting, brightly coloured interior walls, and street-level walkways, is designed to attract the attention, and curiosity, of passers-by. It is a four-story, curved, louvered glass hall incorporating two joined but freestanding nearly full-height pods painted purple and red. These are the auditoria. The main house has 750 seats (expandable to 800) and the smaller studio space has 350 seats. The two auditoria are linked at the stage end of the main auditorium by two safety curtains which can be raised to open the main stage into the studio space. Also, there are two 32-ton, L-shaped safety curtains and acoustic walls that form the side walls of the stage house and these can be opened directly onto the public foyers. This can offer visitors, and even people walking by outside, a clear view of all the action in the foyer, café, bars, backstage areas and even across the stage.

Furthermore, the architect positioned the offices, dressing rooms and scenery workshops on balconies overlooking the performance space. So any activity on stage can be seen by office staff, actors in the dressing rooms and even people in the restaurant, providing an intriguing glimpse into the stage preparation from the outside. Also, the strategic placement of the dressing rooms and workshops means that actors and scenery must cross the public foyer space to get to the stage.

While this unique, fully flexible arrangement has attracted world-wide attention, it has also been labelled as a performance space with an 'inside-out design' (Rushton-Read, 2009). This label is of mixed benefit to the theatre. With it comes an audience expectation that the theatre productions will be experimental and cutting edge. While it holds that at every performance the actors must cross the foyer space to get into position, the theatre also brings in outside productions as a receiving house and takes tours of its own productions out to other, more conventional, theatres. So productions cannot always be specific to this space. What the building does offer is the choice for theatre directors to use the flexibility and openness if they choose to.

Since its opening, the theatre has seen an increase in young people coming to the theatre. They have been attracted by the spectacle of the building itself, by seeing the various phases of production and by experiencing an opening-up of the creative process. However, the theatre's staff must also strive to win over audiences and counter the misconception that the theatre's work will always be experimental and therefore not for them.

Case study 2: A redevelopment – The Royal Shakespeare Company's Transformation Project

After nearly 50 years in its historic 80-year-old home, the Royal Shakespeare Company (RSC) faced the need to redevelop its theatre to meet the changing aspirations of the company and the increasing expectations of its audiences.

The Royal Shakespeare Theatre (RST) is a large-scale theatre owned by the RSC and a Grade II listed building. It is located in the town of Shakespeare's birth, Stratford-upon-Avon, an attractive market town in the English Midlands, with a population of about 24,000, which attracts more than three million visitors each year. There has been a theatre in Stratford-upon-Avon to celebrate the works of Shakespeare since 1769. The RST was built and opened on 23 April 1932 (Shakespeare's birthday) after a fire destroyed the original Shakespeare Memorial Theatre, built in 1879. Over the years, a number of minor changes have been made to the theatre – including the addition in 1986 of another theatre space, the intimate 430-seat Swan Theatre, built in the shell of the original Memorial Theatre – but the cavernous, cinema-style auditorium, where the long rows of seats over three levels faced a stage behind a proscenium arch, remained.

So the RSC recently decided to create a new home for the company within the footprint of the 1932 theatre, complete with a new 1000-seat auditorium and a thrust stage. The aim was to marry the best of the original 1932 theatre, retaining the key heritage elements, such as the art deco foyer, fountain staircases and the riverside facade, with dynamic new spaces. The new RST auditorium will have 500 fewer seats and will dramatically improve the actor–audience relationship by reducing the distance of the furthest seat from the stage from 27 metres to 15 metres and seating the audience on three sides of the stage. Crucially, the refurbishment will also improve the backstage areas for the actors and technicians; create an accessible riverside walkway leading visitors to Holy Trinity Church, Shakespeare's burial place; offer a public square to provide a meeting place and an outdoor performance area; add a new theatre tower with a viewing platform; and expand and improve fully accessible facilities and public spaces for audiences, including a rooftop restaurant, and a colonnade linking the RST with the Swan Theatre.

Most obvious from the outside is the 33-metre high Theatre Tower which will mark the new entrance to the building, provide public circulation to all parts of the building and offer clear views over Stratford-upon-Avon and its surrounding countryside. Although there was some local opposition to the refurbishment plans, particularly when it seemed that the exterior of the 1932 theatre was to be demolished, a comprehensive refurbishment plan has been created that offers a more traditional Shakespearean performing area, while also offering a more personal, and overall more comfortable, theatre experience for audiences and an exciting, enhanced visitor attraction.

The £112.8 million cost of the refurbishment was met by public sector support and a fundraising campaign. The main supporters include Arts Council England, Advantage West Midlands (the regional development agency) and numerous gifts from trusts and individual patrons from over 55 countries worldwide. While the driving force of the project was to replace the 1930s style auditorium with one based more on the RSC's own Swan Theatre style 'one room space', where the actors and audience are brought close together, a number of subsidiary aims were also achieved. These include features designed to make the building more open and welcoming. The main entrance now faces the town and is therefore more accessible to both residents and tourists, enticing them into the box office and encouraging them to spend money in the shop, bars and restaurant. The distinctive Theatre Tower is also an important marker for the town, bringing back a sense of the old Victorian theatre to the town centre and acting as a symbol of change and renewal. Equally important, the new design offers excellent facilities for the actors, technicians and members of the theatre company to keep them working together longer and to strengthen the ensemble nature of the company (see the case study in Chapter 11).

Case study 3: Temporary and transportable venues

The Asylum

Kneehigh is an experimental theatre company based in Cornwall, England, a location with few permanent theatre buildings. Kneehigh was founded in 1980 and its early productions were performed in village halls, marquees, castles, on cliff-tops and in quarries. The company's productions combine puppetry and live music with the visual elements of performance.

Kneehigh has recently commissioned the design and construction of its own portable domed tent as a flexible, transportable performance space, which it has called 'The Asylum'. This is because it wants people to think of the space as 'a shelter, a refuge, a sanctuary and a madhouse' (Western Morning News, 2010). It is meant to be a creative space where the performers and audience can feel free and inspired.

The domed tent measures 45 metres long by 30 metres wide and can be set up in one day on any surface. Depending on the five different configurations it which it can be set, it can hold audience numbers ranging from 200 to1000 people. It cost £870,000 to design and construct. The design has been inspired by ancient building methods and is rooted in the ideas of circus, troubadour and folk traditions. With this comfortable tent, Kneehigh is now able to bring its work closer to its audiences and enjoy all the facilities of a permanent building but with fewer overheads and restrictions.

The Screen Machine

The Screen Machine is Britain's only mobile cinema offering a quality film-going experience. It operates mainly across the Scottish Highlands and Islands and aims to bring a mainstream cinema experience to remote rural locations and fragile communities, where the nearest cinema may be many hours (and sometimes even a ferry ride) away. The current Screen Machine, which has been in service since 2005, is the second design. It comprises a 36-tonne lorry, the trailer of which can expand and unfold to provide an 80-seat self-contained cinema. The cinema is operated by one person alone, who drives the vehicle, sets up the cinema on site, sells the tickets and projects the film. The cinema projects in a digital format, offering digital sound and even 3D. Although a temporary venue, the Screen Machine comes complete with ramped access to its main entrance, an infra-red hearing loop system with personal headsets, a subtitling system and an audio description service that is available upon request, while the colour scheme in the auditorium has been designed to assist the visually impaired.

The Screen Machine at Lochmaddy. Image by Ron Inglis, courtesy of Regional Screen Scotland.

The initiative is run by Regional Screen Scotland and its running costs are approximately £230,000 per year, with major funding coming from Creative Scotland and Highlands & Islands Enterprise. To make it viable, at least 50 tickets must be sold for each showing, and although up to 23,000 people each year see a film in the Screen Machine, the pressure on programming and marketing is considerable.

The Screen Machine is all about access, flexibility, inclusion and sustainability. It offers a social and entertaining experience to remote communities, which many people in more populous areas take for granted, and it therefore plays an important social role in developing community cohesion and lessening the depopulation of fragile communities. The lettering on the side of the lorry tellingly states: 'Unfold Your Imagination'.

Pavillon 21, MINI Opera Space

Opera has yet to find a clear position with 21st century audiences. At its grandest, it is a spectacular art form, with each performance requiring the co-operation and talents of hundreds of people. In Europe, at least, it is usually performed in purpose-built venues stemming from the 18th and 19th centuries, many of which were rebuilt after the Second World War in more or less their original form. The Bavarian State Opera, based in Munich, sought to challenge this notion by offering new experiences in its MINI Opera Space at its 2010 Festival.

Its challenge was to design and build a temporary pavilion with a multifunctional stage and 300 seats or 700 standing places. For the architects, this meant addressing the apparent paradox between mobility and flexibility on the one hand and excellent acoustics on the other. So the Vienna architects Coop Himmelblau created a pavilion which was 21 metres long, 17 metres wide and between six and eight metres high and designed the building to act as a sound reflector, rather than a barrier, to lessen the traffic noise from the nearby roads. The venue comprises a performance area, an auditorium, a backstage area and a bar and lounge.

The Bavarian State Opera company wanted the MINI Opera Space to place no limits on artistic forms, so its openness and flexibility provide the necessary room for the imagination, inviting visitors to 'tread new paths of perception and artistic reflection' (Bayerishe Staatsoper, 2010). The venue was visited by 9000 people during the festival and audiences enjoyed a varied programme ranging from opera performance to clubbing, and from experimental theatre to lectures. Perhaps this type of dynamic, temporary performance space is just what opera needs to attract new audiences in the 21st century.

Conclusion

In this chapter we have explored a number of issues that face the architects, designers, funders and managers of 21st century venues. We have seen how aspects of public support, audience behaviour and expectations, changing social values and the incorporation of new technologies must be recognised and balanced in order to offer a high quality, memorable audience experience. It is worth remembering that venues themselves play a crucial role as instruments with which, and in which, art and live performance is actually created.

Contemporary venues fulfil many roles and face multiple challenges. They represent a new type of social space and visitor attraction which, while reflecting their organisations' cultural, social and economic objectives, must equally draw people out of their homes to experience the excitement of live performance and encourage them to return. So the successful venue managers of the future will not just be concerned with *what* people are experiencing: they must give equal attention to, and understand, the *why*, and continue to be innovative with the *where* and *how*.

References

Appleton, I. (1997) *Buildings for the Performing Arts: A Design and Development Guide*, Oxford: Architectural Press.

Bayerische Staatsoper (2010) 'Pavilion 21: MINI Opera Space'. Available from: http://www.bayerische.staatsoper.de/322-ZG9tPWRvbTQmbD1lbiZwcmVzc2V faWQ9MTE2NjA-~presse~presseinfo~presse-information.html, accessed 11 July 2010.

Brockett, O.G. (1987) *History of the Theatre*, 5th edn, London: Allyn & Bacon.

Carlson, M. (1989) *Places of Performance: The Semiotics of Theatre Architecture*, Ithaca, NY and London: Cornell University Press.

Hammond, M. (2006) *Performing Architecture: Opera Houses, Theatres and Concert Halls for the Twenty-First Century*, London/New York: Merrell.

Hatlen, T.W. (1972) *Orientation to the Theatre*, Englewood Cliffs, NJ: Prentice-Hall.

Kay, P., Wong, E. and Polonsky, M. (2008) 'Understanding barriers to attendance and non-attendance at arts and cultural institutions: a conceptual framework', in D. Spanjaard, S. Denize and N. Sharma (eds), *Proceedings of the Australian and New Zealand Marketing Academy Conference 2008: Marketing: Shifting the Focus from Mainstream to Offbeat*, Victoria, Australia: ANZMAC, pp. 1–7.

Pilbrow, R. (2002) 'Channelling emotion', *International Arts Manager*, October, 15–16.

Rushton-Read, S. (2009) 'Inside story', *Auditoria*, (16), 8.

Strong, J. (ed.) (2010) *Theatre Buildings: A Design Guide*, London: Routledge.

Western Morning News (2010), 'Asylum debuts with old favourite Kneehigh shows', *Western Morning News*, 30 July.

Further reading and research

Auditoria, Dorking: UKiP Media & Events.
(Annual publication on entertainment venue design, operations and technologies)

Cole, R.J. and Lorch, R. (2003) *Buildings, Culture and Environment: Informing Local and Global Practices*, Oxford: Blackwell.

Coop Himmel Blau (2010) *Pavillon 21 Mini Opera Space*, Vienna: Himmelprint.

Farnish, M. (2002) 'The venue masters', *International Arts Manager*, October, 17–19.

Ham, R. (1988) *Theatres: Planning Guidance for Design and Adaptation*, Oxford: Architectural Press.

Hewison, R., Holden, J. and Jones, S. (2010) *All Together: A Creative Approach to Organisational Change*, London: Demos.

Leacroft, R. and Leacroft, H. (1984) *Theatre and Playhouse*, London: Methuen.

MacKintosh, I. (1993) *Architecture, Actor and Audience*, London/New York: Routledge.

Nagler, A.M. (1952) *A Source Book in Theatrical History*, New York: Dover.

Strong, J. (2009) *Building Excellence in the Arts: A Guide for Clients*, London: Arts Council England and CABE.

van Uffelen, C. (2009) *Cinema Architecture*, Salenstein, Switzerland: Braun.

Wood, K. (2006) 'Constant change', *Arts Professional*, **130**, p.7.

8 The Future of Home Entertainment

James Roberts

Introduction

The aim of this chapter is to explore the current scope and character of home entertainment in its many electronic forms (including television, video games and music) focusing particularly on the changing nature of consumer interaction with it. Through an examination of the various forces that have driven its development, the chapter will look at the more significant aspects of its evolution in the decade since 2000 and make some informed judgements about how it might develop in the next.

The term 'home entertainment' has covered a vast range of activities during its long history. The first well-documented evidence of people spending significant time and resources on entertaining themselves at home emerge from Sumerian, Roman and Greek texts. As Juvenal notes, it seemed that all Romans were interested in was 'bread and circuses', and from a relatively early time, wealthier ones saw the opportunity to have both at home, hosting their own dinner parties and banquets. Along with dinner could be music, singing, and dancing by professionals. Such group activities might also be accompanied by more solitary pursuits such as reading, and individuals making their own entertainment through playing musical instruments or reciting poetry.

Even from these earliest times, we see evidence of the impact of three fundamental drivers on the amount and types of home entertainment prevalent in a society. Broadly these can be categorised as follows:

♦ Social/cultural: the availability of free time; prevailing views of the social importance of home entertainment and cultural views on what that entertainment might constitute; views of appropriate behaviour and how entertainment is used in a social context.

♦ Economic: the availability of disposable income, the emergence of providers of home entertainment content or equipment and the business models to support their activities; the emergence of appropriate methods to distribute and consume entertainment.

♦ Technical: the range of products and services enabled by the existing technological infrastructure.

Each of these forces will interact with the others, hence social and cultural issues interact with economic ones around issues such as censorship, copyright control and the protection of perceived cultural integrity within a country through devices like quotas.

Throughout the history of home entertainment these forces have been at work to create the context for the growth and emergence of dominant forms of home entertainment. Figure 8.1 indicates the confluence of events and developments that led to the emergence of printing as a major manufacturing activity in the 1600s, and the subsequent development of reading as a major form of entertainment in the home.

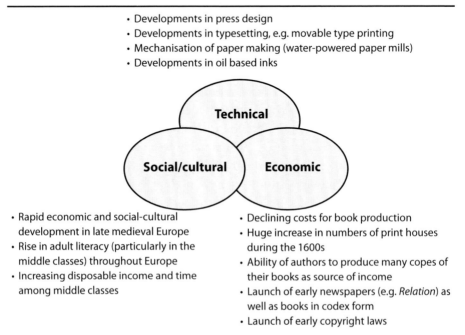

• Developments in press design
• Developments in typesetting, e.g. movable type printing
• Mechanisation of paper making (water-powered paper mills)
• Developments in oil based inks

Technical

Social/cultural   Economic

• Rapid economic and social-cultural development in late medieval Europe
• Rise in adult literacy (particularly in the middle classes) throughout Europe
• Increasing disposable income and time among middle classes

• Declining costs for book production
• Huge increase in numbers of print houses during the 1600s
• Ability of authors to produce many copes of their books as source of income
• Launch of early newspapers (e.g. *Relation*) as well as books in codex form
• Launch of early copyright laws

Figure 8.1: Early enablers of the growth of reading as a form of home entertainment

Only when all three forces work in sympathy does a major new form of home entertainment typically emerge. And when such a form does emerge, particularly mass media such as TV and radio, they in turn can have a significant impact on shaping the character of technology, economics and society. Hence the growth in the medium of television has unarguably had a hugely significant effect on the social, cultural and political environments of most countries. Equally, the mass commercialisation of television services after the Second World War created new opportunities for the re-invention of existing business models like advertising, and allowed large numbers of new companies to enter the economy, generating significant incomes and profoundly impacting on the economic character of many countries.

Hence the forces that are fundamental in shaping entertainment in the home are in turn influenced and modified by the entertainment forms they create. The rest of this chapter explores this central and complex relationship in the context of current developments in the home entertainment field, specifically those involving electronic forms of entertainment.

The evolution of home entertainment since the turn of the century

As we entered the new millennium, the home entertainment industry was established as a significant, technologically sophisticated driver of the global economy and as a key contributor to many of the most significant changes in the social and cultural landscape of many countries since the 1950s. By 2000, the home entertainment market had become hugely complex and fragmented, comprising a plethora of sectors, producers and often highly sophisticated consumers.

For each of the major sectors, a wide range of organisational types are typically involved in the provision of a vast range of services and products. In the television sector alone, the provision of a limited analogue service by a small number of broadcasters in the 1970s, which offered limited channel choice and very little else, has blossomed into a complex, multiplatform environment, offering hundreds of channels, interactive services and a wide variety of associated products, as outlined in Figure 8.2.

Within each of the sectors, a variety of competing technologies and products are striving to eke out consumers' attention and spending. To a degree, competition between platforms for audiences' time and attention (for example between reading and watching television or between TV and listening to music) has moved to competition within sectors (between cable, satellite or digital terrestrial transmission systems, between delivery to the TV or PC, between traditional programmes and interactive content or packaged media). What then are the major trends that have driven this proliferation of home entertainment in the last decade?

Business to business sectors	Types of electronically based home entertainment	Business to consumer sectors	Consumer products
Consumer electronics manufacturers	Radio	Broadcasting	FTA broadcasting, Pay TV including cable, satellite, digital terrestrial, IPTV
Content developers	Television	Hardware provision	Televisions, PVRs, receivers, audio products, screens, networking tools, cables, stands
Infrastructure providers	Music		
	Games consoles		
Merchandise providers, e.g. toy manufacturers	Online	Packaged media	VHS, DVD, Blu-ray
Support organisations (advertising agencies, management companies, law firms, funders, etc.)	Publishing	Merchandising	Toys, games, books, magazines, live shows
		Interactive services	Information services (weather, stocks, news) voting on game shows, play along channels

Figure 8.2: The increasing complexity and diversity of the television sector

Note: see end of chapter for list of acronyms used in the diagram and text

Technology

The influence of technology on the development of home entertainment has been pervasive, enduring and highly significant. It has influenced development through three major mechanisms: the further evolution of existing home entertainment devices and networks; non-entertainment devices and networks being converted to entertainment based use; and the emergence of completely new home entertainment devices and networks. These in turn have been driven by developments in a variety of technologies, but particularly expansions in the capabilities and penetration of electronic networks, developments in display technologies, the evolution of accessible and diverse compression technologies and the shrinking form factor for memory and batteries.

Traditional devices associated with home entertainment, such as the TV, have evolved consistently and have been readily taken up by consumers. The wide-scale rollout of flat screen devices and the emergence of new technologies such as LCD and organic light emitting diode televisions are good examples here. These are augmented by an array of dedicated hardware to receive, record, play back or enhance the audio visual experience (e.g. what are generally known as home cinema systems). Increasingly, it would seem, consumers prefer a truly cinematic experience at home when they watch TV.

Delivery platforms for content have also continued to develop, most recently with the rollout of limited high definition broadcast services in the USA and UK. Packaged media has kept pace with the launch of Blu-ray discs, offering higher onscreen detail, enhanced sound and a range of on and offline interactive content.

Whilst incremental evolution of hardware has been dominant in the television sector, some devices have evolved beyond all recognition. The bulky portable music players of the 1980s and 1990s have been replaced with stylish fashion accessories like the iPod (first introduced in 2001), which offer high quality audio and ultimate portability for people's music collections, and are now owned by over 76 per cent of those aged between 8 and 18 in the USA (Kaiser, 2010). In combination with the mobile phone, they have become a vital lifestyle accessory for many, enabling music, video and games playback; messaging and productivity applications like contact and diary management; and web surfing, all in a single portable device. Masaru Ibuka, Akio Morita, and Kozo Ohsone of Sony could not have imagined that their early efforts with a cassette player in 1980 would have evolved into such a sophisticated device in such a relatively short time.

Devices not traditionally associated with entertainment have also been widely co-opted as extensions of the home entertainment sphere, particularly PCs and mobile phones. Indeed the combination of the rollout of broadband networks with developments in file compression technologies (like mp3 and mp4), means that it is possible to move large amounts of data, at speeds high enough to allow effective content delivery (either streamed or downloaded) through the existing telephony infrastructure. An entirely new delivery network for entertainment has thus evolved, delivering content to mobile phones, PCs and, increasingly, to the TV.

Forms of content, traditionally limited to packaged media or broadcast delivery, have also been freed up for delivery and consumption on a range of non-traditional devices. Hence music once limited to packaged media (vinyl discs, cassettes, CDs) and radio delivery, can be consumed via the TV, radio, PC, mobile phone, portable file player or home hi-fi, in file format or packaged media, streamed or downloaded, bought, rented, copied or stolen (see Figure 8.3).

		1920s	1980s	2010
Do it yourself	**Playing/ recording**	Simple intruments	Instruments and basic recording equipment	Sophisticated computerised home studio systems, access to professional grade instruments
	Distribution	No distribution opportunities	Few distribution opportunities	Access to extensive distribution network via internet
Commercial services	**Packaged media**	Vinyl	Vinyl and cassette, VHS	Vinyl, CD, SACD, DVDs, Blu-ray
	Broadcast	Radio, few channels	Radio, many channels, AM/FM Limited coverage on TV	Radio: many stations, now including DAB, internet radio TV:dedicated channels, significant coverage on terrestrial channels, PPV offerings
	Other			Music files delivered to TV, PC, mobiles, portable players via downloading and streaming

Figure 8.3: The evolving consumption of music in the home

Entirely new devices have also emerged, often attempting to enhance the functionality of an existing entertainment device or method of media consumption. Electronic readers began to be seriously commercialised in 2005. Early offerings by Sony have subsequently been complemented by hardware from Amazon (Kindle) and Apple (iPad). In doing so, they have introduced a range of new functionality to the activity of reading, simply not available in the traditional book form, including automatic bookmarks, interactive content, integrated dictionaries and, perhaps most fundamentally, the ability to access hundreds of books from a single book-sized device. And as developments in networks and devices have continued, content and application producers have taken the opportunity to extend their range of offerings in a wide variety of entertainment sectors.

During the 1980s and 1990s, devices in the home were typically associated with and limited to a specific range of activities and applications. TVs were typically associated with entertainment, PCs with productivity related activities and the telephone with communications. Today, however, each of these devices has taken on a new range of functions and applications, and roles have become much more blurred. Laptop PCs can be used simultaneously to download content, watch a film, finish an assignment and communicate via social network sites. As already indicated, mobile telephones are increasingly used for a variety of entertainment, communication and productivity related tasks, both within and outside the home. Application developers have also taken advantage of the opportunity to develop new offerings based on the merger of various types of activity, as shown in Figure 8.4.

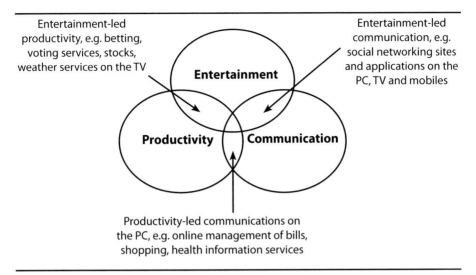

Entertainment-led productivity, e.g. betting, voting services, stocks, weather services on the TV

Entertainment-led communication, e.g. social networking sites and applications on the PC, TV and mobiles

Entertainment

Productivity   Communication

Productivity-led communications on the PC, e.g. online management of bills, shopping, health information services

Figure 8.4: Opportunities for new application types

Finally, technology has had a significant effect on how content is created. Making a film in the past that called for the 'massed nations of the Persian empire' to be on the screen would have involved huge sets, a literal army of extras and weeks of on-location shooting – a hugely expensive and complex enterprise. Today, a similar (if arguably not better) depiction can be created with 60 people and a green room (see Legendary Studios/Warner Bros, film, *300*). Equally, films are made with new technologies in mind (e.g. delivery in 3D or HD) requiring the deployment of new, highly sophisticated cameras and effects.

The home entertainment sector has therefore been a fundamental driver and beneficiary of developments in technology throughout its history, though perhaps this relationship has intensified to a degree never before seen during the last two decades. The next major challenge to technologists revolves around how all of the diverse devices, networks and technologies interact with each other, whether there will be a move to dedicated equipment for dedicated applications or the delivery of content over integrated home networks, with a variety of devices used for a variety of applications at different times by different members of the family. This in turn prompts the question of whether consumers are willing to sacrifice the best experience on one device (the TV is probably still the best place to watch sport), for a lower quality but perhaps more convenient one on another ('it's easier to watch TV and e-mail at the same time on the PC than the TV', 'I can't wait to get home to watch the touchdown; I'll watch a clip on my mobile').

Cultural and social developments

Whilst the cultural and social context for home entertainment is a vast area of study, including consideration of issues around how we interpret the content we receive, and how cultural forces influence the content that is created, this chapter will focus on specific issues around user and consumer interaction with home entertainment forms and technologies. When new forms of home entertainment emerge, consumers can react in a variety of ways: they can ignore it; they can use it in a substitute form for another entertainment activity; they can add it to the existing list of forms they use; or they can use it to modify their use of an existing form.

No matter how technologically advanced, some new products are largely ignored, due to a mismatch in consumer, product and market characteristics. The Phillips CD-i introduced in 1991, which foreshadowed many elements of modern games consoles and packaged media players, never found a satisfactory mass market despite its innovative proposition and constant marketing. It was abandoned five years later, with, some estimates suggest, a $1bn loss to the manufacturer.

Other new products tend to cannibalise existing forms, that is they do not add to the total size of market, but eat away at an existing portion of it. The launch of the DVD format by Warner Bros has arguably cannibalised the use of VHS. Use of social networking sites by teenagers has, according to some, cannibalised their use of TV as an entertainment device.

Perhaps more significantly, new products and forms can add to the total time spent on home entertainment. This is perhaps the key story of the last ten years in terms of home entertainment. With the maturation of the games sector and the increasing use of computers as entertainment devices, the number of hours dedicated to home entertainment, particularly amongst younger demographics, has steadily increased. A recent piece of research (Kaiser, 2010) has suggested that the total number of minutes devoted to home entertainment by children aged 8–18 in the USA has risen by 44 per cent between 1999 and 2009, from 449 to 645 minutes on average per day.

The same research suggested that in terms of growth, the biggest contributors were time spent on the PC (with a 230 per cent increase in entertainment minutes) and games (181 per cent increase). It is also worth noting that time dedicated to music increased by 40 per cent, perhaps due to the launch of a variety of new music devices and services like the iPod.

Along with this rise in overall usage, we have seen increasing evidence of the simultaneous use of a variety of different media. Simultaneous use of media is nothing new, although in the past it has been typified by a combination of a more active medium (like reading the paper) with a more passive one (like listening to radio). In such a scenario, the passive medium commands relatively little attention, acting as a form of background noise, only securing the user's attention when a relevant piece of content appears.

Today, however, we increasingly see the use of a variety of active media simultaneously. Recent research by the Nielsen Company (2009) suggests that during 2009, 59 per cent of their sample used the TV and Internet simultaneously at least once per month. Commentators have noted that a significant proportion of this simultaneous usage is typically engaged in activities around the programmes being watched, e-mailing or instant messaging to discuss it, voting, or researching relevant programme information. In this case, then, the media are being combined to enhance the overall experience of using both. Such interaction does however raise questions about the degree of attention being devoted to any one media and the efficacy of traditional methods of advertising, something that we will return to in a later section.

Another issue raised by such multi-media usage is how it compares with traditional home-based viewing or usage habits. With the diversity of ways in which content can be delivered, combined with people's desire to enhance their experience of it by using multiple platforms simultaneously, it appears that we are far more likely to consume content alone, or in small groups, than in previous years. With 29.9 per cent of TV-owning households in the USA having four or more televisions (Nielsen Company, 2009) and the majority owning at least two, the likelihood of groups within the home watching content on a central TV is limited, and is increasingly restricted to major TV events. However, use of other communications media simultaneously does allow groups to be re-aggregated, to establish immediate communities of viewers or users, albeit over distributed, electronic networks that stretch far beyond the home.

The final theme that has emerged as a particularly significant and contested issue during the last ten years is the issue of consumers' control over the content they consume. Early proponents of the idea that consumers were wrenching control from providers pointed to the emergence of various consumer-based tools designed to manage how content was delivered in the TV environment, including the evolution of recording devices from VHS recorders to hard-disc-based PVRs, customisable electronic programme guides on television and the evolution of pay-per-view services.

And indeed there did appear to be early evidence of changing consumer behaviour, with advertisement skipping and programme time shifting seen as particularly radical and potentially threatening new developments. But penetration of new recording devices has been relatively slow and usage is still limited. The Nielsen Company (2009) suggests that of the 35 hours of television watched on average by Americans per week during the first quarter of 2009, only 2 hours (5 per cent) were time-shifted. Pay-per-view has yet to achieve significant penetration (or impact on the economics) of the industry. Whilst penetration and usage of such services will probably grow, the question of the degree to which all TV viewers are entirely willing to take on the responsibility of programming their own viewing, rather than leaving it to expert schedulers, remains unanswered.

A more convincing element of the argument that consumers want more involvement and control is perhaps the move to the consumption and creation of user-generated content. Even the most cursory glance at any list of top Internet sites reveals the vast amount of user generated content that exists online. In any major category of activity, it is likely that user generated content will make its presence felt. In the entertainment field, sites like YouTube, Second Life and Flickr are hugely popular. In terms of productivity applications, eBay, Wikipedia, Epinions and Ehow command huge numbers of page views. And for communications, Facebook, Friends Reunited, Twitter and Blogger are all highly popular methods of interacting with friends, families and colleagues.

Whilst the quality of such user-generated content varies enormously, for some, content creation is taken very seriously, and users are able to fully embrace even their most demanding creative visions thanks to the decline in the cost of equipment, which until relatively recently was the province of professionals. At around $100, digital camcorders like the Toshiba Camileo P30 (able to record in 1080p at 24fpm) are now available for less than a decent stills camera cost in 2000.

For those with a musical bent, the ability to produce music in the home has moved from ephemeral bedroom or garage jams that do not outlast their delivery, or the accumulation of a large amount of relatively expensive equipment (instruments, microphones, special effects units, channel mixers), to the use of highly sophisticated and inexpensive computer-based mixing and recording suites like GarageBand (Apple) and Cakewalk Sonar (Roland). These software packages are able to produce professional results at a fraction of the cost involved in going into a professional recording studio. And with the evolution of audio broadcast software like Shoutcast, the output of bedroom music producers now has the potential to be heard by anyone with access to the right application on the PC or mobile.

Finally, the production of fan art and fan writing has also emerged as a significant activity for many, with specialist sites like Fanfiction.net allowing authors to post their writing, get critical feedback from other authors, and be read by a potentially vast online audience. But whilst getting your content distributed may be easier than ever for aspiring home artists, finding an audience and commercialising the interaction is, as ever, more problematic. And it is at this point that we turn to some of the more significant economic developments in the field of home entertainment since 2000.

Economic issues

Whilst we consume ever more entertainment in the home, the economic prospects of those supplying much of the content on a commercial basis are troubling for a variety of structural and contextual issues. For companies in most sectors, the years between 2000 and 2010 will be best remembered for the global banking crisis and major recessions. Traditionally, the entertainment sector is seen as countercyclical, that is it tends to fare well in recessions (cinema attendance went up dramatically during the Great Depression in the USA, for example). But whilst we do appear to be consuming more entertainment, the recession has had a significant impact in a variety of less desirable ways.

Separating out the direct effects of the recession is difficult, as they are mixed up with a variety of other ongoing developments, and evidence can be contradictory and inconsistent. There are some suggestions, for example, that consumer adoption of new devices and applications has been encouraged by the need to save money in difficult times. Hence consumers have been encouraged to use newspapers' and magazines' free websites rather than buying hard copies. Equally, it has been argued that consumers have put off buying new, high-end entertainment technology (high definition televisions, top-end mobile phones) by the same motivation, though many hardware suppliers, particularly in Europe, enjoyed a boom in sales driven by the 2010 World Cup in South Africa.

Certainly, funding of core business activities is likely to have been more directly and consistently affected by the recession. Borrowing has become more costly, and for some highly leveraged media companies, the new, more onerous, terms from lenders may be proving highly debilitating to their expansion plans. In some cases, this has had a direct impact on content creation. As of April 2010, production of the 23rd James Bond film was put on hold as questions mounted over whether the company that own the rights to the franchise (MGM) could pay back over $2bn of company debt.

This squeeze on borrowing is particularly painful in a time when advertising revenues (another key source of funds for growth) have declined in many sectors.

This is partly contextual, as corporate advertisers slashed their marketing and advertising budgets during the recession. More significantly for some sectors, it may also be as a result of more fundamental structural changes in the media economy. For whilst end users are consuming more entertainment, they are doing so over an ever wider range of different devices and platforms; and in some cases, they are not paying for it and finding ways to avoid the advertising that providers increasingly rely on.

The golden age of television, when a small number of broadcasters controlled access to a limited number of channels delivered to a single device is over according to many, as is their ability to deliver to advertisers the large captive audiences that resulted. Programming is now delivered over a variety of broadcaster systems (cable, satellite, digital terrestrial, IPTV), by a large number of providers to audiences who watch it on a variety of devices and have a potentially huge number of channels to view. The technology even exists to skip the advertisements (for example via PVRs) that many channels and broadcasters rely on for their revenues.

Hence the large audiences which traditionally secured significant advertising revenues for TV providers have become spread over a much larger range of devices, platforms and channels and it is both difficult and expensive for providers to secure a meaningful presence on all of them to re-aggregate these audiences. Advertising revenues for television companies are under threat. At the same time, the cost of creating and marketing content in a highly competitive environment has generally risen. But new sources of revenue to fill this emerging gap have been in short supply.

Early attempts to launch interactive services delivered to the TV revealed that whilst consumers thought they were nice to have, they would certainly not pay an additional fee for them. Sales of associated packaged media have been increasing, but then again so has online and packaged media piracy, and increasingly the rights to such exploitation opportunities (and others like voting revenues) are not owned by the broadcasters, but by the independent production companies who supply them with programming.

For many broadcasters, these developments will effect a number of significant changes in focus. A number are considering the 'fewer but bigger' approach, i.e. investing in a smaller number of bigger productions that are more likely to succeed, and ensuring they secure some of the revenue that might accrue in other markets, like packaged media, merchandising and viewer participation activities. Others will probably focus their attention solely on the most valuable day-parts for advertising (primetime for example), cutting programming budgets for less valuable segments.

In other sectors, the threats posed by developments in the last ten years have been even more dramatic. The music sector has seen turbulent times, as the major record companies, who have traditionally retained their dominance as a result of their control over global distribution and marketing of artists, have struggled to find a new role and value proposition for their customers (see Chapter 2). Having failed to carve out niches for themselves at the beginning of the online boom in music consumption, they have seen their profits eroded as significant price pressure on the CD has led to falling average prices, and a decline in overall demand as piracy satisfies an ever larger proportion of consumer demand for music. For some companies, these developments have brought them to the brink of financial disaster (EMI for example); for others, the harsh reality of mergers is never far away.

Content piracy is not just the province of the music downloader. Increasingly, film content is subject to the attention of file sharers thanks to compression systems like mp4 and applications like bit torrent. Combined with physical piracy (the illegal production of packaged media), piracy of video content was estimated to be worth $7.3bn in 2005 (IPI, 2006). But this was just the loss of revenue for the companies directly involved. The same study estimated that the total cost of piracy, including lost output of US industries, lost employment and loss of earning to US workers, was closer to $38bn.

More positively, new technologies have created opportunities for content providers to reach audiences at a fraction of the cost of traditional marketing campaigns. In 2007, the average cost of marketing a Hollywood film was around $40m, and for some high profile films like *Avatar*, the figure is much higher, with some estimates suggesting Fox's marketing budget for the film was around $150m (*New York Times*, 2009). In the face of rising marketing costs, many studios are turning to lower cost tools like social networking applications and viral marketing to supplement campaigns and reach viewers at less cost. For companies like Sony, who used Twitter as a way to reach consumers for films such as *District 9*, *Julie & Julia* and *The Ugly Truth*, securing the interest and involvement of fans and early adopters is seen as the best way of delivering persuasive messages to the mass market at the least cost.

But perhaps the biggest economic challenge to all organisations in the content creation and distribution business revolves around the issue of 'free' content (see Chapter 5). Traditionally, business models in the entertainment sector have revolved around three major streams of revenue: payment per item of content (e.g. for a CD or DVD), aggregation of audiences for sale to advertisers, and subscription models. But these models have often struggled to establish themselves in new entertainment markets.

Early attempts to directly charge consumers for content online were met with strong resistance. Where similar content was readily available offline (often associated with entrenched user habits like buying and reading a newspaper when commuting) or online for free, it appeared almost impossible to generate significant revenues from charging for content. Even with the offer of 'premium' content, both micro payment approaches (payment per piece of content) and subscription models struggled to attract the interest and spending of consumers. So during much of the 1990s, content providers, particularly in the publishing business, appeared willing to provide content for free, backed by often minimal advertising, as it was seen as necessary to complement offline offerings and to occupy space that might be occupied by competitors.

In other media sectors, things were little different. Television companies did not initially offer their traditional content via online networks, partly because of bandwidth restrictions. Information might be offered to complement content on main delivery channels to further engage the viewer, but little more. Now, however, a variety of free services is being offered, like BBC's iPlayer in the UK, which streams programme content to PCs and TVs, offering catch-up TV for recently broadcast content. Even commercial channels like NBC in the USA are willing to offer free programmes as long as consumers are willing to watch a very brief (and easily skipped) advertisement at the beginning the show. Others are attempting to introduce pay-per-view models, but such premium models have been trialled in a variety of sectors, often unsuccessfully. If content is already available on YouTube, or via bit torrent sites, the question is: will consumers be willing to upgrade to a premium pay service?

Perhaps the biggest challenge (but also opportunity) is in the music sphere. Compressed music files lend themselves readily to movement across increasingly fast networks. A large number of front-end applications has emerged to search for, download, store and manage such files. File-based content also enables the delivery of content to a wide variety of different devices, and allows users to disaggregate what were increasingly seen as expensive album formats, and just deal in single songs.

This has led to the emergence of a highly efficient and effective (at least for the user) pirate economy, with a large number of consumers posting and sharing content online. The early response of the music companies was to put everything on hold and not license their content until reliable digital rights management software became available. Unfortunately, this meant that the only place to get premium content was the pirate network. Ultimately this may have inculcated a belief in at least some music consumers that content can, and perhaps should, be free. Bands are seen to get sufficient revenues to compensate them for their efforts through merchandising and concerts.

This puts a question mark over the role of record companies in the future. Traditionally, their function has been twofold. On the one hand, to act as venture capitalists, investing in a range of new projects (bands) in the hope that one of the hundreds they invest in becomes sufficiently popular to compensate for their losses on the others. In order to maximise their returns on that one success, they traditionally have dominated distribution and marketing, spending money on advertising to create demand for bands, then supplying packaged media to retailers to satisfy it and taking a large proportion of the resulting revenues.

Yet their ability to extract profits from the distribution and marketing of successful artists has been eroded by the emergence of an online pirate economy and by the pressure put on the prices of CDs. Artists have also proved unwilling in many cases to share their merchandising and concert revenues with them. So the position of the record companies remains uncertain, but would be a significant loss to the music economy, should their model fail. Ultimately, they need to develop a new value proposition for music, which engages consumers, but also allows the generation of sufficient revenue to support their businesses.

And this, perhaps, is the most significant economic issue facing all of those companies in the home entertainment business, particularly those who supply content. How can they change their internal organisation and how should their value propositions evolve to remain attractive in an environment where consumers are becoming more sophisticated, media are becoming more fungible in their use, and existing business models are being challenged?

Case study: Home video, an exercise in cannibalisation? Key issues facing providers

The following case study on the home video sector highlights a number of the key issues mentioned in the chapter. As already noted, consumers have more access to video-enabled devices than ever before, and their penetration is growing quickly, with online video probably the fastest growing sector. For industry providers, a key question is the degree to which these new delivery devices are cannibalising or adding to existing use. And if cannibalisation is happening, which particular activities and are being most damaged (for example watching broadcast TV, playback of packaged media, video on demand, etc.)?

Answering these questions requires taking all of the major forces we have already discussed into account. One the one hand, providers need to get very close to their consumers. They need to understand how usage habits inside and outside the home are changing and consider the social and cultural implications for video consumption. If old ways of watching video are being replaced with new ones, how can the old forms be enhanced to protect viewers' loyalty? How can platforms be used to direct consumers to other platforms to be monetised or generate attention? And in terms of the new platforms like online video, how do the content forms and business models need to change to accommodate a new set of viewers with potentially different requirements and differing willingness to pay.

In terms of technology, one of the biggest issues for providers is to decide which formats to back and which to avoid. If new formats and platforms are to be adopted, often content needs to be re-versioned to fit with the specific technical demands of that platform. This can be an expensive business, particularly if you get it wrong.

Earlier in the decade we witnessed a climactic battle between two new incompatible packaged media formats, HD DVD and Blu-ray Disc, very much like the battle in the 1980s between VHS and Betamax. A number of studios (including Universal Studios, Paramount Studios, and DreamWorks) backed the wrong horse, converting their material to HD DVD, only to find in 2008 that Toshiba, its main hardware proponent, was dropping the format in favour of the more popular Blu-ray. Inevitably content had to be re-converted to the Blu-ray standard.

So challenges and choices abound. Combating piracy is a key issue. Finding ways to monetise (through advertising or consumer payments) content delivered on non-traditional platforms is another. As far as the organisations supplying the content are concerned, there are real challenges in how they run internally. Warner Bros, for example, has operations in broadcast media, packaged media, pay-TV and increasingly on new platforms like online. In theory, adding them all together offers the greatest chance for Warner Bros as a whole to maximise the value of its investment in video. In practice, it creates a complex set of problems including measuring the value of each platform to the overall video proposition; handling internal cannibalisation of platform activities; motivating and rewarding senior management in each of the divisions; and complex strategic decisions around the best way in which to maximise the value of any one property.

The future

Whilst it is difficult to speculate how the environment will evolve in the long term, we can make some informed guesses for how the next decade will play out, bearing in mind a quote from one of the fathers of modern technological development, Bill Gates, who suggested that 'we always overestimate the change that will occur in the next two years and underestimate the change that will occur in the next ten' (Gates, 1996).

On this basis, whilst some commentators predict the death of traditional TV viewing, an overwhelming move to viewing content on PCs, the maturation of the mobile phone as the central entertainment, communications and productivity device for all of us, and consumers dedicating ever more of their spare time to the consumption of home entertainment, we are not going to see this in the next few years. Things just don't change that quickly and when they do it is often in counterintuitive ways. It is arguable, for example, that rather than signalling the death of TV, social networking may end up sustaining the position of linear TV as the predominant home entertainment form, as new applications emerge to foster the interaction of the two and TVs start to be produced 'online ready'. The same may be said for radio, a medium that appeared to be ailing in the last decade. New opportunities to consume radio from all over the world on a variety of different devices and to interact on a global scale with presenters, shows and channels may lead to a surge in radio listening, rather than an often forecast decline.

In terms of social and cultural developments, it is questionable whether the total amount of time spent on home entertainment will rise radically over the next ten years; there are after all natural limits on disposable time and income. As consumers continue to allocate their home entertainment time over an increasing variety of devices and networks, device and content providers will continue to try and find ways in which to re-aggregate this increasingly diverse audience. One of the key ways in which they are likely to attempt this is by developing applications to secure attention during the simultaneous use of a variety of different devices and media.

In order to achieve this, new business models will need to be developed, though arguably this will not help their mid-term prospects. Entertainment providers are in a period of complex challenges, with the ongoing economic turbulence affecting the speed of recovery of the advertising market and the willingness of consumer to embrace new technology and pay for content. Hence whilst further penetration of existing technologies like broadband, PVRs, high definition TV and enhanced mobile phones will continue, developments are likely to be incremental (for example 3D TV, mobile phones with better screens/memory, new form factors of PCs, increased broadband capacity) over the next decade, rather than revolutionary.

Where we may see the most exciting technical developments is in the area of connectivity and the evolution of entertainment networks within the home. Microsoft has already attempted to position itself at the centre of any such network with the launch of Windows 7, which claims to simplify the process of setting up a home network and moving content around it. Yet it remains a complex task for many, confused by different hardware standards, network protocols, playback codecs and file formats; and at least part of this confusion is directly as a result of providers' desire to protect their content.

As networks get faster and compression technologies improve, it is arguably going to be easier than ever before to access the content you want, when and where you want it, without having to pay for it. Piracy will not disappear in the next ten years and will probably only decline if providers find a new an attractive value proposition for content, offering something that the pirates cannot, rather than relying on legislation to stop it. Criminalising your most ardent fans has never been a good model for developing consumer loyalty. This is particularly so in the music sector.

This seems to suggest that as we enter the second decade of the 21st century, the home entertainment landscape will not be radically different from the existing one on the user side – the prospect is for more diverse and cheaper ways to consume content, but also potentially the development of an ever more confusing environment in which platforms and technologies within platforms compete even more intensely for consumers' time, attention and money.

On the supply side, change may be more radical as a result of the ongoing turbulence in the global economy and structural changes in industries. Challenges are likely to be particularly acute for organisations like record companies, public service broadcasters and large multi-platform operators like Warner Bros as they deal with external challenges and internal re-organisation.

We can be sure, however, that the forces that have been influencing the evolution of home entertainment since its inception, socio-cultural, technological and economic, will continue to direct its growth and development. Only through an enhanced understanding of how all of these forces collide and interact can we hope to understand the changing nature and scope of entertainment in the home.

Acronyms used in the text

Codec: a piece of hardware, or more typically software, capable of encoding and decoding a digital data stream.

DAB: digital audio broadcasting.

FTA: free to air broadcasting.

HD DVD: high definition video format, initially supported by Toshiba, Universal Studios, Paramount Studios, and DreamWorks, now abandoned in favour of Blue-ray Disc format.

IPTV: internet protocol television.

PVR: personal video recorder (generally hard-disc based).

SACD: Super Audio CD, an enhanced optical audio disc format.

1080p at 24fpm: hi-definition format for recording/playback of video.

References

Gates, B. (1996) *The Road Ahead*, 2nd edn, London: Penguin.

IPI (Institute for Policy Innovation) (2006) *The true cost of motion picture piracy to the US economy*, 186, www.ipi.org.

Kaiser (Henry J. Kaiser Family Foundation) (2010) *Generation M2: Media in the Lives of 8- to 18-Year-Olds*, http://www.kff.org/entmedia/8010.cfm

New York Times (2009) 'A movie's budget pops from the screen', 8 November.

Nielsen Company (2009) *Three Screens Report (Q1 2009)*, www.nielsen.com.

Further reading and research

Caves, R.E. (2000) *Creative Industries*, Cambridge, MA: Harvard University Press.

Picard, R. (2002) *Media Firms Structures, Operations and Performance*, London: Lawrence Erlbaum Associates.

Wilson, B. (1998) *Media Technology and Society: A History from the Telegraph to the Internet*, London: Routledge.

However, keeping up with developments in home entertainment does not necessarily mean turning to academic books and articles. Getting a historical perspective on the evolution of technical and social issues from writers like Wilson (1998), or economic developments from researchers such as Picard (2002) or Caves (2000) can be useful, particularly if you have a paper to write. Often however, there is a significant lag between developments and their description and analysis in such academic sources.

Staying on top of current developments requires additional resources. Some of the best include the research bodies mentioned in this chapter, like the Henry J. Kaiser Family Foundation and the Nielsen Company who will often publish their latest research findings on things like media usage in the home on their websites. Downloads of reports are often free.

A careful review of leading news sources can also reveal useful insights into current developments in the home entertainment field; hence newspapers like *The Times* or *Wall Street Journal* can be a good source of information. Two points are worth making when using such sources. First, as we have already established, the home entertainment space is influenced by a wide range of economic, technological and societal factors, so read widely, don't just focus on the news pieces or sections that seem most obvious. Second, treat such sources with a good degree of scepticism, newspapers have a vested interest in promoting the 'next big thing', even if in retrospect it turns out to the next Betamax or HD DVD.

9 The Future of Broadcasting

Simon Mundy with Esmée Schilte

Introduction

At the end of the last century, a dictionary could confidently define broadcasting as the transmission of a signal for television or radio. Within a decade, every element of that definition had changed. Transmission had branched out from the cumbersome business of placing masts bearing receivers and transmitters at the highest vantage points across the countryside.

A signal was no longer confined to the band waves that the air could carry – invisible streams snaking their way across the landscape: Ultra High Frequency (UHF) carrying television, as long as the hills weren't in the way; Very High Frequency (VHF or FM) carrying wonderful quality sound, as long as the same hills were not joined by chimneys, bodies, the wrong sort of cloud or stonework; Long Wave, unstoppable by anything except distance, it seemed, carrying cricket and the shipping forecast across Europe and far out to sea; Medium Wave (AM), the carrier of choice for hosts of daytime local music stations and great for listening in the car, but hopeless when night fell and the waves went bouncing around the ionosphere bringing martial music from Albania where the football commentary should have been; and Short Wave – the touchiest of the wave bands, that made catching the words as hard as catching fish, but finally gave national broadcasters a global reach.

Instead, the old analogue signals and the copper wires of telephone lines were replaced by fibre optic cable and digital bytes. The slow, romantic waves were now just pulses of light with the possibility of being either on or off. But what freedom that simplification gave. Freedom came in many forms: there was suddenly room for dozens of new radio stations between the television signals, equally digital – though ironically needing more, if smaller, transmission masts than the old system. The quality achieved is such that picture definition is as close to perfect as is possible in two dimensions. Sound definition is ahead of television in being able to transmit not just in stereo (which has been available for radio since the 1960s) but in surround sound. With the potential for 3D, the introduction of a sense of depth into TV images, watching at home will increase markedly in its sense of realism in the course of the next two decades.

The variations now are more due to the slight differences in the way microphones and ears, and cameras and eyes, hear and see, than to the inadequacies of transmission. And the receivers have developed in parallel: a television used to be a huge box, distended at the back, with a radioactive tube firing particles at a relatively small curved screen. A decade into the 21st century, the technological fashion moved to huge flat screens that could dominate a room, showing liquid crystal pictures in high definition only previously possible for the poster size still photograph.

Signals now come through the air (whether from satellites, dedicated transmitters or mobile phone masts) through cables and telephone lines. The effect on broadcasters themselves, however, has been caused as much by the diversification of the ability to receive, as by the means of delivery. The opportunity to use broadband digital telephone lines and wireless (wi-fi) extensions of them in domestic and public spaces to offer an almost unlimited range of content by computer is revolutionising not just the industry itself, but the expectations of audiences. The Netherlands became the first country in the EU to switch off completely from analogue transmission in 2006. The EU aims to complete the process in 2012, but is unlikely to meet such a stiff target. The Netherlands was also one of the first countries to embrace TV and radio via the Internet. In 2005, 26 per cent of audiences there used it. That figure doubled in three years.

The Internet is becoming as important in delivery as the old infrastructure, and it is global, not local. Broadcasting has been joined by narrowcasting, netcasting and podcasting. Perhaps one should just forget the prefixes and call it all 'casting'; for it does indeed live up to the original metaphorical image of machines casting the seeds of ideas to the winds without knowing where they will fall or what will grow from them. But let's stick to broadcasting. It still has resonance and to call oneself a broadcaster confers a professional cachet that the new terms can't quite invoke.

This chapter suggests ways in which the whole sector may change in the next quarter of a century. It explores the changing expectations of the public and the implications for producers, manufacturers, creative contributors (and their copyright) and, not least, governments. It will largely focus on Europe, and within that Britain and the Netherlands, in terms of regulation. But because the effects of technical delimitation don't stop there, neither will our discussion.

Who will the future broadcasters be?

In the middle of the 20th century, every nation (with the exception of the USA) assumed it would have at least one national broadcaster, contributed to – although not always wholly financed – from taxation and regulated by the national government. The European Broadcasting Union, which has members entirely drawn from that fraternity, is the institutional expression of that assumption. Onto this single national entity were gradually grafted commercial operators, mostly emerging in the third quarter of the century. But these still operated under licence, as the waveband frequencies were scarce enough to have to be allocated, first through international negotiation and then nationally. Where there is allocation there can be control, and though governments varied in the extent to which they exercised it, broadcasters still had to obtain their, or their agencies', permission. As long as radio and television are beamed through the air, governments will have a policy to regulate them.

The Internet is in the process of tearing all that down, however. While national broadcasters may only be allowed to make aspects of their content available in some territories – defined usually by copyright and commercial licensing deals, more than state restrictions – small independent companies and individuals can bypass the geography, whether political or physical. As long as the receiver has Internet access, there is access to the broadcaster. It was hoped in the 1980s and 1990s that satellite broadcasting might achieve this flexibility of access. In the event, the expense of uploading and the complexity for customers of deciding which satellite to tune to meant that, for the most part, it merely allowed some major media corporations to become global in reach and some niche operators (like Eurosport) to establish themselves.

Internet broadcasting is still in its infancy. Most individuals are using sites like YouTube, MySpace and Facebook to post material, but few are yet taking the next step and founding their own station. There are some truly interactive experiments, like Qoob TV in Italy, run by Telecom Italia Media, which enables programming to be generated by the user rather than the broadcaster. Broadcasting is becoming more democratic, not just in the interactivity between broadcasters and audiences, but in the ability of anybody with minimal equipment to make their own material available. While this has huge implications for professionalism and media organisation structures (which will be discussed below), it also lends a dynamism to individual expressive potential which is almost comparable to the growth of literacy and the availability of cheap paper and ink.

Where new niche 'normal' broadcasters are establishing themselves on the Net, for example the co-operative Novi Radio Beograd in Serbia, it is often in response to the inability of traditional national broadcasters to provide sufficiently adventurous formats and content. Ironically, though, the places where the national broadcasters are most inadequate have been those where the small number of people speaking the language means that efforts to provide free global Internet radio tend to be limited in listenership to the host nation and its diaspora. This does not matter too much as long as the broadcaster has an income stream. Getting the Internet to produce money, though, as those wanting to publish anything from magazines to music recordings have found to their consternation, is much more difficult on the Internet than from traditional sales or advertising. The underlying principle of the Internet is free access and users resent paying unless they are buying physical goods. And Internet audiences are nowhere near as predictable for advertisers as local ones.

There is a battle ahead and it will have four sides:

1. Old-style national or state broadcasters;
2. Big commercial media companies;
3. Small local but traditional stations;
4. The new breed of Internet-based, small global audience providers.

Trying to influence this battle will be the regulators, whether national or multilateral (like the European Commission, World Intellectual Property Organization and the World Trade Organization). In the end though, the audiences will decide, based on content, convenience, technical access and cost.

Devices

At the start of the century, technological advancement was the driving force, changing the way content was available and stimulating equally profound changes in the expectations of the public. The way people watch and listen has been changing at a similar pace to the technology. But the basic patterns are still there. People still listen to the radio when they are getting up in the morning, when they are in the car and when they are working (builders' radio still flourishes, for example). Some switch the TV on when they get home in the evening or have it playing permanently (and often silently) in the room while they are at home.

However, the commonality of domestic viewing and listening has changed. This is not just because there are more channels and people now expect to find something to fit their individual taste. It is more because the machines for receiving are cheaper, multifarious and more portable than ever. For communal viewing, large liquid crystal display (LCD) sets now mean that televisions are effectively home cinema screens – able to reproduce high definition images that bring home viewers into a sense of proximity that is at times almost too direct.

The real change, however, is that Europeans are now beginning to take back the initiative from the device designers and demand that change keeps up with a new generation's demands, a generation who have been brought up to think that anything is technically possible and who cannot imagine a time before the World Wide Web and mobile phones with multiple functions. They expect to have access to programmes in any part of the house, and increasingly out of it as well. This was always true of radio, where the 1950s development of transistors meant that the last three generations have grown up expecting sound to be their constant companion. It is only with digital technology and LCD that television has become available in the same way. The usual content that used to be available only through broadcast or a cable can now be accessed at the desk computer, on a laptop, a phone or any device combining them.

In fact, it is this merging of equipment that is really altering the future of broadcasting. The old forms are changing but are not disappearing. But they are being joined by systems that make no great distinction between the information they offer. Just as the viewer or listener does not care much how the programmes are delivered, the hardware matches that freedom. Audiences expect to be able to find arts and entertainment wherever they are, and they are becoming increasingly irritated by licensing agreements and copyright that prevents them from finding what they want, when they want it (see Chapter 5).

The result for manufacturers is clear too: they can no longer afford to be producing equipment for just one platform. Soon the major corporations will need to produce across the whole range of devices; those for the home, the pocket, the car and the office. It is beginning to happen. The borders between the audio-visual and computer or mobile phone providers have broken down considerably in the last decade, but there is still a long way to go. Some major companies have merged – Sony and Ericsson, for example – and some, like Phillips, Samsung and Toshiba, have tried to retain a foot in all camps. However, the time is fast approaching when computer hardware specialists like Dell will be wondering, along with audio-visual specialists like Hitachi, whether more concentration of the industry is necessary. With Apple constantly pushing the boundaries of technical function merger, the pace of change has plenty of scope for acceleration.

New services are sprouting up every few months and the costs of access for the viewer and listener are decreasing – though not as fast as they should be. The apathy of consumers in failing to demand simpler and fairer packages is allowing many multinational media companies to retain customers in pricing structures which reflect neither the quality nor the value for money that they should.

Some of the excitement and momentum of this process is being dissipated in reality, too, by the present inability of broadband and wi-fi speeds to live up to their advertised efficiency. Eurostat, the European Union's statistical agency, has reported that there is an overestimation of speeds as providers pick their best performing services in order to justify the price of packages. In reality, a combination of infrastructure inadequacies, amount of traffic and variations in conductivity mean that the experience of those watching or listening is often of inconsistent quality. In public places, where a laptop computer is dependent on a shared wi-fi service for a signal, the streaming of information (and with it the coherence of sound and picture) can be slow and haphazard to the point of serious frustration. The earth's geography and the topography of buildings are proving as stubborn an obstacle to the new generation of technologies as it did to the old.

Similarly, the inadequate coverage of mobile phone signals, particularly bad in the UK, means that it will be many years before the claims of providers are matched by the reality. With traditional radio and television in most domestic settings, audiences have become used to receiving clear, uninterrupted pictures and good stereo sound as a matter of course. While new services have the potential to go far beyond the standards of the end of the 20th century, they are not yet as uniformly available as their creators would have us believe. The EU is revising its comparator statistics so that it can measure delivery standards more accurately and this is likely to lead to regulatory pressure on pricing and advertising claims. Because this will happen across the 27 member states of the market, it is likely to push technical developments forward far more quickly than could be achieved by national governments acting alone.

Great Expectations

The revolution in delivery and audience habits raises expectations all round. Audiences revel in the new equipment and experience. The magic that is promised does not always quite come off, though. The same can be said for the strategies of the corporate world. The giant media corporations – Time-Warner, News Corporation, *et al.* – and the new generation multi-function phone manufacturers were convinced in the first years of the century that the new era brought with it unlimited global opportunities and freedom from the regulation that they regarded as stifling their free global market.

There was a series of flaws in the assumption, though. The first and biggest was the fact that consumers were already becoming used to the way the Web allowed them access to the services they needed without charge. For every subscription site, there would be plenty offering something similar for nothing, even if technically inferior and limited in scope. More damagingly, the major public service broadcasters around the world, who did not have to fund themselves entirely from earned income, could make their huge back catalogues and some of their live coverage available free. Not everything was offered for downloading, but quite enough was to make the exclusivity presented by purely commercial operators lose its appeal. Enough people took the decision that they could live without the extra facets of expensive programme packages. This made it uneconomic for the niche markets that remained to provide for them. It was a problem faced not just by broadcasting corporations; the competition from free downloads nearly destroyed the market for music recordings too. So far the same has not happened for books, despite the technology for reading online or on handheld screens, but the ease of ordering books from Internet traders has in many countries caused a major crisis in traditional bookshops, while the improvement in search engines and online reference tools has hit the use of public libraries.

Monetising services has become a considerable headache for companies marketing content. The old models of distribution and sales, based on rights in national territories, seem increasingly obsolete and the expectation of the global public is to have global access without respecting the lines of closely fought territorial demarcations over intellectual property that were negotiated through the 20th century (see Chapter 5). The expectation of the local public is to have all their traditional services and to be able to join in the global system whenever it suits them at home and whenever they travel away from it.

The market is struggling just as much as political systems to match aspiration to its ability to adapt as quickly as citizens expect – which is as fast and as cheaply as the technology allows. In this case, though, the market is not just the corporate interests of media companies or the propaganda interests of governments; it is the livelihoods of all those who provide contemporary information and entertainment – journalists, performers, writers, composers and publishers are all finding their means of sustaining an income severely curtailed.

This has crucial implications for modern economies, many of which (having all but abandoned their manufacturing bases) are increasingly hoping to rely on the cultural industries to kick-start growth after a period of financial blight. The trouble is that the cultural industries are precisely the ones most likely to be destabilised by the assault on their profitability by free or very inexpensive online services. Much of the argument for culture as an agent and instigator of development would be threatened if the main props of cultural industrial growth were knocked away. International organisations (WIPO, World Bank, UNESCO, UNCTAD) and regional groupings (such as the EU, CARICOM and OAS) will need to address seriously the problem of how to reinvigorate cultural earnings if a crucial plank of economic stability in post-industrial and pre-industrial countries is not to be removed. For developing countries, eager to find environmentally neutral and culturally sustainable ways of generating income, the new opportunities for promoting themselves and their artistic resources are considerable, but only if methods can be found to turn activity into money. Similarly Europe and North America will lose earnings that have kept important sectors of their economies vital for the last 60 years if new ways of recouping costs and making a living are not found quickly.

The benefactor of this process is democracy. As its founders hoped (but corporations and governments feared), the Web has allowed people to cater for their own interests as individuals, not as part of predetermined market segments or defined citizens. Democracy is being enhanced, not just for those wanting to make their ideas, images and voices available to the world without waiting for a broadcasting company to give them the opportunity, but by allowing viewers and listeners the chance to bypass the mediation of state-run and commercial interests and to make their own judgements of the massive amount of material on offer. For those with access to it (still a worldwide minority but one which is growing massively, according to UNESCO), the process is becoming the greatest source of personal empowerment since printing.

National Public Service Broadcasting

Despite the growth of commercial local, national and satellite broadcasters during the last 30 years, the basic building blocks of the provision of radio and television in Europe remain the publicly owned or regulated national servers. Their financing, control and ambition vary massively from country to country. However, where standards are high (and even where they are not, as in Italy), the public has remained remarkably loyal to them throughout all the changes outlined above. Especially in times of economic strain or national threat, European citizens seem to fall back on their national broadcasters for a sense of commonality and security. Generally, they tend to believe the news and comment carried by traditional stations more than those which are wholly commercial or multinational, except at times when the government itself is deemed untrustworthy – and even then, the faith in the national broadcaster will long outlive faith in ministers.

The *raison d'être* for the formation of European national broadcasting organisations in the third decade of the 20th Century was simple enough. The then new wireless technology allowed people to be spoken to, entertained and educated on a mass basis for the first time. The infrastructure to do so was expensive, but offered governments both prestige and the ability to convey news and convenient messages more effectively than ever before. Frequencies suitable for early broadcasting were limited and, so as not to interfere with those in other languages, had to be allocated through negotiations between governments. It would, technically, almost have been possible to have services provided across geography designated by language predominance rather than national boundaries. But in the nationalist and fading imperial period after the First World War, when the League of Nations was the only multilateral agency in its weak infancy, anything other than national networks was unthinkable in Europe, even though the USA (with its vast territory and mistrust of federal agencies) came to a different conclusion. This was not forgone, though, because it could have established individual state-funded broadcasters on the model that emerged in Europe. However, unlike the USA, Europe had a history of accepting that innovation which increased the public good was best paid for out of public taxation.

In emerging democracies, wary of old aristocratic and industrial interests, it seemed both fairer and more practical to aim for a national consensus on the content. Most, if not all, Eastern European broadcasters remained little more than government mouthpieces in news coverage and analysis until the end of the century. Others, though, evolved into public bodies proud of their distance from daily politics and of their ability to innovate in other areas. The cultural contribution of national broadcasters, their ability to fund and disseminate the arts and to bring together communities through shared knowledge and entertainment, was arguably one of the defining features of 20th century social development.

Such certainties no longer apply. While traditional frequencies still need to be allocated, most of Europe will be covered by digital frequencies by the middle of this decade and satellite and web delivery obviates the need for boundaries of any sort. If public sector broadcasters (PSBs) are no longer technically necessary, however – and many of those in the commercial sector who regard them as unfair competitors argue that they are not – there is considerable reluctance among either the public or politicians to see them abolished. There are calls, though, for them to relinquish some services, not to assume that their access to taxation means that they have to do everything that a commercial operator does, and to deliver their services more cheaply and with less bureaucracy. There is also a sense that, if regulators demand public service standards and functions from commercial broadcasters, they are entitled to a proportion of the revenue that is devoted to the 'flag carrier'.

There is no technical or market purpose in retaining national broadcasting corporations. However there are strong cultural, political and artistic reasons for doing so. This means that even if they ultimately change their character considerably, PSBs are likely to remain significant players in the industry until at least the middle of the century. Their significant contribution to political stability and to regional diversity; the public expectation to be able to see and listen to major national and global sporting events for free; and the vital part they play in the arts all mean that there will be just as powerful lobbies arguing for their retention as for their break-up.

It seems not to be the old, established taxation-funded national broadcasters that are under immediate threat but rather their commercial competitors. In many countries, there has long been a mix of funding between advertising and subsidy for national stations. In Britain, the division has been that the BBC's domestic services are funded through a licence fee on TV sets (extended now to anybody who downloads content online at home too, though that is proving virtually unenforceable without serious infringements of personal privacy), while other channels are funded through advertising. However, as the number of receiving platforms has risen, and as the number of channels available on those platforms has multiplied, market share for individual TV and radio stations has dropped sharply.

While the time an average European spent watching television overall remained remarkably constant between 2005 and 2009 at around 200 minutes per day, it did not rise to meet the explosive growth of channels on offer. The result is that the number of people who watch an individual programme, to which advertising is attached, on a commercial station has dropped sharply. Companies have retained good shares for major sports events and occasionally for national talent shows, which have been relentlessly marketed through the tabloid press, but for very little else. It was assumed that the novelty of fly-on-the-wall and competitive reality shows would generate perpetual interest; but the fashion, like any other, was wearing thin within a decade as producers became ever more desperate for new formats. Nothing could hide the fact that real life, even for the most exalted celebrities, makes for rather dull viewing after a while.

The results are predictable (see Figure 9.1). Between 2004 and 2008 the combined viewing share of Britain's five main PSB TV channels dropped from 75 per cent to 61 per cent, with an even more destructive 18 per cent drop in peak time viewing. Traditional companies depending on advertising revenues in a single national market are highly vulnerable. While the non-commercial BBC1 only lost 3 per cent of its peak viewers, ITV1 lost 6 per cent. Some commercial channels, like Britain's ITV and Channel 4, have public service limitations less onerous but comparable to the publicly funded networks, which either hamper their ability to maximise their income at certain times or require them to carry necessary but unprofitable news services and national events. Other companies, who always saw themselves as niche providers and assumed that the rewards would start flowing as soon as analogue broadcasting made way for digital, have found that people are slower to change their viewing habits than they expected.

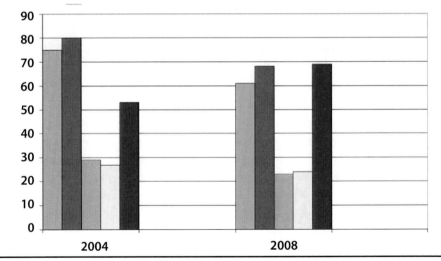

Figure 9.1: Public Service TV Viewing Shares in the UK 2004–2008

(*Source:* BBC Annual Report 2008/09)

Despite the downturn in market share, the traditional companies still retain a relatively high proportion of the audience. If all Britain's PSB TV channels are combined, their share between 2004 and 2008 actually rose from 53 per cent to 69 per cent. So there is no dent in their ability to attract audiences in general –

only a fall in the viewing for individual channels within the portfolio. The same is true in some other European countries. PSB reach in the Netherlands rose by 3.6 per cent in the decade before 2008.

There is no doubt that there is a need for public service broadcasting if the aim is to have high quality programmes in all genres available to all the viewing population, regardless of disposable income. This has been the historical basis for government regulation of the industry beyond the need for the dissemination of public information. The BBC's original remit, 'to inform, educate and entertain', remains the basic purpose of public service broadcasting. While such an aim might be possible in the totality of a commercial system, it would neither be at the centre of any one company's policy or interests, nor available to all the population with access to the signal. So the issue of how to make money out of broadcasting in a digital age, such that programme diversity and quality can be maintained, is still open.

Case study: The Arts in Broadcasting

From the 1950s onward, the arts became increasingly dependent on broadcasters. In the case of classical music, the dependence on radio began 20 years earlier. This was not just a matter of the airtime given to the arts which, as a proportion, remained relatively slight on television and, apart from dedicated channels, on radio too. The real benefit was the hidden subsidy broadcasters provided through the employment of actors, musicians, composers, writers and all the supporting skills. Without programme making by public service broadcasters, notably but not exclusively the BBC, it would have been impossible in many regional centres to earn a living in the arts. It was the BBC, not any cultural ministry, which started London's first orchestra with full-time players on staff contracts and the BBC Symphony Orchestra remains the only one out of five in London with that structure. Its continued partnerships with Arts Councils in Cardiff and Belfast provides Wales and Ulster with orchestras they would be hard pressed to afford otherwise.

The same is true of theatre. Many commercial theatres rely on the name recognition which their actors acquire from television. One might argue that this would happen whether the broadcaster is public service or not, but the counter argument is that without the regulatory pressure for broadcasters to produce a relatively high proportion of home grown drama, there would be far fewer opportunities. Some countries in Europe, notably Germany and Sweden, maintain actors in their city theatres on full time salaries, but for most that never happens. The broadcasting work makes it possible for actors in occasional employment to stay in the profession. Similar arguments apply to all others in the performing arts and to many writers too.

Without the continued vitality and production investment of public service broadcasters, the future of the arts sector in the majority of European countries – but especially Britain, the Netherlands, Spain and smaller countries like Slovenia and the Czech Republic – will be even more precarious than it is now. To retain anything like the same size, coverage and depth would require either a far higher level of direct funding from central, local and regional government, which becomes increasingly unlikely, or a model closer to that of the United States, where a mixture of local public money and donations from business, foundations and individuals is relied upon. The trouble is that in the USA, arts organisations are fewer per head of the population and just as unstable – with a tendency to fold during economic recession unless they have built up significant endowments. Such endowments could secure the future work on this side of the Atlantic too, but they take at least half a century to build into a sum significant enough to support the portion of an organisation's budget that in Europe usually comes from the public purse.

For most European countries, the effect on the arts of removing public service obligations from broadcasting organisations would be the same as withdrawing from industry: a massive fall in capacity, a rise in unemployment, the gradual erosion of national particularity and a swift surrender to imports from larger markets: in the case of Britain, directly from the USA; in the case of other European countries, the same, but with many more programmes dubbed. It is not a development that the European Commission, for one, wishes to see.

The Future of Broadcasting

It is likely that the futures of television and radio will be very different.

Television

Television has high production costs but its programmes can be recycled and repackaged many times. US Television has for decades worked on the principle of making a relatively small number of high production value, long-running series and then recouping the cost by selling widely and cheaply. US networks are ruthless with shows which fail to find the right commercial formula, although they are quite prepared to fill in the gaps between the headline series with low production value, indifferent quality shows that still bring in enough audience to pay their way. European television companies have traditionally invested less, allowed individual writers to develop short series and, with the exception of daily soaps, have veered away from the American practice of scripting in large teams. Even long-running detective series, with characters as predictable and satisfying from week to week as instant coffee, tend to have single writers per episode.

With few exceptions (such as UK–USA co-productions) markets for TV programmes in Europe are relatively small in comparison to North and South America, the Arab world or China. Language limits their production to their home countries, even though dubbing and surtitles extend their reach to audiences who are accustomed to the technique. Britain, however, remains impervious to almost all programmes from outside that do not originate in the USA or Australia, even co-productions. For the moment, its production industry has the good fortune to be operating in a majority market so that its lack of interest in co-operation will not affect its ability to reach wider audiences in the short term. Other countries, especially those with the smallest linguistic footprint, will have to be more inventive, or continue to make programmes for an ever diminishing share of the market.

Within 20 years, it is likely that all content will be able to be viewed on multi-function devices. This may mean that current Internet content will be digitally broadcast as much as television will be viewed online. Television scheduling is likely to change more than the content itself, with programmers concentrating on live or topically limited shows which lose their novelty and zest if watched later than the event itself or a few days afterwards. First showings, for which channels are able to generate the sort of public excitement that is felt at the first night of a new opera or theatre show, should be part of the scene. Repeats, though, and screenings of old films and documentaries will in theory be thoroughly pointless once TV and Internet casting are integrated. Those channels that specialise in re-runs are likely to change to being closer to video libraries, with material permanently available for selection. There will still be room for a few old style channels, however, because viewers may not always want to go through the laborious task of selecting for themselves. In the same way that it is sometimes easier to switch on the radio instead of searching one's iPod or CD collection, it will often be more convenient to let someone else decide. In reality, the scheduler will become more of a curator – highlighting aspects of the material on offer, pointing the way to sequels, or to programmes with something in common – an actor, a writer, a theme.

Production companies will not always need networks to commission and show their material. Residual audience loyalty may make it desirable to be screened first by one of the big names, but there will be no reason why producers cannot have their own online channels and download libraries, as record companies are learning to do. Some may charge subscriptions, though that is easily resisted by consumers. Others may charge per download or integrate advertising in the package as newspapers and Internet service providers do now. The fact that these will be global rather than dependent on territory will mean rethinking the rights contracts. But again, this has not prevented the music business from reinventing itself, although it has been a painful process for many rights holders as much as for traditional publishers.

The 'TVscape', will be divided between originating broadcasters, mostly with a public service or regulated remit; production and 'library' companies offering their own or recycled material online; and multinational packaging conglomerates exploiting formats and operating in remaining cable and satellite markets. The losers will be national commercial companies which have tried to continue as traditional television companies, albeit on several platforms, without the benefit of public service subsidy.

Niche sports and news broadcasters, whether local or global, should remain largely untouched by any change in delivery method because their product is governed by topicality in gathering an audience, not by attracting it in the same way that film and book publishers have to. Effectively, the arts (including drama, comedy and documentary) will be merged into the film and book world model of opening presentation followed by library availability. However it is likely that the big American media conglomerates will try to make sure they control significant numbers of outlets on every platform that uses English. They will argue against the 'competition distortion' of public service broadcasters while fighting their real opponents, the Internet service providers, for control of new online operations. In the process they will be happy to use their ownership of the written press to unsettle national governments where regulation stands in their way or limits their ability to use TV to present only their political perspective. While Britain, Canada and Australia will find that tiresome, the real prize will be China.

Radio

Radio, though, has a different likely path. Audiences are immensely loyal to their favourite radio stations, often only shuffling between three or four of the hundred or so available on traditional frequencies. They look to the radio not just for information or entertainment, but for comfort, companionship, conversation (radio has been 'interactive' ever since the introduction of the 'phone-in') and sometimes just an argument. Unlike TV, much of radio's audience listens while travelling, working or relaxing away from home. The listenership and viewer patterns reverse, with most radio being listened to in the daytime and TV being watched at night. Radio is most successful when it is live, but increasingly, audiences are opting to listen to particular programmes when they want, either through podcasts or download listening packages.

Although radio programmes cost only a fraction of the amount of their TV equivalents, they are much harder to make money out of. As a result, except in the lucrative US local radio market, there is less interest from media giants, more emphasis on PSBs, and potentially many more opportunities for small independent and semi-professional broadcasters to operate, not all of them 24 hours per day. This, at least, has always been the hope of community broadcasters, student radio enthusiasts and advocates of the democratisation of expression. The truth is a little more inconvenient, though, for sustaining the income for a radio station, on whatever platform it is delivered, is somewhat harder than generating the content. Audiences are even less tolerant of advertising breaks on radio than on TV, and only in rare cases in each country is the audience large enough for each station to interest mass advertisers consistently against other media. In the Netherlands, advertising revenue for radio dropped almost 17 per cent in the financial crisis year of 2008/09.

The global audience via the Internet is even more diffuse and there is a suspicion that the Net is waiting in vain for a web-only station to emerge that is a world-wide sustained commercial success. Nonetheless, there is no sign that the appetite for radio, whether powered by clockwork or computer, is diminishing. There is real and largely unexplored scope to develop European radio stations via the web, satellite and digital transmission, directed at niche audiences, which might be relatively small in individual countries, but which are significant across the continent and beyond. The key to these will be language flexibility, which means that, at first, those aimed at well-educated audiences may fare better, perhaps as not-for-profit foundations so that they can attract funding from trusts and trans-national public bodies.

It will always be a battle for large national PSBs to justify their expensive radio orchestras and high quality scripted talks against the twin attacks of government penny pinchers and commercial opponents. But there is a reasonable chance that political pressure from listeners will prevent their destruction until the century is considerably older.

Conclusions

♦ There is no reason why PSBs should not continue for many years to come in most European countries, as long as they do not have to rely on national or local advertising revenue.

♦ Machinery will become more multifunctional but is unlikely to replace radio sets and televisions completely in the medium term because of the many different places and circumstances in which people watch and listen. Multifunction receivers will add to the range, not replace it, in the same way that the aeroplane did not kill off the bicycle.

♦ Opportunities to broadcast will outstrip the revenue available, making it harder for traditional medium-scale general stations to thrive.

♦ Regulation will change and become more multilateral, as in all other political spheres, but will still only be effective against corporations and national broadcasters, not those who use only the Web. However legal norms and international standards are likely to be no more and no less enforceable than in any other area of activity.

♦ There is real scope to expand web-based radio, especially for those looking for global or continent-wide audiences.

Further reading and research

Aside from the annual reports of public broadcasters, and reports of the European Broadcasting Union, you may find the following useful:

Council of Europe (2009) 'Public service media governance: looking to the future', Discussion Paper, 1st Council of European Conference of Ministers responsible for Media and New Communication Services, 28–29 May, Reykjavik.

European Commission (2009) 'Benchmarking digital Europe 2011–2015: A conceptual framework'. Available from http://ec.europa.eu/information_society/eeurope/i2010/benchmarking/index_en.htm, accessed 20 October 2010.

Hallett, L. and Hintz, A. (2010) 'Digital broadcasting: challenges and opportunities for European community radio broadcasters', *Telematics and Informatics*, **27** (2).

Katsirea, I. (2008) *Public Broadcasting and European Law: A Comparative Examination of Public Service Obligations in Six Member States*, Alphen aan den Rijn, The Netherlands: Kluwer Law International

Keith, S., CBS and BWS (2010) 'Comparing war images across media platforms: methodological challenges for content analysis', *Media, War and Conflict*, 1.

Nikoltchev, S. (2006) 'Audiovisual media services without frontiers: implementing the rules', *Iris*, September 2006, Strasbourg: European Audiovisual Observatory.

Nikoltchev, S. (2007) 'The public service broadcasting culture', *Iris*, March 2007, Strasbourg: European Audiovisual Observatory.

Nissen, C.S. (2006) 'Public service media in the information society', report prepared for the Council of Europe's Group of Specialists on Public Service Broadcasting in the Information Society.

Toletti, G. and Turba, L. (2009) 'Sofa-TV: the new digital landscape', *International Journal of Digital Multimedia Broadcasting*, August. Also available online from: http://www.hindawi.com/journals/ijdmb/2009/186281.html, accessed 5 January 2011.

10 Cultural Entrepreneurship

Stuart Moss

An introduction to entrepreneurship

We are all entrepreneurs … to some extent. As humans, we are gifted with imagination and the ability to think creatively, and we are sometimes inclined to take risks by making choices that have uncertain future outcomes and implications. Zaharudin (2006) likens entrepreneurs to adventurers, in the sense that they often embark upon journeys into the unknown. Like adventurers, entrepreneurs need to be prepared for their journeys so as not to come to any harm along the way. By researching the journey ahead, and taking into account risks along the way, entrepreneurs are more likely to succeed upon their chosen path.

We are often inclined to consider entrepreneurs as 'business people' and the reward for entrepreneurial activities as financial gain. There is an ongoing debate as to what the true meaning of entrepreneur actually is – between those who focus exclusively on the economic function of entrepreneurship and those who consider it the personal behaviours of the individuals who undertake the economic activity (Willax, 2003). In Ford's (1998) article examining entrepreneurial stereotypes, he states: 'I searched the dictionary, which defines an entrepreneur as "one who organizes, manages and assumes the risks of a business or enterprise". While this definition describes the entrepreneurial function, it somehow misses the attitude and philosophy of the matter'.

In classic business literature there is certainly a skew towards the economic definition of entrepreneurship without properly considering the behaviours, traits and characteristics which are common to entrepreneurs. This bias is highlighted by Davidsson (2005: 1), who finds numerous definitions relating to the economic function of entrepreneurship. A stance focusing upon the importance of behaviour is more apparent in contemporary texts such as Chell (2008) and Nieuwenhuizen (2008), which have followed a foundation of employability and management skills literature published over the past two decades. Such texts capitalise upon the personal rewards that can be gained from entrepreneurial activities and aim to highlight behaviours and improve the entrepreneurial capabilities of individuals by developing their entrepreneurial 'skills'.

In support of the economic function of entrepreneurship, Timmons (1994) states that entrepreneurship involves building something of value from virtually nothing. From a business perspective, entrepreneurship is essential in order for the start-up, survival and growth of companies and organisations. Through a creative process, new products, ways of working, and *enterprises* emerge. An enterprise is the creative extraction of value from environments (Bridge *et al.*, 2003); and in a highly competitive business environment, entrepreneurship is all the more necessary to ensure success for enterprises in the face of competition. Stottlemyer (2007) notes the impact of the political and social environments upon entrepreneurship and demonstrates how economic entrepreneurship has thrived in Western democracies where political and economic freedoms are ingrained into cultural norms, leading to greater levels of risk-taking behaviour. This is particularly true of the arts and entertainment industry, where freedom of expression has encouraged rather than suppressed new and often controversial entrepreneurial undertakings.

Entrepreneurship in the arts and entertainment industry

As key components of the creative and cultural industries, the arts and entertainment are synonymous with entrepreneurship because they involve idea generation, innovation, processing, strategy and creative outputs. Willax (2003: 17A) states that the word 'entrepreneur' comes from the French words 'entre prendre' meaning 'between taking', which signifies the activities undertaken by an entrepreneur in their endeavours to 'make something positive happen'.

According to the *Oxford English Dictionary*, one of the earliest uses of the word 'entrepreneur' in the English language was to describe a person who put on staged performance events for money. A person who undertakes such an endeavour recognises that people are willing to hand over their money if they believe that they will be rewarded with an experience that they feel is gratifying to them. This is the basis upon which the entire arts and entertainment industry operates, and the industry is extremely competitive as more entrepreneurs become involved with it, offering new and imitation products to rival existing products to would-be audiences and consumers. When competition is fierce, innovation is essential to ensure competitive advantage and survival.

The arts and entertainment industry is founded upon both the creation and economic exploitation of products (both tangible and intangible) for audience consumption. In terms of creation, these may be products that were created specifically for audience consumption, e.g. a song performed by a popular band or artist, which was created specifically for financial gain. In terms of economic exploitation, this could be a product that wasn't specifically created for the purposes of attracting audiences, but which nevertheless attracted audiences and capitalised upon this by providing facilities to cater for them. An actual example of this from the built environment is an airport viewing gallery such as Manchester Airport's 'Runway Visitor Park'. Manchester Airport was created as a regional transport hub, not to entertain audiences, but many people with a curiosity about aviation would gather around the airport. This was recognised by the airport's management, who developed an area adjacent to the runway specifically designed for the purposes of allowing audiences of onlookers to view aircraft. This area now includes viewing, catering and retail facilities, and has become a visitor attraction in its own right to entice fee-paying customers.

Say (1800, in Morrison *et al.*, 1999) considers the economic function of entrepreneurship as a situation where entrepreneurs respond to an outside force which can impact upon the market system. In this case, the outside force was people with an interest in aviation and audiences were being entertained by something that was not specifically put there for the purposes of entertainment. By targeting this interest, the visitor park has been acknowledged as a source of entertainment and developed in a manner that is absolutely entrepreneurial, in essence generating income at arguably little extra effort from something that was largely already there – thus supporting Timmons' notion of entrepreneurship discussed above. There are numerous other similar examples of entrepreneurial economic exploitation to create visitor attractions from within both the built and natural environments throughout the arts, entertainment and tourism industries.

Entrepreneurial influences and characteristics

It is the consensus of many authorities that entrepreneurs often share particular characteristics, personal traits and attributes. These are often shaped by the manner in which entrepreneurs have been raised, and by the environment in which they live. Many successful entrepreneurs become involved with entrepreneurial endeavours at a young age, via activities such as having a paper round, earning money from doing odd jobs and helping run a family business. Such activities can serve to foster an appreciation for the value and importance of money.

Other common early influences upon successful entrepreneurs include: having a competitive upbringing, either through sibling rivalry, pushy parents, or ambitious teachers; having supportive parents; having to learn to adapt to change at an early age; exhibiting high achievement in either schooling or sports teams in their younger lives; and participating in a varied programme of activities outside school, such as being a Scout or a Guide.

Common personal attributes that may be developed by the backgrounds of entrepreneurs include the following qualities:

♦ Leadership – possessing natural leadership abilities is a common trait amongst entrepreneurs. Teams need to be managed and decisions need to be made, so entrepreneurs need to be prepared to take actions that might not be popular, and delegate where necessary.

♦ Creativity – artists who produce original work of any kind are highly creative, and entrepreneurs who are not artists need to be creative thinkers in order to solve problems, and examine alternative and often imaginative approaches to working.

♦ Futurism – there is a need for entrepreneurs to be able to make informed judgements about things that will impact upon, and be impacted by, the future and events outside the immediate control of the entrepreneur. The ability to be able to do this in a strategic manner is a necessity for an entrepreneur to thrive.

♦ Risk-taking – many entrepreneurial activities carry an associated risk, be that a financial risk, a reputational risk, or even a legal or contractual risk. Entrepreneurs tend to take more risks in their endeavours than non-entrepreneurs, partially because of a great amount of self-belief and the conviction that failure is not an option.

♦ Locus of control – that they alone control their destiny is something that entrepreneurs often believe. Along with this often comes an illusion of invincibility, occasionally even in the face of insurmountable odds.

♦ Non-conformism – entrepreneurs are free thinkers who do not like doing things a particular way because they have always been done that way, and they tend to question current ways of working. Entrepreneurs are therefore not always easy to manage, as their non-conformist nature often makes them do things the way they want to do them, rather than the way that others want them doing.

♦ Energy – undertaking entrepreneurial activities is hugely demanding, often involving very long hours that can seemingly take over a person's life. Entrepreneurs need to be willing to do what is required of them, whatever that is, and at all times needs to keep motivated, particularly when leading others.

It should however be noted, that whilst the above is true of many entrepreneurs, not all can be stereotyped in this way. O'Brien (1998) recognised that entrepreneurs, like all other 'groups' of individuals, can differ enormously in their skills, personal attributes and behaviours.

Entrepreneurial motivation

Put simply, motivation is the will to act. It is the force that drives us throughout our lives to achieve goals and accomplishments. Motivation can be intrinsic in that it is something driven by a personal interest or enjoyment, and it can also be extrinsic in that it is driven by something externally such as reward (often, but not just, financial), praise or promotion. Bridge *et al.* (2003) recognise the need amongst entrepreneurs for *achievement*, something which is a key driver for entrepreneurial individuals.

Economist and theorist Joseph Schumpeter wrote extensively on the motivational theories of entrepreneurs, coining the term '*Unternehmergeist*', which is German for 'entrepreneurial spirit'. Schumpeter (1934: 93) theorised entrepreneurial motivations at various levels, including those that are:

1. Centred around creating wealth: 'the dream and the will to found a private kingdom, usually, though not necessarily, also a dynasty';

2. Concerned with social standing and superiority: 'the will to conquer: the impulse to fight, to prove oneself superior to others, to succeed for the sake, not of the fruits of success, but of success itself';

3. Engaged in for the pleasure of self expression: 'the joy of creating, of getting things done, or simply of exercising one's energy and ingenuity'.

Schumpeter considered entrepreneurs as carriers and facilitators of innovation and change. He is also responsible for coining the term 'creative destruction', a term used to demonstrate how innovation can lead to new and improved design, rendering older designs obsolete in a continual cycle, something which is easily demonstrated by the rise and fall of numerous audio-visual media formats in favour of media-less digital electronic formats. This clearly demonstrates how creativity, invention and innovation all feed into the entrepreneurial process.

Particularly in the arts, and possibly to a lesser extent in the entertainment industry, there is a wealth (excuse the pun) of entrepreneurs who take intrinsic pleasure from self-expression, and who are concerned with either not-for-profit endeavours, or who gain satisfaction through means that may not necessarily be financial. The appreciation that consumers of their work may demonstrate, or particularly in the case of the arts, discussion and controversy that might arise through audience reaction to their work, can help 'feed' the motivations of creative people. There is of course a tipping point between the financial and non-financial motivations of entrepreneurs; it is an old adage that 'every-body has their price', and this notion can also be witnessed, but not proven, throughout the arts and entertainment industries.

Avenues to extrinsic financial rewards via the Internet have led to a motivational shift from a number of once largely intrinsically motivated entrepreneurs by 'monetising' their creative output. A contemporary example of this phenom-enon can be found with YouTube, which is intended to allow members to create and share their own videos with a potentially global audience. Once upon a time, YouTube was the domain of video enthusiasts who wanted to share their creations with the world, thus demonstrating intrinsic motivation through the enjoyment of their endeavours and the pleasure of giving. This would also lead to minor extrinsic rewards such as gaining 'channel' subscribers, and having videos commented upon and ranked by viewers.

However, since the takeover of YouTube by Google in 2006, Google AdSense, a scheme that allows subscribers to have potentially revenue generating pay-per-click adverts superimposed on YouTube videos, has been available to a large number of YouTube members. AdSense provides an income generation stream, from something that may not have originally been created for this purpose. This potential has been seized upon by a large proportion of YouTube members, many of whom are now gaining a regular income from their videos.

The potential for creative people to make money from their endeavours in this way could work in two ways. Financial reward could motivate entrepreneurs to generate more innovative content to drive traffic volume (and therefore revenues) upward. Alternatively, quality and innovation could be sacrificed in order to increase the volume of videos produced, upon which adverts might be placed. There is of course a middle and in-between ground. Peters *et al.* (2009) describe entrepreneurs who are both intrinsically and extrinsically motivated by their undertakings, and who do it for the enjoyment and financial reward as 'lifestyle entrepreneurs'.

A well-known creative entrepreneur, whose original motivations were arguably intrinsic, is Banksy, who has been creating politically motivated stencilled street art since the early 1990s. Banksy's art is typically found in public places on surfaces that are not his property and this has allowed property owners to profit from the sale of Banksy art. Art pieces such as that of a naked man dangling from a window ledge painted on the side of a Bristol sexual health clinic have become famous world-over, thanks to both the media and the communicative power of the Internet.

Whilst work such as the dangling naked man has attracted critical acclaim, much of Banksy's work is highly political in nature, particularly with a slant on anti-capitalism and anti-imperialism. One such piece was a life-sized figure of a Guantanamo Bay detainee wearing an orange boiler suit, which Banksy managed to smuggle into California's Disneyland and construct next to the Big Thunder Mountain Railroad ride. The piece was only in place for 90 minutes before being removed by Disneyland security, but this was long enough for it to appear on news websites globally. This work courted much controversy due to its political connotations at a time that coincided with the fifth anniversary of the September 11th attacks, and at a time when nations including the United States were at war.

Figure 10.1: – A stencilled Banksy painting above an art shop, Bristol, UK
Image courtesy of Dan Gritzman.

In the words of Irish dramatist Brendad Behan, 'there is no such thing as bad publicity except your own obituary'; and whilst Banksy's creative endeavours at Disneyland earned the artist little in terms of financial reward, what it did serve to do was further expose the 'Banksy' brand to a global audience. In this case, controversial art became a 'sellertainment' promotional tool for other art products. Banksy is not unique in this sense, and there are numerous other creative entrepreneurs who have also profited due to the exposure given to their controversial works – Damien Hirst being another prime example.

Defining culture and cultural entrepreneurs

According to the *Oxford English Dictionary*, the word 'culture' first appeared in the English language in the 15th century, where its Anglo-Norman origins were associated with the tillage of the land – later to become known as agriculture. Culture, in popular usage, has two broad meanings: it can relate to people and society, and it can relate to the performing and creative arts. A society's culture comprises its values, behaviours, beliefs and traditions represented through everything from play, recreation, arts, sports, fashion, festivals, religion, gastronomy, architecture, health, and language to industry, travel and tourism. We are a world with a plethora of cultures, and culture is a complex concept constructed and embodied through race, religion, gender, sexual orientation, vocation, lifestyle, age, and artistic taste, to name but a few. The potential number of separate cultures that could exist globally is vast, possibly infinite.

Like culture, the arts vary hugely throughout various regions of the world. Some well established and nationally specific art forms include the following: Indian cinema (Bollywood), Jamaican reggae, English Brit-pop, Spanish flamenco dancing, and Australian Aboriginal art. These art forms may all be labelled as being cultural, as they are deemed representative of the society from which they are from, so somebody who creates a product (tangible or intangible) in relation to any of the above and profits from this is in theory a cultural entrepreneur.

However, if we move away from the arts and look at something else which may vary from one region to another – such as motor cars – we can also see that many countries have their own car manufacturers. Again some well-known examples include Volkswagen (Germany), Chevrolet (United States), Nissan (Japan), and Fiat (Italy). These may also be labelled as being cultural, as they are deemed representative of the society from which they are from, but is somebody who creates a product (tangible or intangible) in relation to any of the above a cultural entrepreneur? The consensus would most probably be that they are not, and a clear distinction needs to be made between a cultural entrepreneur and any other kind of entrepreneur.

The United Nations Educational, Scientific and Cultural Organization (UNESCO) defines the cultural industries as being 'the result or product of individual or collective creativity, and include printed matter (newspapers and literature), music, the visual arts, cinema and theatre, photography, radio and television, games and sporting goods' (UNESCO, 2000). Whilst this definition serves to inform us of some of the aspects of the cultural industries, it fails to distinguish exactly what makes up the cultural industries, and perhaps more importantly to inform us exactly what is *not* included within them, leaving it somewhat open to interpretation. This is one of the reasons why it is difficult to define what a cultural entrepreneur actually is.

This confusion has also been complicated by the rise of the term 'creative industries', a term whose true meaning lacks any global consensus with the result that the terms 'creative industries' and 'cultural industries' are often used interchangeably. There is an ongoing debate between national governments and global bodies such as UNESCO, the United Nations Conference on Trade and Development (UNCTAD) and the World Trade Organization (WTO) as to whether the cultural industries are a part of the creative industries (or vice versa); whether they are essentially the same thing; and if not, where the overlap between them might start and finish. The one certainty is that both the cultural and creative industries are driven by people with ideas and vision, who can carry their ideas forward and make something original or different from them – these people are cultural entrepreneurs.

Food varies greatly from region to region around the world, and is very representative of where it has come from, yet gastronomy is not mentioned as a part of the cultural industries by UNESCO. An authentic Indian themed restaurant with Indian music, food, staff, aromas, textiles, décor and furnishings is undoubtedly a cultural venue, as it is the product of individual or collective creativity. Therefore it should be considered a part of the cultural industries as what it provides for consumers is a rich and immersive cultural *experience*.

Indeed it is the word 'experience' which is significant when considering the meaning of the term 'cultural entrepreneur', particularly from an arts and entertainment perspective. By allowing ourselves to participate in an experience, we become subject to forces that affect our senses and have a profound emotional impact upon us, often resulting in a physiological output. Examples of this include listening to a piece of music for the purposes of relaxation, or watching a horror movie so as to feel (and react to) the terror of the story and special effects, albeit from the safety of our seats or in our own homes. Considering this, the following is offered as a definition of a cultural entrepreneur: somebody who creates and/or provides products (tangible or intangible), which have the primary purpose of influencing the emotional state of consumers, often through sensory stimulation.

The complexity of the infrastructure and supply chains of the cultural industries often mean that there is not one sole entrepreneur involved in the provision of a cultural product. In other words, the cultural industries tend to rely on a process of collective creativity. Using the example of a film, this involves writers, producers, directors, editors, specialist technicians and a plethora of others involved in all aspects of commissioning, creation, production and distribution. The one person who is typically credited with the creation of a film is the producer, as they are responsible for the overall management of the project. However without the assistance of their team, many members of which are also working entrepreneurially, the end product would never come to fruition. This is the same throughout all sectors of the creative arts, including music, the stage and curated works. This demonstrates the necessity for cultural entrepreneurs to demonstrate strong team-working and leadership skills.

In the industrialised world, there has been unprecedented growth in the number of avenues by which people can spend both their increasing levels of disposable income and free time. The arts and entertainment industry has witnessed unprecedented levels of growth, and has never in point of fact shrunk, surviving wars and recessions alike. Competition amongst organisations to supply consumers with products to keep them occupied, interested and emotionally involved has never been fiercer, both within the home and outside it. The recognition of this and the industry's value to the economy has led to a global reverence of the industry by governments, making it an attractive proposition for imitators and followers and a 'hotbed' of cultural entrepreneurship.

Cultural entrepreneur Morgan Khan

Morgan Khan is a cultural entrepreneur and music mogul, who owns a specialist dance music label called Street Sounds, which specialises in compilations of hip hop, electro, house, hip house and R&B. According to Street Sounds (2011) Morgan is accredited as 'pioneering electro/hip hop, house, hip house and acid music in Europe'. Morgan has been involved in the recorded music industry in various capacities since 1978, and originally founded Street Sounds in 1982. In 1988, the label went into liquidation, but was re-launched in 2009.

During the 1980s, Street Sounds released numerous series of dance music compilations, as well as one-off releases. It was perhaps most well known for its 'Electro' series of compilations, which fused a synthesised electro sound with hip hop tunes at a time when hip hop was in its infancy in the UK. The unique selling point of Street Sounds compilations was that they included full-length rather than single versions of each track, and that each track was mixed into the next track without gaps and silence between them. Whilst tracks being mixed together on CD albums is now commonplace, in the 1980s this was a very novel approach, which soon attracted imitators.

Morgan's upbringing provides an insight into the influences that shaped his entrepreneurial spirit in later life. Key factors that have played a part in shaping his entrepreneurial characteristics from his childhood are outlined in Table 10.1.

Figure 10.2: Morgan Khan

Table 10.1: Factors influencing entrepreneurship in Morgan Khan's childhood.

Events in Morgan Khan's childhood	Influences towards entrepreneurship
Morgan was born and raised in Kowloon Hong Kong, to an Indian father and Scottish mother.	From an early age, Morgan was aware of different cultures and issues of cultural adaption.
Morgan was the youngest of three brothers.	Being the youngest child gave Morgan role models. It also meant that he had to strive hard in what he did, as sibling rivalry was strong.
Naturally left-handed, Morgan was beaten over the knuckles at school if he did not write with his right hand.	Morgan was forced to adapt at an early age, and do something that did not come naturally to him.
Morgan's mother stood by him for being left-handed and furiously demanded the beatings to make him write with his right hand stopped, which they did.	Morgan's mother demonstrated strong parenting skills and provided strong emotional support for him.
Aged 9, Morgan and his family moved from Kowloon, Hong Kong, to Kew, London.	Morgan again had to learn to adapt – to a new climate and new cultural norms.

Music was always close to Morgan and his family: his parents would listen to Mantovani and Frank Sinatra, while his brothers listened to rock 'n' roll, Deep Purple and Black Sabbath.	Exposure to music at a young age stimulated Morgan's passion.
Morgan later attended a boarding school, which was a strict Catholic college run by Jesuit monks where discipline was a key cultural element. However he had a rebellious streak, and was regularly disciplined.	Morgan learned about risk and the price of punishment. He also understood how far he could go before being punished.
At school, Morgan was a member of the Presentation College Combined Cadet Force (CCF). He relished activities such as orienteering and stood out as somebody who shone in such activities and led others successfully along the way.	Such endeavours allowed Morgan to appreciate the need for leadership, particularly when working in teams. It also helped foster the competitive spirit within him.
At school, a 'house' system was in operation whereby pupils were put into 'houses' in direct competition with each other. Points were awarded to houses for positive accomplishments, and deducted for misbehaviour. This meant that one person could have a negative impact upon a whole house, which would harm others in the house.	The house system instilled peer-discipline amongst pupils, each of whom wanted their own house to succeed. This again enforced the values of teamwork and leadership, so as to ensure that nobody would let the house down by making mistakes.
When he was 13, Morgan's parents separated, and the consequence of a reduced family income meant that Morgan had to attend a secondary modern school where racism and bullying were rife. However, Morgan overcame the bullies and helped to stamp the bullying out.	Overcoming emotional trauma and difficulties demonstrated to Morgan that even in the face of adversity, it was still possible to succeed and achieve a positive outcome.
Morgan's oldest brother was working long hours as a mini-cab driver and at a flying club so that he could bring money into the home and also to pay for flying lessons. His dream was to become an airline pilot, and his determination helped him to fulfil this dream.	Having such a strong role model within the family reinforced in Morgan the values of hard work and determination and proved that these can lead to personal success.

Early career

By the time Morgan had left school, he had planned to become a doctor and had made applications to several London universities to follow this career path. He had a small transistor radio, which his mother had bought him, and he found that he particularly liked the sound of black artists. Morgan decided that he wanted to work in the music business, and his mother, although surprised, supported him in his decision.

In order to support himself financially, Morgan had to take low-paid and mundane jobs. He worked double shifts for an employment agency, cleaning out petrol cans and working in kitchens preparing breakfasts. Ultimately, Morgan knew that this would be for a limited period and that he would get through it, with the ends justifying the means.

In 1978, Morgan formed a small company called Megafusion Promotions and went about promoting a record called 'Magic Mandrake' by the Sarr Band, which was released on the Calendar label in the UK. This was poorly paid work that paid less than his previous agency jobs, but Morgan realised that this role opened up doors to him that otherwise would have been closed. He would visit radio stations, vendors, and various figures throughout the music industry promoting this and subsequent titles. Through rubbing shoulders with such figures, Morgan learned about many aspects of the music industry and quickly learned the power of networking. He also learned about the importance of the 'blag' to open up further doors to create fresh opportunities.

Fate was to play the next step in Morgan's career path. He was walking home late one night past Cherry's nightclub on Coventry Street in London when the doorman looked at Morgan and asked if he was a DJ, as he was carrying a box of records. Moments later, Morgan found himself in the DJ booth, without a clue about how to operate the equipment, but he had to learn quickly, and he did so. Risk-taking behaviour was proving to be fruitful for Morgan.

A career in music

Whilst working as a DJ, Morgan met Dave McAleer, a music business veteran and a senior Label Manager at Pye Records. Morgan asked Dave if he could work for him at Pye, and was given the position of 'Disco Promotions Manager'. This was not exactly what Morgan wanted, but at least it was a foot in the door of the music business. However, the position itself had a more glamorous title than the reality of the job, which was in fact more of a post-boy position. Morgan spent most of his time mailing out records to radio stations and DJs and sometimes visiting them in person. Morgan was keen to learn more, so he spent time shadowing senior figures, and from these experts he learned about the creative side of the music business, contracts, negotiations and general business and management practice.

After being at Pye for six months, Morgan was given several of the company's subsidiary labels to manage. This was a steep learning curve, but he quickly adapted to this role and soon excelled at it. But still keen to learn more about the business, Morgan would spend his nights in the recording studios watching, listening and learning – he did this in his own time, and would often even sleep there.

In reward for his endeavours, Morgan was allocated the challenging task of going to New York to sign up to Pye a US label called Sugarhill Records. He believes that one of the reasons he was given this opportunity was because he had helped a certain influential individual who was now repaying his debt. Musically, this would forever shape his future, as what Morgan discovered with Sugarhill Records was people talking in rhyme over music -- rap. The deal was made upon Morgan's recommendations and the first Sugarhill / Pye release in the UK was 'Rapper's Delight' by 'The Sugarhill Gang', catalogue number SHL 101. In 1979, Morgan Khan thus became the first person to officially bring hip hop to the UK, and since then he has never looked back.

The following year, Morgan parted company with Pye and joined forces with a company called Red Bus to create a record label called 'R&B Records' with Morgan as its Managing Director. Morgan's vision was for this label to become the UK's answer to Motown by signing black British talent, which was something that had never been attempted before in the UK. The first release for Red Bus was 'Body Talk' by Imagination, which reached number four in the UK Singles Chart in May 1981, selling 250,000 copies in the UK and spending 18 weeks in the UK Top 50. Morgan eventually parted company with Red Bus over a financial dispute; two years later, he won a court case and received a substantial pay-out from Red Bus. This was the trigger that would allow Morgan Khan to realise his long-term ambition of owning a record label outright.

The rise, fall and rise again of Street Sounds

From this point, Morgan formed the record label Streetwave, and then Street Sounds, releasing over 80 compilation albums over the next six years along with numerous singles and six major box-sets. At the time of the launch of Street Sounds, a twelve-inch single was priced around £2, with imports costing more than double that. The Street Sounds compilations offered between eight and 12 full length twelve-inch tracks for less than £5, making them immediately popular amongst dance music fans.

Figure 10.3: The Street Sounds logo

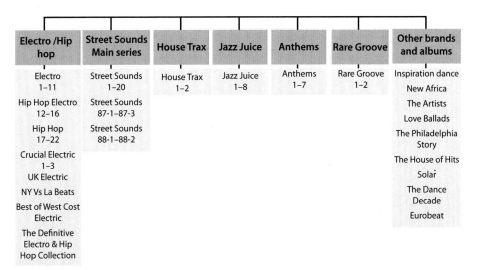

Electro /Hip hop	Street Sounds Main series	House Trax	Jazz Juice	Anthems	Rare Groove	Other brands and albums
Electro 1–11	Street Sounds 1–20	House Trax 1–2	Jazz Juice 1–8	Anthems 1–7	Rare Groove 1–2	Inspiration dance
Hip Hop Electro 12–16	Street Sounds 87-1–87-3					New Africa
Hip Hop 17–22	Street Sounds 88-1–88-2					The Artists
Crucial Electric 1–3						Love Ballads
UK Electric						The Philadelphia Story
NY Vs La Beats						The House of Hits
Best of West Cost Electric						Solar
The Definitive Electro & Hip Hop Collection						The Dance Decade
						Eurobeat

Figure 10.4: Street Sounds Brands 1982–88

In 1986, Morgan organised Europe's first major hip hop festival entitled 'UK Fresh', which completely sold out Wembley Arena in London, with artists who at the time were relatively unknown and had largely never been in the 'pop' charts. He is largely credited with helping spread hip hop music across the Atlantic to the UK and mainland Europe. From music, Morgan decided to go into publishing, creating a magazine dedicated to street music and fashion called *Street Scene*. Unfortunately, this was to prove the downfall of Morgan's empire. In the face of stiff competition for shelf space in retail outlets, the magazine failed, forcing Morgan to put Street Sounds into liquidation in 1988.

Two decades later, and after countless requests from Street Sounds fans, Morgan decided to re-start the Street Sounds brand. The rise of the Internet, and in particular of social media such as Facebook, meant that Morgan had access to consumers easily and cost-effectively. This has subsequently proved to be invaluable as a marketing tool, allowing Street Sounds to reach out to both new and existing audiences. Several websites and social networking pages were created to promote the re-launch of Street Sounds, and in 2009 'Nu Electro vol. 1' was released, which has been followed by three sequels, with numerous other compilations including the new 'R&B Street Anthems' series. Morgan is also developing new artists, and is involved in several other creative projects, including a written piece. The iconic Street Sounds brand has also been used to create a range of merchandise including clothing and other products.

Morgan Khan has demonstrated through his endeavours that he is a serial entrepreneur, by putting his energies into numerous creative undertakings. His intrinsic love for what he does is undeniably a driver to Morgan, as undoubtedly are the extrinsic rewards for the entrepreneurial success of his undertakings. Street Sounds is on the rise again, but continuous innovation will be necessary for it to maintain its position in the face of fierce competition.

Conclusion

We are all entrepreneurs to some extent, but few among us are willing to take the risks in pushing ourselves, our ideas, and our abilities forward in order to create something new. Those who are willing to take the risk are likely to have life-long influences that have shaped them into somebody who is prepared to face enormous future uncertainty. It is that very uncertainty that holds the majority of would-be entrepreneurs back.

Entrepreneurship is essential for the survival of any industry, but for the arts and entertainment industry, it is what its very foundations are built upon, in the form of human creativity. With cultural entrepreneurs, intrinsic passion is often a driver to creativity which in turn leads to new ideas and products. Extrinsic rewards typically come as a later benefit for their endeavours. Entrepreneurial success attracts imitators, competitors, inventors and innovators, creating rewards for some in the face of failure for others in what is a cycle of continual creative destruction. Where uncertainty is the only certainty on the path ahead, only the brave will tread.

References

Bridge, S., O'Neill, K. and Cromie, S. (2003) *Understanding Enterprise, Entrepreneurship and Small Business*, Basingstoke: Palgrave Macmillan.

Chell, E. (2008) *The Entrepreneurial Personality: A Social Construction*, Hove: Routledge.

Davidsson, P. (2005) *Researching Entrepreneurship*, New York: Springer Science.

Ford, T. (1998) 'Breaking the entrepreneurial stereotype', *Business Press*, **10** (3), 20.

Morrison, A., Rimmington, M. and Williams, C. (1999) *Entrepreneurship in the Hospitality, Tourism and Leisure Industries*, Oxford: Butterworth Heinemann.

Nieuwenhuizen, C. (2008) *Entrepreneurial Skills*, Cape Town: Juta & Co.

O'Brien, G. (1998) 'Entrepreneurship: can it be taught?', *Business West*, **15** (4) 33–35.

Peters, M., Frehse, J. and Buhalis, D. (2009) 'The importance of lifestyle entrepreneurship: a conceptual study of the tourism industry', *PASOS*, **7** (2), 393–405.

Schumpeter, J.A. (1934) *Fundamentals of Economic Development*, Cambridge, MA: Harvard University Press.

Stottlemyer, T. (2007) 'Celebrating the freedom to be entrepreneurs', *Business Journal*, **21** (27), 25.

Street Sounds (2011) *About Morgan Khan*, London: Street Sounds. Available from: http://www.streetsoundsmusic.co.uk/page.php?i=50, accessed 5 January 2011.

Timmons, J. (1994) *New Venture Creation*, Boston, MA: Irwin.

UNESCO (2000) *International Flows of Selected Cultural Goods, 1980 – 1998, Executive Summary*, Paris: UNESCO Institute of Statistics / UNESCO Culture Sector

Willax, P. (2003) 'Sorting through the definitions of an "entrepreneur"', *NH Business Review*, 27 June–10 July, p.17A.

Zaharudin, H. (2006) *A to Z Entrepreneur in Practice*, Jakarta: CV Dian Anugerah Prakasa.

Further reading and research

Du Gay, P. and Pryke, M. (eds) (2002) *Cultural Economy*, London: Sage.

Johnson, L. (2009) *Cultural Capitals: Revaluing the Arts, Remaking Urban Spaces*, Farnham: Ashgate.

Risker, C. (1998) 'Toward an innovation typology of entrepreneurs', *Journal of Small Business and Entrepreneurship*, **15** (2), 27–41.

Thomas, A. and Mueller, S. (2000) 'A case for comparative entrepreneurship: assessing the relevance of culture', *Journal of International Business Studies*, **31** (2), 287–301.

Websites

http://culturalentrepreneurs.com/

http://www.culturalentrepreneur.org/

http://www.mediaenterprise.co.uk/2008/02/29/what-is-a-cultural-entrepreneur-anyway/

11 Current Issues in Cultural and Strategic Leadership

John Holden

Introduction

Leadership in the cultural sector involves negotiating changes that are taking place continually at three levels:

1. At the **macro**-level of society, where social attitudes constantly evolve, technology opens up new possibilities, and fluctuations in the economy present opportunities and constraints;

2. At the **median** level – that is to say the specific operating context – where the leader must take into account art-form developments, shifts in arts practice, changes in law, policy, and funding;

3. At the **micro**-level of the organisation, where relationships, resources, energy, intelligence and emotions combine to produce organisational effectiveness.

These are, of course, all interrelated. For example, when new technology enables arts and entertainment organisations to enter into a two-way relationship with audiences, the role of marketing changes. Instead of simply being about selling a predetermined product, marketing becomes a dialogue, with the audience helping to shape the direction, and sometimes the programming, of the organisation. In turn, the organisation will respond by changing its structure – in this case possibly by combining marketing and programming and appointing a webmaster – and that will inevitably affect the behaviour of people working there and bring into being a new set of relationships between them.

Given the pressures of running an organisation, it is easy to get bogged down in the minutiae of everyday life, particularly when leaders face difficulties in their immediate operating context, such as funding cuts, staff issues or governance problems. But one thing that leaders must do is to lift their eyes from the everyday and scan the horizon. They should be looking out for long-term trends, anticipating how these will affect their own organisations; and they should also be looking to see what other people are doing. In other words, leaders should be constantly learning and thinking, as well as doing and directing.

If cultural leaders do start to examine the long-term trends, I believe they will find many reasons to be optimistic. In this chapter, we will first look at the way that the meaning of the word 'culture' has been changing in the very recent past, because in turn that will show how culture is likely to become more important to people, and consequently, how it will be viewed differently by government. Next, we'll consider the particular questions that cultural leaders face in serving the various, and sometimes competing, interests of artists, funders, businesses, politicians, the organisation's staff and the public – all those many individuals and groups who have an interest in what goes on in the cultural world. Who has authority in that world – is it cultural leaders themselves, or do others also get to decide what culture really is and how it develops? Cultural leaders in the UK should be congratulated because they have led the debate about how competing priorities and the concerns of different interest groups, can be reconciled or accommodated in the everyday practice of their organisations.

Finally, we will discover how technology, social change, and globalisation are altering the way that all organisations, within and beyond the sector, are functioning, and hence how they are led. How can the leaders of cultural organisations – which are often quite small – develop the personal and organisational capacities they need?

In all this, I will draw on two pamphlets published by the London-based think-tank Demos. These are *Democratic Culture* (Holden, 2008) and *All Together*, a case study of leadership and organisational change at the Royal Shakespeare Company that I co-authored with Robert Hewison and Samuel Jones (Hewison *et al.*, 2010).

In writing about cultural leaders, I have in mind primarily the people who are running or who are aspiring to run both whole organisations, and the departments within them. This covers all art forms and all scales from small to large. Leadership roles are becoming more distributed around organisations, so it is important to grasp that leadership is not just about titles. Being given a label such as Director or Chief Executive may confer authority, but leadership is a capability and a way of being, rather than a badge of office. Leaders are followed when they develop trust on the part of their followers, and this has to be achieved on a continuous basis. Leadership these days exists, indeed it *has* to exist, at many levels within an organisation.

Culture today: a practical definition

The Demos pamphlet *All Together* contains the following definition of effective leadership: 'What "effective leadership" now means is the ability to marry rhetorical power with practical innovations so as to create a sustainable, resilient, well-networked organisation, capable of growing its own capacity to act, and providing high-quality results for its customers, staff and funders' (Hewison *et al.*, 2010: 117). This definition has a sense of leadership being a continuous process of adjustment, one that helps an organism to survive and thrive through adaptation, rather than being a fixed set of tasks based on a linear and mechanical model where cause and effect are easily predictable. It recognises that the cultural leader of today is operating in a very fluid world.

This is just as well, because the most basic idea of what culture means – a fundamental concept – has been changing significantly within a short space of time. Not that long ago, back in the 20th century, the word 'culture' was principally used in two senses. On the one hand it meant 'the arts'– an established canon of art forms including opera, ballet, poetry, literature, painting, sculpture, music and drama. These arts each contained their own hierarchies, and they were enjoyed almost exclusively by people who were well educated and well off. This social group was small in numbers, but had great political and social influence. It defined its own social standing not just through money and education, but through the very act of appreciating the arts, which meant that artistic consumption and social status became if not synonymous, at least highly correlated. In turn, the arts were labelled as elitist, a conclusion drawn as much from the make-up of the audience as it was from the limited appeal, sometimes expressed as the 'difficulty' or 'inaccessibility' of the work itself.

But 'culture' also had a different meaning from 'the arts', an anthropological meaning that extended to include everything that we did to express and understand ourselves. This encompassed how we enjoyed ourselves, what we produced and what we consumed. It included watching *Coronation Street*, eating fish and chips, and reading thrillers. This all-encompassing idea of culture is familiar from the lists of icons and activities quoted as markers of 'Britishness' by Prime Ministers from Stanley Baldwin (1935) to the fictional PM played by Hugh Grant in the film *Love, Actually*.

The problem with having two different meanings for the word 'culture' is that they are in conflict. Culture in the sense of the arts and popular culture are often thought to be mutually exclusive: the arts are 'high culture' and the rest is 'popular' or 'low', so that a hierarchy of value is built into the language. The cultural difference becomes a social difference: the high arts and superior people on the one hand; popular culture and inferior specimens on the other. On top of that, the two camps of 'the arts' and popular culture are forever divided by a twist of logic – if a particular artwork becomes admired and loved by everyone, it ceases to be 'high culture' and becomes 'popular culture'. Witness the passage of 'Nessun' Dorma' from opera houses to football stadia and compilation CDs.

The confusion caused by these contradictory notions of culture extends into politics, where approaches to culture have cut across the Left/Right divide. The publicly funded arts have been attacked from parts of the Left for being reliant on regressive taxes that take money from the poor to pay for middle-class pleasures, and attacked by the monetarists of the Right for being an interference with the market. But the arts have also been defended on the Left for being one of those good things in life that everyone should have access to, and defended on the Right as being a civilising and calming influence on society.

This old, twentieth century model of culture then is an either/or model, but there is now a new cultural reality that is not based on a set of oppositional binaries of high/low, refined/debased, and elitist/popular. The new reality demands a different way of looking at what culture means, which in turn has many practical ramifications: business models, funding patterns, distribution channels, and relationships with audiences are all affected. Not least, it changes the dynamics and demands of cultural leadership as new challenges and opportunities emerge.

For practical purposes, culture can now be thought of as three distinct but deeply interrelated families: publicly funded culture, commercial culture and home-made culture. Instead of being in opposition to each other they are symbiotic. They simultaneously compete and co-operate, and no one part of this ecology could thrive, or possibly even survive, without the others.

Publicly funded culture is defined by practice: what gets funded becomes culture. This pragmatic approach has allowed an expansion of what culture in this sense means, so that it can now include things like circus, puppetry and street art as well as opera and ballet. In addition, official responses to the cultural production of different community, social, ethnic and faith groups carry deep significance in terms of validating or accepting different cultures within the definition of what government, and by extension society, sees as culture. Who makes these decisions about how to fund, and hence to define, this type of culture, is therefore a matter of considerable public interest. This affects cultural leaders because it places a responsibility on them: what they decide to allow on their stages, whom they book and who gets to use their facilities become social as much as artistic questions.

Commercial culture is equally pragmatically defined: if someone thinks there is a chance that a song or a show will sell, it gets produced; but the consumer is the ultimate arbiter of commercial culture. Success or failure is market driven, but access to the market – the elusive 'big bucks record deal' that Bruce Springsteen sings about in 'Rosalita', the stage debut, or the first novel – is controlled by a commercial administrative class just as powerful as the bureaucrats of publicly funded culture.

In publicly funded culture and commercial culture, then, there are gatekeepers who define the meaning of culture through their decisions. But the third cultural 'family', home-made culture, is different. Here, the definition of what counts as culture is much broader; it is defined by an informal, self-selecting peer group, and the barriers to entry are much lower. A great deal of skill, knowledge and experience can be brought to bear in home-made culture, whether in the making of a video for YouTube, singing in a community choir, or writing a poem. But the crucial point is that the results can now be put into the public domain without institutional back-up, and without the interposition of gatekeepers. In a break with the past, people can not only create their culture, they can also collaborate and communicate freely. Decisions about the quality of what is produced are then taken by all those who see, hear or otherwise experience the finished article. As we saw in Chapter 1, culture no longer lies solely in the hands of professional critics and the gatekeepers who have traditionally interposed between the performer and the audience.

The Internet is credited with driving the mass creativity that is found in home-made culture, but in reality it is only one of the factors that explain it. Cheap musical instruments, the availability of digital camcorders instead of expensive film, new public investment in galleries and theatres, the education system – all these things have played a part. As a result, the public, the commercial and the home-made have become inextricably linked and interconnected, riffing off each other and feeding off each other. We now have an overall culture where the three spheres are intensely networked, and where cultural leaders can no longer confine their attention to one small part of the mix.

The new importance of culture and cultural leaders

The switch from a binary model of the arts and popular culture, to a triple model of funded, commercial and home-made culture is profoundly important. Under the old model, culture was something marginal to society, a leisure pursuit, a nice-to-have ornament that was not as serious as business or work or foreign relations. Hence culture had a very low value in the pecking-order of governments, as the erratic and very limited funding of the arts amply demonstrated.

In the old model, popular culture could be left to its own devices. Governments might have wished to put some limits on the content of books and films, and censor them; and they might want to license the playing of live music in pubs; but popular culture could more or less get on with it. As for the arts, so-called high culture, well there governments might have wanted more people to have access to it, because they thought that was a good thing; they might have argued that as a matter of status, a country or city should have a gallery and an opera house. But culture would still have been conceived as something essentially peripheral, something to be afforded and indulged in once the hard business of the day was done.

This view is no longer tenable, because cultural policy is no longer confined to a small budget line and a narrow set of questions about art. On the contrary, if culture is understood in the terms here outlined – as a networked activity, where funded, home-made and commercial culture are deeply interconnected – then the wider value of culture in and to society can be appreciated.

Instead of publicly funded culture being thought of as elitist, commercial culture dismissed as mere entertainment, and homemade culture looked down on as amateur, when all three are considered together, culture becomes, to use the words of Jordi Marti, the Head of Culture in Barcelona, 'the second ecosystem of humankind'.

This changes the position of the cultural leader, because now her or his job has become much more important. As well as providing entertainment or a pleasant experience that compensates for the pain of daily life, cultural leaders are becoming central both to the way that the people they serve understand who they are, and to the way that their societies function – economically, politically and morally. As a result, cultural leaders of the future can expect much more scrutiny from all quarters.

There is a further important consequence of the change in the meaning and relevance of culture. Since culture has become more important to people as a means of creating, defining, and experimenting with their identities, their investment in culture – emotional as well as financial – is increasing, so they will care much more about what cultural institutions do, and how those institutions interact with and treat the public. As they become more confident consumers and co-producers in the rest of their lives, so too will they expect a greater voice, and more control, over what happens in their cultural lives. Speaking about how consumers are changing, Shoshona Zuboff and James Maxmim have pointed out that 'the new individuals seek true voice, direct participation, unmediated influence and identity-based community because they are comfortable using their own experience as the basis for making judgements' (Zuboff and Maxmin, 2004: 112). If that is true in business and public services, why would it be different in the case of culture?

Again, the consequences for cultural leaders are profound. They can expect their public, the people who used to be known as the audience, to become much more interested in participating, joining in, and influencing what happens to their organisation, including its programming. No longer will the cultural leader be an expert whose views cannot be challenged. Instead, their expertise will have to be applied by working *with* people, not just for them.

The public have a much bigger stake and interest in culture than they used to. So too do politicians, because culture is fast becoming significant across a range of policy areas that governments are interested in. Three brief examples – the economy, education and international relations typify this new importance.

Culture and the creative industries have become economically significant in their own right – in the UK over 7 per cent of GDP comes for the cultural and creative industries, and the sector has been growing much faster than the rest of the economy for at least the past decade (DCMS, 2008).

Culture also has a greater importance in education, where evidence is mounting that engaging with the creative arts not only helps children develop specific skills, but also encourages them to develop many of the capacities that they need to operate successfully in a modern economy – things like an intelligent approach to risk-taking, the ability to think creatively, the application to make things work, greater confidence and better communications skills.

Finally, governments are taking more account of culture even in the sphere of foreign relations. Because of cheaper travel, mass tourism, migrant flows, 24-hour news and the Internet, people right around the planet are having much more contact that they used to with other cultures. The cultural world provides opportunities to create greater understanding between people, but it also generates many misunderstandings between people as well, so governments are having to take greater account of it.

Indeed, it is already happening. As Michael Kaiser, President of the Kennedy Center in Washington DC recently wrote:

> Most people do not know that no fewer than nine government agencies provide support to arts in the US. That is not a typo. In addition to the National Endowment for the Arts, the National Endowment for the Humanities, and the Institute of Museum and Library Services, arts money is also granted by the Departments of Commerce, Education, State, Agriculture, Defense, and Transportation.
>
> (Kaiser, 2009)

This trend will continue, and governments can be expected to take more and more interest in the cultural world.

The same applies to business. As culture becomes more important in people's lives, business will surely follow, in an attempt to stay ahead of consumers. Luxury brands such as Louis Vuitton have been doing this for some time, and have allied themselves particularly with the contemporary visual arts; other companies have seen the value of the arts in community settings. Both these trends are likely to continue as more mainstream businesses get involved with the arts and culture in a very wide range of online, media and physical settings.

The new role of cultural leaders

What all of this adds up to is that the cultural world will become ever more contested, with the interests of different groups coming up against each other. One of the jobs of cultural leaders will be to create opportunities and spaces for those competing interests to come up against each other. The days when cultural leaders could expect to take a government grant, or a sponsorship cheque and then go off and do exactly as they pleased are over. Negotiation and partnership will be the watchwords of the future.

But as they face scrutiny, influence and interference, cultural leaders must retain the understanding that they are above all *cultural*. Their task is to create cultural as well as financial value, so they face a set of issues that are particular to the cultural field itself, and often to individual art forms. Cultural leaders should be asking themselves and their staff whether they are showing work of good quality, whether they are developing their art form, whether they are educating and satisfying their public and increasing the cultural capital of the society that they operate in.

In striving to achieve these distinctly cultural aims, cultural leaders are nonetheless confronted by a set of social and technological changes that affect the way that *all* organisations operate, whatever sector they belong to. To begin with, technology is making communication quicker, and increasing the connectivity – that is the number, strength, speed and frequency of connections – between people within and between organisations. One consequence is that the speed at which organisations need to function, in order to remain competitive in the face of changing consumer expectations and rapidly changing externalities, means that there is no longer time for decisions to flow up and down hierarchies. Leaders therefore have to find ways to devolve decision-making whether they like that or not.

Another reason why decision-making has to be devolved is that as roles within organisations have become increasingly specialised and ever more complex within those specialisms, it has become impossible for leaders to know everything about their organisations. They can no longer be the ultimate source of all knowledge. And because knowledge has become more narrowly specialist, there is an increasing tendency to put together teams and ad hoc groupings of people from both within the organisation and outside it to solve specific problems, or to address specific issues that require particular combinations of knowledge, skill or access to networks for their solution. Moreover, in order to reduce costs and to use expertise efficiently, organisations are outsourcing more of the functions that used to be managed and developed in-house and instead are buying-in bits of expertise as and when they need them.

A further consequence of increased specialisation is that particular skills and competencies become highly valued, and 'talent retention' can then become difficult. People are motivated to stay with organisations not only for financial reasons, but also when they find satisfaction and emotional reward in their work and their working relationships.

Finally, organisations now operate in virtual as well as physical spaces. Consumers can interact with organisations, and staff members can be managed, out of hours and without face-to-face contact. This not only places new demands on staff in terms of their knowledge, skills and behaviour, but also means that more people within organisations are now 'frontline' because they have direct contact with the outside world. A classic example of this is staff contributing to organisational blogs, Facebook and Twitter sites. This development presents challenges for leaders in terms of communications, brand management, logistics and investment.

These changes combine to create a situation in which organisations need to build systems that are not just optimally efficient in a specific set of circumstances, but also capable of changing to meet new circumstances: in other words, organisations need internally generated resilience. This resilience comes about through constant learning. It is essential to develop the knowledge and competence of staff on a continuous basis. But resilience is also developed by creating shared terms of engagement that govern the relationships between different people and functions.

Leaders, networks and interconnectedness

The changes discussed above present leaders with two fundamental challenges. The first is how to lead across networks rather than within hierarchies. When so much is being achieved nowadays through partnerships, subcontracting to freelancers, using outside consultants and so on, traditional management authority that flows down from a leader and cascades into a hierarchy is less important than the ability to operate as part of a network through persuasion, compromise and focusing energy. As the renowned business professor Henry Mintzberg puts it: 'A robust community requires a form of leadership quite different from the models that have it driving transformation from the top. Community leaders see themselves as being in the centre, reaching out rather than down' (Mintzberg, 2009: 142).

Case study: Royal Shakespeare Company

The Royal Shakespeare Company's developing understanding of the changing role of leadership is reflected in two diagrams that show how the RSC's leaders visualise the organisation. Seven years ago, it took the form of a traditional organogram with the leaders at the top. This showed linear, vertical relationships with the implication that authority and power flowed in one direction only (see Figure 11.1). But in 2010, the organisational diagram takes the form of a series of interconnected functions, with the leaders at the centre of a network, not at the top of a pyramid. This more fluid structure is illustrated in Figure 11.2 .

The second fundamental challenge is that leaders have to develop interconnectedness *within* the organisation, increasing the capacity and the capability of individuals and departments to work together. Instead of attempting the now impossible task of micromanaging specialised, knowledge-driven functions, leaders must pay attention to developing the norms of responsibility, honesty and trust within the organisation that enable people to work together.

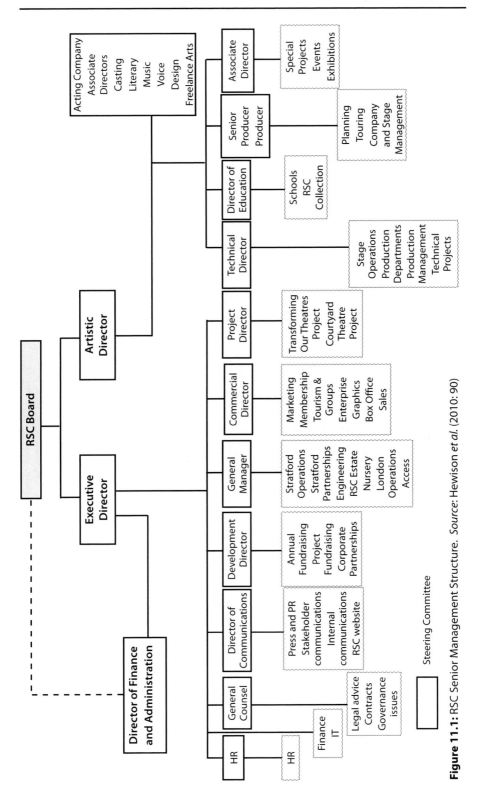

Figure 11.1: RSC Senior Management Structure. *Source:* Hewison *et al.* (2010: 90)

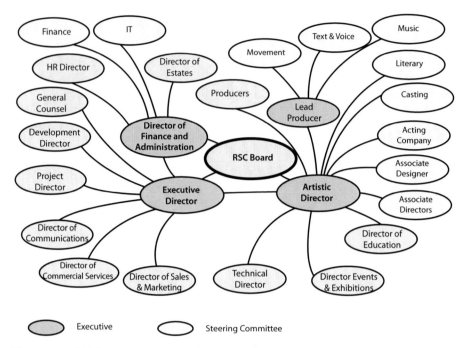

Figure 11.2: RSC Senior Management Structure, since 2010.

Source: Hewison *et al.* (2010)

This is no easy task, involving, as it does, finding the right balance between first, instilling behavioural norms through strong values; and second, reconciling the individual's needs for creative expression, reward and autonomy, with the equally important need to be part of a social system that is efficient, responsive and liberating rather than conformist, restricting and inefficient. There is something of a paradox here, because the organic development of a co-operative and empowered organisational culture nevertheless depends on the direction and coherence provided by effective leadership.

Leadership lessons

In the case of our study of the Royal Shakespeare Company (Hewison *et al.*, 2010), a number of lessons about the leadership of cultural organisations emerged. Lesson one was that leadership should be shared. The RSC story shows that it is not the titles and conventions of leadership that matter, but what leaders do and how they do it. Much of the rhetoric around leadership concentrates on the individual ('the right person at the top'). But research shows that companies (in the creative sector at least) may have a single individual as the public face, but have strong teams acting as collective leaders. At the RSC – and in theatre and the arts more widely – the model of explicit shared leadership between artistic and managerial roles is far from novel: the National Theatre in London, for instance, has both an Artistic Director and an Executive Director. Leadership, then, is embedded within a wider group, and is a flexible activity that can be successfully shared in many ways. The generally accepted term for this in leadership theory is '*distributed leadership*'.

The second lesson is that leaders need to use the right language and metaphors, not just to communicate within their organisations, but to inspire and persuade. We found that in the process of the RSC's change, it was important to find some word or term that both acted as a metaphor for distributed leadership and fitted with the organisational culture. At the RSC it was the term 'ensemble'. Ensemble is a French word that means 'together', but it also has a particular resonance within the theatre, going back many generations, and applying to a group of actors who collaborate and work together over a long period of time, sharing roles, understudying each other's parts, and contributing to the artistic development of a play in tandem with a director. At the RSC, the leadership plan was to turn the whole organisation of more than 700 people into an ensemble, achieving that fine balance of co-operation, respect and recognition of everyone's contribution with the need for direction, efficient decision-making, and the public's demand for theatrical stars. Other organisations will need to find a way to express their values that fits their own culture and sector, but everyone needs a shorthand that sends the same set of messages: that people will have a voice, will take responsibility for each other and themselves, and will work to a common end. Whatever form it takes, it needs to be adaptable to the way that the organisation develops, and leaders must be alive to when the language needs to change.

Next, leaders need to embody the values that they promote. The RSC's Artistic Director, Michael Boyd, has repeatedly emphasised the need for honesty, altruism, tolerance, forgiveness, humility and magnanimity. One of the main tasks of leaders is to articulate and reiterate organisational values and link them in one direction to the individual and in the other to the wider world. Any disparity between the rhetoric of values and what happens on the ground damages organisations. Equally, values need to connect inwardly so that they are apparent in everyday practices and the quality of relationships. When values expressed are disconnected from the norms of behaviour within an organisation it leads to cynicism and therefore poor morale and performance.

But leaders cannot simply communicate values – they have to do much more. In an organisational context, the discussion of values can often seem artificial and remote from everyday life. Lofty pronouncements from the Board or the

Chief Executive seem divorced from the daily pressures of getting things done. Leaders have to provide the spaces, places and time for values to be explored, discussed, disputed, agreed and internalised. They also have to 'walk the talk' and be personally responsible for living up to the organisation's values. Sustainable organisational change can only come about if the rhetoric of the way the organisation operates is matched by the quality of relationships that it produces.

The next lesson is that leaders must acknowledge the existence of, and the important role played by, emotions in organisational life. A remarkable, and highly unusual feature of the RSC's leadership and management style has been the regular and explicit reference to emotions. Michael Boyd is forever using words like terror, daring, fear, empathy, compassion and even love. Very few leaders in government or the corporate sector speak so openly about the emotions that everyone knows are a major feature of organisational life. In fact, leaders usually avoid talking about the emotional life of an organisation – it is seen as odd, embarrassing and 'soft'. But emotions exist and, when harnessed in the right way, act as a powerful force. As Linda Holbeche, an expert in organisational change argues: 'Managing change effectively requires more than an intellectual understanding of the processes involved. It requires … real emotional, political and some would say spiritual intelligence on the part of those leading change' (Holbeche, 2005: 8).

The final lesson is that one of the main jobs of leaders these days is to provide conceptual simplicity in response to organisational and contextual complexity. We live in a mind-bendingly complex and fast world. Difficult and demanding tasks need to be underpinned by clear and comprehensible concepts that everyone understands and can feel part of, both intellectually and emotionally. A good example of getting this right happened when President Kennedy visited the NASA Space Center. He asked a cleaner what his job was, and the cleaner replied: 'Putting a man on the moon'.

Conclusion

Running a cultural organisation sometimes feels just as difficult and complex as putting someone on the moon. This chapter has set out how cultural leadership is evolving, driven by changes in the meaning of culture itself, and by developments in technology and social relations that are forcing organisations to alter their structures and their behaviours. The relationships between leaders and staff, and between organisations and their publics, are at a point of fundamental re-negotiation. Successful organisations – and successful leaders – will be those that are able to adapt to the new circumstances.

Leadership itself will continue to be an essential element in the pursuit of the noble aim of creating a culture that involves everyone – a culture that combines an understanding of the past with the creativity of the present and a culture that hopefully passes on a richer inheritance to the next generation.

References

Baldwin, S. (1935) 'England: An address by the Rt. Hon. Stanley Baldwin'. Public lecture at the City of Birmingham School of Printing.

DCMS (Department of Culture, Media and Sport) (2008) 'Creative Britain: new talents for the new economy', London: DCMS.

Hewison, R., Holden, J. and Jones, S. (2010) *All Together: A Creative Approach to Organisational Change*, London: Demos.

Holbeche, L. (2005) *The High Performance Organisation: Creating Dynamic Stability and Sustainable Success*, Oxford: Butterworth-Heinemann.

Holden, J. (2008) *Democratic Culture*, London: Demos.

Kaiser, M. (2009) 'Needed: a federal arts policy', *Huffington Post*. Available from: http://www.huffingtonpost.com/michael-kaiser/needed-a-federal-arts-pol_b_226041.html, accessed 30 June 2010.

Mintzberg, H. (2009) 'Rebuilding companies as communities', *Harvard Business Review*, **87** (7/8), 140–143.

Zuboff, S. and Maxmin, J. (2004) *The Support Economy: Why Corporations are Failing Individuals and the Next Episode of Capitalism*, London: Penguin.

12 Responsible Entertainment: Greening festivals and events

Chantal Laws

Introduction

This chapter explores the contemporary issue of responsible production within the arts and entertainment industries, focusing on live music events and festivals in particular. In its broadest context the entertainment industry is vast, encompassing 18 unique sectors (Moss, 2009), each providing a plethora of tangible and intangible products that, according to Vogel (2007), is estimated at US$1 trillion annually. This makes it the largest industry in the world, generating more revenue and growing at an exponential rate as leisure time becomes increasingly important as an escape from, or antidote to, the pressures of modern life.

Live events bridge the distinction between high art products which are considered as a 'merit good' (Pratt, 2005) and forms of popular culture and leisure that can be consumed both at home and in designated public spaces. Hughes (2000) states that live performance of both art and entertainment is a distinct area for management, as such events require active participation on the part of an audience. As pop/rock consumers can now choose from 'an almost limitless number of events' (Mintel Group, 2008) at any given time, the viability of continued growth in the industry becomes of real concern, and the impact of such intense consumption levels can no longer be ignored.

In this chapter, the notion of sustainability is introduced and applied to live arts and entertainment, and the various drivers for event producers to adopt sustainable and responsible management are considered in detail. The debates surrounding the 'greening' of events are outlined, and the various models and concepts introduced. A number of examples are given to illustrate the range of approaches to sustainability adopted within the music industry, and an extended case study of Jack Johnson's music production and touring is provided to exemplify how entertainment can aspire both to achieve a 'closed-loop supply chain' – a holistic approach where production, consumption, customer service and post-disposal disposition of products are managed sustainably (Linton et al., 2007) – and to motivate consumers for social good.

Furthermore, in common with the overarching theme of this book, the relationship between producer and audience is given particular consideration, and sustainable entertainment is considered as a space and place for both producers and consumers to practise and engage in dialogue about responsible consumption. In line with Pine and Gilmore's (1999) notion of the 'experience economy', responsible entertainment is therefore conceived as a form of co-created leisure, and this concept of entertainment as social justice is examined as a pointer to the shape of arts and entertainment events in the future.

Responsible entertainment: concept and context

Music has a long tradition of social commentary, with recording artists exploring the human condition or using their songs as a platform to promote particular concerns. As such, entertainment often acts as a mirror to reflect contemporary issues and the impact of humans on the natural world has been a prevalent theme across many genres of music for some time. From the counter-culture protest songs of Joni Mitchell and Marvin Gaye, to The Beloved's 'Sweet Harmony', redolent of Britain's rave-inspired second summer of love; and from the personal lament of Julian Lennon through Michael Jackson's more bombastic 'Earth Song' to the political activism of Sting, U2, Coldplay and Band Aid/Live Aid, the use of music as a political medium is clear.

Social and political concerns are also present in the organisation of live music events: festivals that are now considered mainstream, such as the Glastonbury Festival of Contemporary and Performing Arts, have their roots in the counter-culture movement of the post-Second World War period. Free festivals (as Glastonbury was in its second year of operation) were a natural expression of disaffiliation with the dominant culture, as according to Whitely (1992: 2): 'Progressive rock was acknowledged as the major communicative organ of the counter-culture'. Music provided a channel for explorations of self within society that authors such as Partridge (2006) would argue can be traced through the 1970s through to the rave movement of the 1980s–1990s and on to present-day festivals that in turn are inspired by electronic dance music. Here, we can see the origins of the spiritual, ideological, philosophical and political aspects of green living that still comprise an essential part of the sustainability ethos today (Figure 12.1).

Figure 12.1: Carved wooden figure of Pan in the Green Field at Glastonbury Festival, 2003

Source: Chantal Laws

However, as festivals and live music events matured to constitute an industry in their own right, the necessity of professional event organisation, in the face of increasing legislative and political oversight, altered the hedonic nature of free festivals towards a more commercial (and some would argue certainly a more viable) operational strategy. Indeed, in the years since 2000, festivals have increased phenomenally: according to a recent survey by industry website efestivals.com (2008), 530 festivals took place in 2008 against 12 in 2000; whilst research by the Mintel Group (2008) further identified that live popular music events account for 60 per cent of consumer activity, totalling 36 million visits in the surveyed year. Another key trend emerging from Mintel's research indicates that 'much of the upward trend in audiences is being fuelled on the supply-side', with the majority of these events taking place at new outdoor provincial greenfield sites. This highlights the logistical complexities for the modern music festival industry.

It is of little surprise, therefore, that concerns about the sustainability of staging events on a global scale have come to dominate the discussion. Now, when it takes as much power to supply Glastonbury Festival over the duration of the event as it does the nearby city of Bath (according to supplier Aggreko, who serviced the 2007 festival), and when legendary organiser Michael Eavis can state that 'the greenest thing to do is not to run the event' (Hasted, 2008), the debate has well and truly shifted from the ideological to the practical.

Sustainability, corporate social responsibility and the greening of events

For many people (producers and consumers alike) the terminology surrounding the greening of events management can be confusing. The terms 'sustainability', 'corporate social responsibility' (CSR) and 'greening' themselves are often misunderstood and used interchangeably despite their separate, yet interrelated, meanings. To further complicate the issue, stakeholders may have a range of perspectives, requirements and demands that entail different responses from the producer which may not be mutually contingent. What follows are simple definitions to aid the reader in differentiating these concepts and in understanding how they will be employed here; for those wishing to pursue the debates more fully, some sources are included in the further reading section at the end of this chapter.

The term 'sustainability' and the related concept of 'sustainable development' were defined in 1987 by the WCED/Brundtland Commission of the United Nations as 'development that meets the needs of the present without compromising the ability of future generations to meet their own needs' (UNNGO Sustainability, 2010). This is the most widely utilised interpretation, although it is by no means uncontested. The concept was further refined in 1992 to accommodate the concept of the three dimensions of sustainability (Figure 12.2), which links to the model of triple bottom-line (TBL) metrics analysis conceptualised in 1994 to account for the impact of wealth creation on people, planet and profit, also known as the 'three pillars' of sustainability (Elkington, 2004).

Corporate social responsibility or CSR has become a ubiquitous phrase in recent years, with major businesses and international corporations promoting their ethical management practice as a form of brand differentiation to attract and retain new ethical consumers. Again, there are many interpretations of the meaning and practice of CSR, but the ISO (International Organization for Standardization, 2002) defines it as 'a balanced approach for organizations to address economic, social and environmental issues in a way that aims to benefit people, communities and society': we can clearly see the link here with the TBL and three pillars concepts outlined above.

Figure 12.2: The Declaration of Rio on Environment and Development Three-Dimension Concept

Source: UNNGO Sustainability (2010)

'Greening' is much less clearly defined as a process, but it describes the practical steps that any individual, group or organisation can take to transform their lifestyle and environment in line with environmental principles. It covers a broad range of activities from recycling to the intelligent design of space and products. Whilst professionals working in the industry may be comfortable with the idea of greening as a strategic management tool (Jones, 2009) for some stakeholders, in particular consumers, the concept may smack of tokenism, leading to criticisms of 'greenwash' or 'green sheen'.

We are working here with concepts that are still fluid and carry multiple meanings so understanding the perspective of stakeholder groups may help to clarify the drivers for greening entertainment events.

Stakeholder perspectives

Events are traditionally considered to operate across a range of sectors and at varying levels of scale and impact from local through to mega events (Bowdin *et al.*, 2006), with the impact increasing exponentially as the event grows in scale. At the hallmark and mega end of this spectrum, government has a clear interest in the sustainability of the event and may indeed be a key stakeholder in its delivery. For example, the London 2012 Olympics claims to be the first summer host city to embed sustainability into the planning process from the bidding stage onwards, and the UK Government is keen to ensure that this legacy is secured well beyond the duration of the event itself. In the cultural sphere, hallmark projects such as the European City of Culture or established events such as the Edinburgh Festivals receive funding from the public purse to achieve social and economic gains, and the instrumental use of cultural events to lever social benefits is well documented (see, for example, Langen and Garcia, 2009).

Commercial events, such as festivals and gigs, have received relatively less attention from political stakeholders, but scrutiny is increasing with the awareness that the cultural, creative, leisure, tourism and entertainment industries are increasingly important to the health of national economies (DCMS, 2010). In a climate of changes to UK licensing legislation, the introduction of standards for sustainable events (such as BS8901 and the soon to be introduced ISO20121) and the establishment of ethical guidelines from professional organisations such as the International Festival and Events Association (IFEA), this scrutiny will only intensify.

Indeed, in countries where environmental awareness has a longer history, or where the locations for music events are marginal and resources therefore need careful management, event producers have set the agenda for responsible management that has since been taken up by government, for example the Peats Ridge Festival in Australia (Jones, 2009).

The rise in schemes and programmes funded and monitored by government has necessitated the careful measurement of any claims of sustainability and greening. This kind of quality management in the form of key performance indicators (KPIs) is providing a good amount of quantitative data for benchmarking activity and leading to the development of models of best practice which, with their clear evidence base, will ultimately be simpler for managers to instigate.

Organisations such as Julie's Bicycle are key in driving forward this grounded research into the greening of the entertainment industries. Established in the UK in 2007, Julie's Bicycle describes itself as 'a broad coalition of music, theatre and scientific experts committed to making our industry green' (Julie's Bicycle, 2010a). Working with a wide range of associates, from practitioners to major corporations and active researchers, it produces timely and relevant information on the sustainability agenda. This type of collaborative partnership is an increasingly prevalent model of green activity in the entertainment industry, where a range of groups from the public, private and third sectors come together for mutual interest and benefit. The charitable work of many festivals and events is testament to the success of partnership working, with Orange RockCorps gigs demonstrating an effective social enterprise model.

Consumers could be considered as the largest stakeholder for green festivals and events, and perhaps the most essential. The movement of large audiences is a requirement for festivals and events to succeed, and yet their journeys to and from an event frequently constitute the single most impactful activity on event sustainability (Julie's Bicycle, 2010b; Jones, 2009; Best Foot Forward, 2007), with a recent survey by AGreenerFestival.com (2008) finding that 61 per cent of attendees travel by car. Audiences can also be difficult to manage in terms of their consumer behaviour and expectations of the event environment once on site. The sheer scale of some festival audiences inherently encompasses a broad demographic: well known 'green' festivals such as Bonnaroo Music Festival in the USA and Woodford Folk Festival in Australia have upwards of 80,000 participants and Glastonbury is the largest greenfield festival globally with a capacity of 175,000 for the 2010 festival. This demographic will inevitably include committed festival fans, who are likely to have an interest in sustainability outside their music consumption and who will be well-informed about the debates and actions for green living, as well as more casual participants, such as the 'lads on tour' identified by Slater (2010), who are likely to put their hedonic enjoyment well ahead of responsibility concerns.

There are many typologies to explain the range of consumer behaviours at music events, and we are increasingly moving beyond crude demographic statistics to understand the meaning of event experiences for consumers in a more holistic manner. Recent research by Arts Council England (Bunting *et al.*, 2008) proposes 13 categories of engagement in arts activity, and two modes of participation – active and passive. It is suggested that active consumers with a strong pre-existing interest in green issues will be willing to pay more for sustainable products, whereas those in passive mode may need additional incentives whilst on site. According to *The Guardian*'s 'Green Living' blog, Festival Republic tailors its recycling strategy to suit the audience, so at Reading and Leeds festivals, for example, the typically younger crowd are offered beer or money in return for recycling items on site (Edwards, 2010).

One of the key challenges for event managers is that the very process of ticket purchase at a relatively high price may itself encourage a feeling of permissive licentiousness, a kind of hypothecation along the lines of 'pay to pollute', where because consumers believe the larger intentions of the event are to be green, they are somehow exonerated from personal responsibility for their individual contribution to the impact of the event.

Glastonbury has struggled with this in previous years, leading to the establishment of the 'Love the Farm, Leave no Trace' campaign in 2008, which educated festival attendees about the polluting impact of urination into the site's streams and the dangers to cattle of metal tent pegs left in the ground once the farm was returned to agricultural use. The annual Burning Man Project event in Black Rock, Nevada, USA, similarly introduced an educational campaign to communicate the gift economy status of the temporary Black Rock City, which is established for the duration of the event (Jones, 2009). Gifting is 'both an ethos and an economic system' that rejects marketplace economics, allowing 'no vending, no advertising, no buying or selling of anything' and discourages 'bartering because even bartering is a commodity transaction' according to founder Larry Harvey (2002). Reading Festival experienced issues on the Sunday night in 2008 and 2009 with incidents of looting and burning of tents to fuel bonfires – an example of the negative side of the carnivalesque behaviour which modern festivals can sometimes embody (Arcodia and Whitford, 2007).

In steering the behaviour of consumers towards positive choices before, during and after the event, there is a balance to be struck between a potentially didactic, authoritarian or 'preachy' tone and the need to alter behaviours for the long-term. Linking back to Pine and Gilmore's (1999) theory of an experience economy, sustainability strategies at festivals and music events can act as a form of 'edutainment' (Moss, 2009) with the immersive atmosphere reinforcing education messages and addressing the higher order needs of sophisticated and sustainability-aware consumers. But as can be appreciated from the example above, the strategy adopted depends on the character of the event itself and can be enhanced or compromised by the nature of the audience, any existing partnerships, and oversights by public agencies. Whilst the techniques for facilitating sustainable behaviour are in themselves fairly simple (Jones, 2009), the often complex contexts in which that behaviour occurs are not.

Theories of responsible entertainment

Given the ambiguity that surrounds some of the key concepts in sustainability, and the complexity of the operational contexts for festivals and music events, it is perhaps not surprising that clear definitions of sustainable event management have only recently emerged.

Events management as an academic field is still moving towards maturity, and in common with any emerging discipline it has been somewhat preoccupied with setting the parameters for *what* is involved and *how* to do it, rather than *why* events are significant, although Getz (2007) has recently progressed the debate with an event, and subsequently festival (Getz and Andersson, 2008; Getz *et al.*, 2010), studies paradigm. Where those researching into the phenomena of events are fortunate is that there is a good deal of information from 'parent' and related disciplines on which to draw: tourism, particularly, has a longer tradition of concern for sustainable development, and there is much useful literature in leisure, arts and marketing management to support a discussion of responsible entertainment.

Possibly because the literature on events management is dichotomised into academic theory on one side and practical application on the other, it has proved difficult to locate a clear definition of 'responsible entertainment'. Smith-Christensen (in Raj and Musgrave, 2009: 23) proposes that sustainable events are those 'managed as an autonomous cyclical process through the interaction between event management, host community and event-goers'. Developing this further to acknowledge the three pillars and TBL, Smith-Christensen characterises responsible events as 'sensitive to the economic, sociocultural and environmental needs within the local host community and organised in such a way as to optimize the net holistic (positive) output' (p. 25).

Awareness of this potential positive output has developed iteratively over time, according to shifting priorities in the wider context that Raj and Musgrave conceptualise as follows (Figure 12.3):

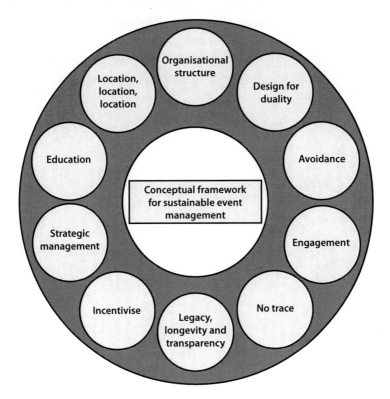

Figure 12.3: The Sustainable Events Management Wheel
Source: Raj and Musgrave (2009: 8)

These authors argue that any sustainable events policy must account for all ten categories in this conceptual framework. However, Jones (2009) states that the challenges are largely operational and require the responsible manager to alter systems of purchasing, waste management, energy production, water management and transport for their event.

The challenge, then, is to combine knowledge of the practical implementation of sustainable operations in terms of planning, project management and logistics with a long-term strategic context as outlined above. Jones (2009: 4) argues that: 'Your event's sustainable management and the way you communicate this along with creative ways to involve and inspire your audience and other stakeholders is as important as making the actual changes'. In this perspective, action and context are seen to be inseparable; and to borrow from Kotler's (2010: 251) classic model of the three levels of product, responsible entertainment comprises a bundle of benefits that are unpacked over the course of a consumer's experience, for example moving from appreciation of the core product (a green festival) through the tangible consumption (sustainable public transport, green tent hire, solar showers, beer for recycling, low energy lighting, etc.) to the augmented, long-term benefits (how the experience positively alters the individual's behaviour after the event, such as changing utility supplier, choosing fair-trade products, etc.). As festivals are no longer time-limited one-off events, but one activity in the calendar of an established community, it has become easier to promote and reinforce these augmented messages. The Burning Man community is an excellent example of a physical and computer-mediated global network that has an event at its hub but is active all year round.

Case studies: Responsible entertainment in practice

However, the entertainment industry is diverse, and there are a number of equally viable approaches to achieving responsible events. The following short case studies provide six different examples of responsible entertainment in practice.

1 Social justice and equity: Glastonbury Festival

Glastonbury is popularly considered to be a green event, but its scale as a global hallmark event in reality means that the environmental impact of the event is largely negative. The operational team work hard to minimise the environmental impact of the event on site, yet for the organiser, it is the cultural influence of Glastonbury and its work with charities that best exemplify the ideal of responsible entertainment:

> The company actively pursues the objective of making a profit, and in so doing, is able not only to make improvements to the site, but also to distribute large amounts of money to Greenpeace, Oxfam, Water Aid and other humanitarian causes, which enhance the fabric of our society. In the running of the event the Festival deliberately employs the services of these organisations, increasing the amounts they can raise towards their objectives.
>
> (Glastonbury Festivals, 2010)

The festival estimates that in the years 2002–04, over one million pounds were donated to named beneficiaries per annum, representing 10 per cent of the total festival turnover in 2002 – a significant resource commitment.

2 Supply chain integration: Live Nation

Live Nation has emerged in recent years to dominate both the recorded and live music industry. It has revolutionised the traditional contract with recording artists, anticipating a new model that demonstrates the 'Rockonomics' principle proposed by Connolly and Krueger (2006) and discussed in Chapter 2. The company describes itself as:

> the largest live entertainment company in the world, consisting of five businesses: concert promotion and venue operations, sponsorship, ticketing solutions, e-commerce and artist management. Live Nation seeks to innovate and enhance the live entertainment experience for artists and fans: before, during and after the show. In 2009, Live Nation sold 140 million tickets, promoted 21,000 concerts, partnered with 850 sponsors and averaged 25 million unique monthly users of its e-commerce sites.
>
> (Live Nation UK, 2010)

According to the Mintel Group (2008), the company has 'developed a vertically integrated approach that handles all the needs of artists including touring, ticketing, album production, merchandise, website and video. It plans to become a single source for all the needs of music fans. It is, by its own estimation, "the future of the music business".'

As producer for the London leg of the Live Earth concerts in 2007, Live Nation was required to implement the BS8901 Sustainable Event Management standard into its operations, with the Production Manager reporting a positive experience, stating: 'Once you've got a grasp of sustainability, it's not that difficult' (Visit London, 2010). Event attendees were encouraged to take an active role in driving forward the transition toward sustainable events through their collective choices. As outlined by Harvey (2009), audiences are a key event stakeholder with a significant environmental footprint, so opportunities were maximised to encourage sustainable behaviour for the one million concert attendees and two billion who accessed the event via broadcast media. All participants were encouraged to make sustainable legacy pledges, and as illustrated by Brymer (2008), Live Earth's global lighting sponsor Phillips facilitated consumer commitment to purchase greener light bulbs via the Live Earth website, which, it is estimated, led to three million sales.

Whilst some are critical of Live Nation's domination of the live entertainment industry, through sheer economies of scale and a global network involving major players in supporting industries, the company is able to deliver on responsible management in a way that smaller, more environmentally-principled organisations are unlikely to achieve.

3 Spiritual transformation: The Big Chill

As discussed earlier in this chapter, with its atmosphere of responsible hedonism, The Big Chill is regarded as the modern successor to counter-culture and rave events in the UK. Along with the Big Chill bars, club and record label, the festival promotes 'a lifestyle dedicated to *transforming the spirit of our times*' (Laws, 2008: 358). The festival further describes itself as offering 'a highly evolved, all-round experience that is completely unique, with a wide variety of music and performance, art, comedy, dance and film; technology and its relationship with nature; identifying artists and nurturing their creativity. It is about energy, community and fun' (Big Chill Fest, 2010). The festival also works closely with its sustainability partners, Julie's Bicycle and 10:10, as well as with eco-aware suppliers such as the Green Tent Company. Through art installations on site, it also promotes the 'Leave No Trace' ethos and embeds the idea of responsibility firmly within the experience of the bucolic festival landscape.

Figure 12.4: Installation at the 2009 Big Chill Festival

Source: Anni Timms

4 Personal integrity: Radiohead and Thom Yorke

The English band Radiohead has demonstrated a deep commitment to sustainable living primarily by commissioning research into the impact of its touring by the carbon footprint consultancy Best Foot Forward. This report found that fan travel contributed the majority of negative energy impacts for Radiohead's 2003 and 2006 North American tours, followed by international and internal US travel to tour venues by the band themselves. The estimates of fan travel and consumption impacts were 86 per cent of the total energy use for theatre performances, and 97 per cent for gigs in amphitheatres. According to Best Foot Forward (2007: 3), 'this makes sense, considering that there are nearly a quarter of a million people turning out on the Amphitheatre tour, and 70,000 on the Theatre tour, mostly driving high-emission US cars.'

When the band commenced touring the *In Rainbows* album in 2008, it was clear that they had taken this research to heart: not only did the tour aim to be carbon neutral, it also booked venues with good public transport infrastructure, used biodiesel for transporting equipment, and employed state of the art LEDs as part of a custom-designed backline and lighting set (see Figure 12.5). The lighting was central to the twenty-fold reduction in air freight achieved for the tour: as outlined by the band's Production Manager, Richard Young, LEDs (or light-emitting diodes) not only draw significantly less power than incandescent lighting but are more reliable, responsive and easier to transport given their small scale (Moles, 2008).

Backstage, the band requested real cutlery on their rider and water flasks for all crew instead of plastic bottles, and local environmental groups were present to educate the audience on sustainability during their appearance at the Daydream festival in Barcelona (Scholtus, 2008).

Figure 12.5: Radiohead's LED lighting for the *In Rainbows* tour 2008

Source: Sarah Fleming

Lead singer Thom Yorke has taken his personal commitment even further, participating in Friends of the Earth events, and lobbying at the United Nations COP 15 summit in Copenhagen in 2009, where he voiced criticisms of the agreements being made to address climate change (*The Guardian*, 2009). The band appears reticent to promote its green credentials for publicity purposes, but its actions clearly demonstrate that it is possible to retain your environmental integrity whilst working in a challenging industry.

5 Edutainment: Eden Sessions

The Eden Sessions is a series of summer performances hosted at Cornwall's Eden Project since 2002 that has garnered a reputation for innovative and eclectic programming. The Eden Project is the world's largest conservatory, housing a range of botanical examples that narrate human 'dependence on, and connection to the natural world' (Eden Trust, 2010a). The Project is a Lottery-funded Millennium attraction that was constructed in a disused quarry, providing an excellent example of sustainable regeneration through tourism.

From its inception, music has been an integral part of Eden's communication strategy, reflecting its objective to engage visitors in the sustainability debate on an emotional level (Blewitt, 2004; Hempel, 2007). This demonstrates synergy with the concepts of imagineering and rich consumer experience identified earlier in this book. Eden has a strategy that aims to use the power of music and major artists 'to draw attention to issues, campaigns and causes' and to unify, showing 'the enormous benefits of participating in shared music experiences and in creating music to build the strong and vibrant communities that are the bedrock of the new social order we need' (Eden Trust, 2010b).

The Eden Sessions comprise a key part of this strategy, with the specific aim to 'encourage audiences to think about the environment and the actions they can take to modify their impacts upon it. All profits from the Eden Sessions go towards supporting our educational charity and programmes' (Eden Trust, 2010c). Entry to the Sessions includes the opportunity to visit the venue's famous biomes, and supporting acts are programmed in these conservation spaces throughout the day to further strengthen the sustainability message through experiential consumption.

6 Holistic responsible entertainment: Jack Johnson

One of this year's Eden Sessions artists, Jack Johnson, demonstrates perhaps the most fulsome engagement with environmental work, echoing the holistic and responsible approach to sustainable production outlined by Smith-Christensen earlier in the chapter. Jack Johnson's music has become synonymous with the surfer culture in which he was raised in his native Hawaii, and his gentle acoustic songs are perceived (at least in the UK on the back of the phenomenal success of his 2005 *In Between Dreams* album) as good dinner-party music: pleasant but inoffensive. However, the sometimes whimsical nature of his song-writing belies a serious and long-standing commitment to environmental and social concerns that informs every aspect of his musical output.

Johnson's commitment to sustainable music has grown over the years, from the eco-friendly studio housing his record label, Brushfire Records, to the organisation of a carbon-neutral world tour for his 2008 album *Sleep through the Static*. He is also very active in philanthropic and sustainable entertainment work in Hawaii.

For his 2010 release *To the Sea*, Johnson took these initiatives even further: the album was recorded in two solar-powered studios in Hawaii and Los Angeles, and the physical release of the CD used 100 per cent post-consumer waste sustainable packaging rather than the jewel cases which have been shown to have a highly negative environmental impact (Julie's Bicycle, 2009). The album also carried the '1% For The Planet' commitment: this involved significant lobbying by Brushfire of the distributor Universal to change its manufacture and distribution process to incorporate the use of FSC-certified recycled paper for music and movie releases, develop the first 100 per cent recycled plastic tray, and pilot a new form of environmental packaging called Eco-Pac. Brushfire is still challenging Universal to adopt a biodegradable corn-based shrink wrap and soy-based inks, and is itself developing a recycled slimline plastic or paper replacement for all its radio singles.

The *To the Sea* tour has been greened in collaboration with All At Once, a social action network that Johnson helped to found. This encourages fans and concert attendees to connect with groups to make a positive change to their communities, connect with non-profit groups, take environmental action, and receive rewards. The 2010 scheme promoted sustainable local food systems and plastic free initiatives as its core themes, and participants could register their action through a passport system endorsed in the special green space established at Johnson's gigs – the Village Green. Analysis of activity for the first five shows on the North American leg of the tour found that:

♦ Over 30 non-profit organizations participated in the All At Once Village Green.

♦ More than 100 All At Once volunteers engaged and educated fans.

♦ Over 3000 people completed three or more environmental actions at the Village Green.

♦ Each night two lucky people who took action won the 'Best Seat in the House' prize and got to watch the show from the stage.

♦ By filling reusable water bottles at the Brita Water Stations concertgoers saved more than 6000 single-use plastic bottles from going into the waste stream.

All 100 per cent of the profits from this tour have also been committed to the Johnson Ohana Charitable Foundation, established in 2008, with a commitment to further match audience donations to All At Once partner groups up to US$2500.

The tour infrastructure has also been greened through the introduction of sustainable logistics for water provision, waste management, recycling, travel, catering, and concessions and merchandise. Once all the energy conservation measures had been directly adopted, the remaining CO_2 emissions were managed through carbon offsets. Johnson acknowledges that the very process of touring his music is impactful, but argues for the necessity of change agents working from within the industry, whilst also recognising that music should be fun.

> It's a step-by-step process. It's a learning experience for me and there's two ways of looking at it: we could make less of an impact by not touring at all, but, at the same time, if you can help change the industry you're involved with, that's a more responsible thing than to just walk away altogether. Because I do have that guilt of flying airplanes wherever we go but it's fun. I like travelling and it's nice to go places.

(Case studies sourced from: All at Once, 2010; Jack Johnson Music, 2010; and Sumner, 2008)

Conclusions

Jack Johnson's efforts to green his music demonstrate the benefits that a holistic approach to event planning can bring. But what is clear is that such activism is a serious and ongoing personal and financial commitment: it goes far beyond the production and performance of the music by attempting to influence everyone involved in the supply chain to alter their behaviour fundamentally.

In order to achieve this, some element of evangelism is required. If you are a fan, then it's likely that this will 'ring true' with your own consumer values. But those less enamoured of a particular artist may in fact be switched off by their explicit green message. At the crux of this problem is the contradictory and shifting nature of consumer behaviour, and it is this aspect of greening events that to date remains relatively unexplored. AGreenerFestival.com has conducted two surveys (in 2006 and 2008) showing an upward curve in audience engagement with green issues, but these studies are limited in terms of scale given the vast scope of the entertainment industry and its continued growth.

We have seen in this chapter that there exists a diverse range of practical greening initiatives that event managers can adopt. As the case studies have illustrated, the strategy selected will depend on the intended outcome. Clearly, it is virtually impossible for an entertainment event to be green in the purest sense of the term, and to focus only on environmental impacts may indeed narrow rather than enlarge the debate.

This chapter has proposed a tailored and synergistic approach to greening festivals and events. It has highlighted the need for responsible entertainment to be designed with a clear mission, achievable event logistics and ambitions to shape behaviour beyond the immediate event. What the industry now needs more of is longitudinal evidence to demonstrate that this approach does in fact succeed, effecting real and lasting change for tomorrow's generations.

References

Aggreko (2007) 'Aggreko powers, Glastonbury rocks'. Available from: http://www. aggreko.com/media-centre/press-releases/glastonbury-festival.aspx, accessed 6 May 2010.

AGreenerFestival.com (2008) 'Music fans want green events!'. Available from: http://www.agreenerfestival.com/summary.html, accessed 11 July 2010.

All at Once (2010) *2010 Environmental Impact Results*, Available from http://. allatonce.org/home, accessed 8 May 2010.

Arcodia, C. and Whitford, M. (2007) 'Festival attendance and the development of social capital', *Journal of Convention & Event Tourism*, **8** (2), 1–18.

Best Foot Forward (2007) *Ecological Footprint and Carbon Audit of Radiohead's North American Tours, 2003 & 2006*, Oxford: Best Foot Forward.

Big Chill Fest (2010) 'About us'. Available from: http://www.bigchill.net/label/info, accessed 5 July 2010.

Blewitt, J. (2004) 'The Eden Project: making a connection', *Museum and Society*, **2** (3), 175–189.

Bowdin, G. Allen, J., O'Toole, W., Harris, R. and O'Donnell, I. (2006) *Events Management*, Oxford: Elsevier.

Brymer, C. (2008) *The Nature of Marketing: Marketing to the Swarm as well as the Herd*, Basingstoke: Palgrave Macmillan.

Bunting, C., Chan, T.W., Goldthorpe, J., Keaney, E. and Oskala, A. (2008) 'From indifference to enthusiasm: patterns of arts attendance in England', London: Arts Council. Available from: http://www.artscouncil.org.uk/media/uploads/ indifferencetoenthusiasm.pdf?, accessed 9 March 2010.

Connolly, M. and Krueger, A.B. (2006) 'Rockonomics: the economics of popular music', *Handbook on the Economics of Art and Culture*, **1**, 667–719.

DCMS (2010) 'Creative industries economic estimates, February 2010'. Available from: http://webarchive.nationalarchives.gov.uk/+/http://www.culture.gov.uk/ reference_library/publications/6622.aspx, accessed 14 May 2010.

Eden Trust (2010a) 'What's it all about?'. Available from: http://www.edenproject. com/whats-it-all-about/index.php, accessed 11 July 2010.

Eden Trust (2010b) 'Music at the Eden Project'. Available from: http://www.edenproject.com/sessions/music-at-eden-project.php, accessed 11 July 2010.

Eden Trust (2010c) 'A bit about the Eden Sessions'. Available from: http://www.edenproject.com/sessions/about.php, accessed 11 July 2010.

Edwards, R. (2010) 'Festivals like Glastonbury and Leeds need to curb their carbon emissions', *The Guardian's Green Living Blog*, 5 May 2010. Available at: http://www.guardian.co.uk/environment/green-living-blog/2010/may/05/festivals-glastonbury-leeds-carbon-emissions, accessed 6 May 2010.

efestivals.com (2008), 'About'. Available from: http://www.efestivals.co.uk/about/ , accessed 15 December 2008.

Elkington, J. (2004) 'Enter the triple bottom line', in A. Henriques and J. Richardson (eds), *The Triple Bottom Line: Does it all Add Up?*, London: Earthscan, pp.1–16.

Getz, D. (2007) *Event Studies*, Oxford: Elsevier Butterworth-Heinemann.

Getz, D. and Andersson, T.D. (2008) 'Sustainable festivals: on becoming an institution', *Events Management*, **12**(1), 1–17.

Getz, D., Andersson, T. and Carlsen, J. (2010) 'Festival management studies: developing a framework and priorities for comparative and cross-cultural research', *International Journal of Event and Festival Management*, **1** (1), 29–59.

Glastonbury Festivals (2010) 'Extract from Glastonbury Festival Event Management Plan; Section 28: involvement with charities and local organisations'. Available from: http://www.glastonburyfestivals.co.uk/_assets/pdf/educational-resources/28BeneficiaryCharities.pdf, accessed: 12 April 2010.

The Guardian (2009) 'Thom Yorke: "I want to be here saying No"', Friday 18 December, 2009. Video available from: http://www.guardian.co.uk/environment/video/2009/dec/18/thom-yorke-copenhagen-climate-summit, accessed 6 May 2010.

Harvey, E. (2009) 'Greening Live Earth UK', in R. Raj and J. Musgrave (eds), *Event Management and Sustainability*, Wallingford: CABI, pp. 195–205.

Harvey, L. (2002) 'Viva Las Xmas', speech given at the Cooper Union, New York City, 25 April 2002. Transcript available from: http://www.burningman.com/whatisburningman/lectures/viva.html, accessed 30 August 2010.

Hasted, N. (2008) 'Going green on the festival scene', *The Independent*, 7 March 2008. Available from: http://www.independent.co.uk/arts-entertainment/music/features/going-green-on-the-festival-scene-792582.html, accessed 12 April 2010.

Hempel, P. (2007) Talk at the Eden Project for University of Gloucestershire students, 7 May 2007.

Hughes, H. (2000) *Arts, Entertainment and Tourism*, Oxford: Butterworth-Heinemann.

ISO (International Organization for Standardization, 2002) **<< referenced in text: details needed >>**

Jack Johnson Music (2010) http://jackjohnsonmusic.com/home, accessed 8 May 2010.

Jones, M. (2009) *Sustainable Event Management: A Practical Guide*, London:

Earthscan.

Julie's Bicycle (2009) 'Impacts and opportunities: reducing the emissions of CD packaging'. Available from: http://www.juliesbicycle.com/about-jb/research/impacts-and-opportunities, accessed 15 May 2010.

Julie's Bicycle (2010a) 'About us'. Available from: http://www.juliesbicycle.com/about-jb, accessed 15 May 2010.

Julie's Bicycle (2010b) 'Moving arts: managing the carbon impacts of our touring – Volume 1: Bands'. Available from: http://www.juliesbicycle.com/about-jb/research/moving-arts-bands, accessed 11 July 2010.

Kotler, P. and Armstrong, G. (2010) *Principles of Marketing*, 13th edn, Upper Saddle River (NJ): Pearson Prentice Hall.

Langen, F. and Garcia, B. (2009) 'Measuring the impacts of large scale cultural events: a literature review', Liverpool: Impacts 08/University of Liverpool/LMJU.

Laws, C. (2008) 'Case study: The Big Chill Festival, England, United Kingdom', in M.K. Smith and L. Puczko (eds), *Health and Wellness Tourism*, Oxford: Elsevier Butterworth-Heinemann, pp. 357–361.

Linton, J.D., Klassen, R. and Jayaraman, V. (2007) 'Sustainable supply chains: an introduction', *Journal of Operations Management*, **25** (6), 1075–1082. Available from: http://dx.doi.org/10.1016/j.jom.2007.01.012, accessed 2 September 2010.

Live Nation UK (2010) 'About us'. Available from: http://www.livenation.co.uk/aboutus, accessed 2 February 2010.

Mintel Group (2008) 'Music concerts and festivals – UK – August 2008'. Available from: http://academic.mintel.com/sinatra/oxygen/display/id=280413, accessed 11 May 2010.

Moles, S. (2008) 'Radiohead on tour', *Lighting and Sound International*, June, 46–56.

Moss, S. (ed.) (2009) *The Entertainment Industry: An Introduction*, Wallingford: CABI.

Partridge, C. (2006) 'The spiritual and the revolutionary: alternative spirituality, British free festivals, and the emergence of rave culture', *Culture and Religion*, **7** (1), 41–60.

Pine, B. J. and Gilmore, J. H (1999) *The Experience Economy: Work is Theatre & Every Business a Stage*, Harvard Business Press.

Pratt, A.C. (2005) 'Cultural industries and public policy', *International Journal of Cultural Policy*, **11** (1), 31–44.

Raj, R. and Musgrave, J. (eds) (2009) *Event Management and Sustainability*, Wallingford: CABI.

Scholtus, P. (2008) 'Radiohead pushes festivals like Daydream to go green'. Available from: http://www.treehugger.com/files/2008/06/radiohead-daydream-festival-led-lighting.php, accessed 7 November 2009.

Slater, L. (2010) 'Festival guide 2010: boutique bargains'. Available from: http://drownedinsound.com/in_depth/4140113-festival-guide-2010--boutique-bargains, accessed 11 July 2010.

Sumner, B. (2008) 'Jack Johnson and global warming'. Available from: http://www. stuff.co.nz/entertainment/265605, accessed 8 June 2010.

UN NGO Committee on Sustainability (UNNGO) (2010) Brundtland definition – three-dimension concept'. Available from: http://www.unngosustainability.org/ CSD_Definitions%20SD.htm, accessed 8 May 2010.

Visit London (2010) 'Staging a sustainable event'. Available from: http://business. visitlondon.com/case_studies/sustainable-event, accessed 2 February 2010.

Vogel, H.L. (2007) *Entertainment Industry Economics: A Guide for Financial Analysis*, 7th edn, Cambridge: Cambridge University Press.

Whitely, S. (1992) *The Space between the Notes: Rock and the Counter-Culture*, London: Routledge.

Further reading and research

ISO International Organization for Standardization strategic advisory group on corporate social responsibility, preliminary working definition of organizational social responsibility, ISO/TMB AGCSR N4, 2002.

http://www.agreenerfestival.com/index.html

http://www.bigchill.net/

http://www.burningman.com/

http://www.glastonburyfestivals.co.uk/information/educational-resources/

http://www.onepercentfortheplanet.org/en/

http://www.orangerockcorps.co.uk/

Conclusion

Ben Walmsley

The underlying thesis of this book was that the arts and entertainment industry is currently witnessing a fundamental change in the way that its content is produced, experienced and consumed, and that this phenomenon is revolutionising traditional relationships between producers, consumers and audiences. It is safe to say that the critical exploration of the latest theories, ideas and legislation presented in this book has vindicated this thesis; and the case studies provided in each chapter have served to illustrate and underline how leaders and organisations in the industry are adapting and leading the way in this unprecedented era of change.

The book began with a discussion of the changing role of the audience. To echo David Bollier and borrow Jay Rosen's unforgettable phrase, the 'people formerly known as the audience' are gradually emerging from the back rows of the stalls and demanding a role in the creative process. This transformation throws up not only semantic quandaries (such as what we should call this new species of audience) but also fundamental philosophical, strategic and operational challenges for arts and entertainment organisations, which are having to rethink their business models and marketing strategies alike. In the final chapter of the book, Chantal Laws invoked Elkington's 'pillars of sustainability', namely people, planet and profit. And having read every chapter of this book, it seems to me that the one key word to characterise this industry is *people*. To that extent, the industry has perhaps changed less than we might fear.

However, the book has clearly demonstrated the major repercussions of the changing relationship between producers and audiences. These include the opening up of venues and the creative processes that drive them; the transformation of business models from an artistic push towards a collaboratively creative pull; and the demand for a new generation of cultural leaders and entrepreneurs, who have the skills and qualities to speak to 21st century audiences. In order to understand and reflect this new dynamic, practitioners and researchers will need to embrace more sensitive qualitative methods, which are capable of exploring and expressing value in audiences' terms.

We have seen in the course of the book how technology is also reshaping the relationship between consumers and content providers and in the process breaking down traditional barriers of geography, culture and class. In this respect, the industry is witnessing a period of huge opportunity to engage with its audiences in different ways and on more equal terms. But with opportunity comes responsibility, and we have also seen in this book the challenges facing the industry in terms of sustainability. It remains to be seen how the industry will adapt to a future where travel may well be prohibitively expensive, never mind unethical. The key to rising to these types of challenges is arguably strong and effective leadership, and we have seen time and again through the case studies in this book how organisations depend on good leadership to achieve change, develop audiences and reform their business models. So to this extent, the future of the industry lies in the hands of a relatively small number of cultural leaders.

I hope that this book has provided an authentic and practice-based picture of an arts and entertainment industry on the cusp of revolutionary change. It will be for a future edition to revisit the issues we have covered here and appraise how the industry has reacted to and coped with this change.

Index